BURIED

IN

THE ARCTIC ICE

BURIED
IN
THE ARCTIC ICE

CYRIL DUNNE

N

Dedicated to my Grandmother Mary Dunne (*née* Hand).
Gran, uncle Jimmy has not been forgotten.

The author's royalties will be donated to
the Irish Guide Dogs for the Blind.

First published 2009

Nonsuch Ireland
119 Baggot Street,
Dublin 2
www.nonsuchireland.com

British Library Cataloguing in Publication Data.
A catalogue record for this book is available from the British Library.

ISBN 978 1 84588 945 6

Typesetting and origination by The History Press
Printed in Great Britain

Contents

Acknowledgements

I owe a great debt of gratitude to Michael Kelleher at the Bray Library. Through his connections he obtained for me from Britain the loan of the two volumes of G.S. Nares's *Voyage to the Polar Sea*, which was the complete record of the 1875 British Naval Expedition. These were unavailable in Ireland, and he tenaciously tracked down copies of the Parliamentary Papers to The University of Manitoba, Canada. I had given up all hope of securing them after my letter to the House of Commons in London was ignored. I also want to thank Michael for all his encouragement and advice. I am deeply indebted to him for the time he spent on the project. Michael – many thanks.

The surviving first-generation descendants of Michael and Mary Hand, the Metcalfes, Dunnes, Cullens, and Dodds, owe a debt of gratitude to Frank Nugent for resurrecting the memory of Jim Hand. His book *Seek the Frozen Lands* was my inspiration to write *Buried In The Arctic Ice*. My thanks to my cousin Jim Metcalfe who drew my attention to Frank Nugent's book; to my cousin Dr Leo Metcalfe, a scientist at the European Space Agency in Madrid, for his assistance as a wonderful problem solver and a wizard at checking out the most obscure factual information; to my cousin Anne Power (*née* Cullen), another strand of the Hand family, for her time freely given in sharing the tedious but essential task of typing; to Mark McCormack for his assistance in research. My thanks also to golfing pal Richard (Richy) Roche, he always obliged when I needed help in solving my computer problems.

A novice author researching a history book which spans a number of countries going back to 1830, can read vast volumes on the subject, can visit countless websites, and view television documentaries and videos but without the human contact of friends and strangers alike for background information in Ireland, Britain, and indeed as far away as Canada, something is missing.

In my situation these contacts were absolutely crucial. I have been overwhelmed by the offers of assistance, guidance, and the generosity of time and energy given by people, some of whom I have never met and in many cases I never will meet. Thank you to everyone who offered their help.

Thank you to Maeve Convery, Commissioning Editor with Nonsuch

Publishing for her encouraging boost of confidence after reading the manuscript of *Buried in the Arctic Ice*, and her wholehearted co-operation in the publication of the book. Special thanks also to the following: Tim Christie of the Canadian Meteorological Service, Toronto; Jeremy Mitchell, Martin Salmon, Colin Startkey, Julie Coughlan and Andrew Davies of the British National Maritime Museum in London; Jennifer Hamilton, Collections Archaeologist, Parks Canada, and her colleagues; Doug McGregor, of Parks Canada Western and Northern Service Centre; Noel Dunne, Benny Dunne, Louis Kearney, and Annie Childs, all in Greenwich; Mary Wills in Devon; Derek Ryan in Aberdeen; John Doyle; Jim Rees; Henry Cairns; Shay Ryan; Michael Suttle; Paddy Gallagher; Brian Murphy; Rita, Gillian, Anne and Robert in the Bray Library, and the Bray Heritage Centre for assistance with photographs.

Compiling an index for a history book of this size is a mammoth task that requires special expertise and infinite patience. Two local historians, Henry Cairns and Jim Scannell both suggested the name Helen Litton. Despite her very busy schedule, and thanks in no small part to her admiration for the Irish Guide Dogs for the Blind, she agreed to help. Helen, on my own behalf and on behalf of the Irish Guide Dogs for the Blind, many thanks for your invaluable contribution.

Also a huge thank you to Miranda Moriarty for her kind co-operation an unending patience. Miranda, who was a great help in the preparation of this text, edited a previous book of mine, *A History of Golf in Bray* (which was, incidentally, the first documented evidence of golf played in the Republic of Ireland).

And finally a huge thank you to my darling wife Sheila, for her patience and encouragement.

A Note on the Images

My research uncovered a series of sketches of the 1875 Royal Navy Expedition to the North Pole published in the *Illustrated London News*. The sketches were published both prior to the expedition's departure on 29 May 1875 and on its return to England in November 1876. However, the source found could only provide photocopies, which I felt unsuitable for reproduction in my book.

In a conversation with Mr John Doyle, the MD of H.J. Byrne, the long-established Bray estate agency, he suggested an introduction to a friend of his, Mr Andrew Bonar Law, who John felt might be able to assist me. Subsequently Andrew invited me to his home at Shankill Castle in Co. Dublin and there to my amazement, among Andrew's vast library collection, he had hundreds of copies of the *Illustrated London News*, dating back to the first issue. Andrew produced the series of sketches of the expedition I was seeking and further to my enormous surprise Andrew made me a present of them.

I contacted my cousin Noel Dunne, who works in a Naval Base in Devon on the south coast of England, the traditional home of the British Fleet, to assist me in my quest for backround information on the list of ships Jim Hand served on prior to enlisting on the George S. Nares Expedition of 1875. While he was seeking these details Noel came across two Jim Hand memorial markers in Canada which he did not know existed and which are on display to the present day.

This discovery opened up a Pandora's box which led to Winnipeg and also led to a Mr Tim Christie in Toronto. This in turn led me to Lady Franklin Bay on Ellesmere Island where the HMS *Discovery* anchored for a year and a whole new chapter was born, 'The Mystery of the Two Memorial Markers'.

Unless otherwise accredited, images belong to the James Hand family collection.

A Note from Irish Guide Dogs for the Blind

Irish Guide Dogs for the Blind is dedicated to bringing mobility and independence to blind and visually impaired people, and also to families of children with autism.

As an charitable organisation we face many challenges but the rewards are great. Our guide and assistance dogs, along with other services, bring about positive life-changing experiences to those in need. These huge accomplishments are brought about by the generous help we receive from members of the public.

Through Cyril Dunne's generosity of donating the proceeds of *Buried in the Arctic Ice* to our charity, Irish Guide Dogs for the Blind will continue to provide essential services in Ireland. Who could have said that Jim Hand's plight during the famine era would go on to help Irish people over 160 years later?

To those of you who purchase this epic book, we thank you.

Peter Franklin

About the Author

Cyril Dunne lives in the town of Bray, in Co. Wicklow,. He is a great-grandson of Michael Hand, the younger brother of James 'Jim' Hand.

Michael Hand was born in 1850, three years after James. Michael married Mary Mooney and together they had six children; four girls, Mary, Julia, Christine, and Agnes, and two sons, Jack, and James. Subsequently, Mary married John Dunne; Julia married William Cullen; Christine married Joseph Metcalfe, and Jack married Theresa Fields. Michael passed away in 1936 at the grand old age of eighty-six, having spent his final days with the Metcalfe family.

Cyril was raised by his grandmother Mary Dunne (1880–1964) and remembers his great-grandfather Michael as the tallest man he had ever seen, with a long white beard.

It was James Metcalfe, a grandson of Michael who first drew Cyril's attention to Frank Nugent's Book, *Seek The Frozen Lands: Irish Explorers 1740-1922*. He also had in his possession James Hand's ships' papers, which recorded the complete list of the Navy ships he served on, beginning with the HMS *Ajax* in January 1862 and culminating with the HMS *Discovery* in 1875. Cyril was intrigued, and began to delve into the history of Arctic expeditions, discovering as he did, that they held a great fascination for him.

On behalf of his great-grandfather Michael and Michael's daughter Mary (Cyril's grandmother) he decided to record the story of the life and times of James 'Jim' Hand.

Foreword

When researching for my history of Irish polar exploration in 2002, I made a thrilling discovery one morning at the Public Records Office (PRO) at Kew. I found in the logbook of HMS *Immortalité* an entry relating to Able Bodied seaman James Hand of Bray, Co. Wicklow. It contained his full naval service record up to his joining that ship. His career record was obviously transcribed from Hand's own service papers. That same morning my wife Carol, in another part of the PRO, discovered the surgeon's report from the North Pole Expedition of 1875. This document gave a detailed account of the final suffering and death from scurvy of the same gallant AB James Hand following his participation in an exploration sledge party from HMS *Alert* along the north-west coast of Greenland. His life ended at Polaris Bay inside the Arctic Circle.

When we met for lunch following such a productive morning among the dusty archives we were able to piece together an outline of the naval life and death of James Hand. Back in Bray a week later we were able to find his baptismal records and trace his parents and home to Bray Strand in the popular seaside resort near Dublin City. Admiralty records also revealed that an Arctic Medal was posthumously awarded to James Hand, which was sent to his father, John at Bray on 19 November 1877.

James Hand took his rightful place in my book *Seek the Frozen Lands: Irish Polar Explorers 1740-1922*. He represented a typical below-deck unsung Irishman in the Royal Navy. I often wondered whether any of his family's descendants kept his medal or other artefacts of his career in the Navy, or would the publication of my book resurrect someone who knew a little more about Hand.

Then one day Cyril Dunne rang me from his home in Bray; he was a distant relation of Hand and he wanted to find out more and write a more detailed biography about him. I was not immediately convinced that he would find much additional material to justify his efforts, but I shared with him my knowledge and enthusiasm for polar history. Cyril explained he had written a history of golf in Bray for the 1997 centenary of Bray Golf Club, where he was a past Captain and President. It is obvious from this well-researched and well-written gem that Cyril knew the history of his town, particularly in the eighteenth century when the first golfers appeared in Bray in around 1762.

I am glad to say Cyril has successfully contextualised the life story of James Hand, identifying his solid Bray roots, linking his life to that place and time in Irish history. He discovered that Hand's service papers were still in safe family hands and he had access to them. He outlines the sequence of Arctic exploration exploits in the area of the Kane and Hall Basins, which was explored as a consequence of the search for the lost Franklin Expedition of 1845. The story then goes on to relate how Hand joined the Navy as a fifteen-year-old boy, his life and career as a seaman, his ships, and his voyages up to his last fateful journey aboard HMS *Alert*, which brought him and his shipmates inside the Arctic Circle. He recounts the hardship of the sledging party using McClintock sledges, clothing, hardware and food. Hand had a tough time on the expedition and finally lost his life, suffering from the debilitation and agony of scurvy while pulling a man-hauled sledge. He was buried alongside the great American explorer Charles Francis Hall who searched for Franklin and was buried in Polaris Bay by his crew, some of whom are suspected of having poisoned him.

Cyril Dunne has unveiled a life story ending in Polar gallantry and sacrifice, and tells the very human story of a young Irishman who chose to go to sea to seek adventure rather than live a life of tedium in a small seaside town. Since writing *Seek the Frozen Lands* in 2003, several significant Irish Arctic biographies have been published including excellent accounts of Captain Francis Crozier and Sir Leopold McClintock by Michael Smith and David Murphy respectively. Both of these Irishmen were Ship Captains from relatively wealthy families, with many sources and references relating to their lives easily found in the archives of the Admiralty and logs of the ships they sailed. Below-deck heroes are easier lost and forgotten over time and details of their lives and contributions to such exploits are quite often lost in a single generation within families, and the only record of their passing is found in lists of officers and men in ship logs.

Cyril has uncovered much relevant material through exhaustive and passionate work and he skillfully tells Hand's story to recreate the life and times of a seaman born on the seafront at Bray who was one of four on Nares's North Pole Expedition who perished in the frozen Arctic in the dedicated delivery of their duty. It is said that all history is local and it is a special honour for me to be asked and to be associated with this excellent contribution to local and national history and the celebration of the life of this honest Wicklow seaman. He, like many other Irishmen in the British Navy (they accounted for one eighth of the Navy strength in the early nineteenth century), are deserving of recognition for their skill, fortitude, seamanship, discipline and heroism as they voyaged to wherever their orders took them. They are a credit to our island nation.

Frank Nugent
Mountaineer and Explorer
Author of *Seek the Frozen Lands: Irish Polar Explorers 1740-1922*

Prologue

There is a stillness in the Arctic wilderness at 81°38'N, L.61°44'W that is simply unimaginable to those who have not experienced it. On the morning of Monday 5 June 1876, this eerie silence was shattered by the sharp crack of a pickaxe striking solid ice. It echoed like a gunshot for miles in all directions. The man attempting to dig a shallow grave in the ice was British Naval Lt Wyatt Rawson. Unable to penetrate the thick ice and complete the arduous task, he decided to return with reinforcements the next day. Several yards away there was another solitary grave over which fluttered the Stars and Stripes of America. At the head of the grave stood an improvised wooden grave marker, on which the inscription read:

In Memory

of

Charles Francis Hall,

Late Commander US Steamer *Polaris*, North Pole Expedition.

Died November 8th 1871,

Aged 50 Years.

I am the Resurrection and the Life; He that believeth in me, though he were dead, yet shall he live.

Embedded at the foot of the grave was a brass plate that had been prepared in England and recently erected with all solemnity. It read, 'This tablet has been erected by the British Polar Expedition of 1875, who following in his footsteps, have profited by his experience.'

Hall had been America's most successful Arctic explorer and Commander of the American *Polaris* Expedition of 1871-3. He was buried on 9 November 1871 after a burial service performed by the ship's Chaplain, Richard Bryan, surrounded by approximately twenty shivering mourners, one or more of whom it was alleged, may have poisoned him.

Almost five years later, on Thursday morning, 8 June 1876, seven men hauled a sledge on which lay the remains of Able Seaman James Hand from Bray, Co. Wicklow, Ireland. They were: Lt Wyatt Rawson; British Naval Lt Reginald

Fulford; British Naval Surgeon Henry Coppinger, from Dublin; Frank Chatel Captain Forecastle; Able Seaman Michael Regan; Marine Gunner Elijah Rayner, and an Inuit hunter from Greenland, named Hans Hendrik. All the men were crew members of Captain Nares's North Pole Expedition.

Lt Rawson, knowing J.J. Hand was a Roman Catholic, requested Dr Coppinger to read the Service. When it was concluded, they placed the twenty-eight-year-old Hand's body, wrapped in a makeshift canvas shroud, into the shallow grave. They covered the grave with broken ice, and Dr Coppinger hammered in half a wooden table top with an appropriate inscription carved on it as an improvised headstone.

The remains of Jim Hand and Captain Hall lie at Thank God Harbour, Polaris Bay, North Greenland. What series of tragic events had occurred to cause America's most successful explorer of that time, the distinguished Captain Charles Francis Hall, and the twenty-eight-year-old Irishman to lie beside each other in the isolated Arctic wastes more than a thousand miles from civilisation?

The explanation is in the narrative.

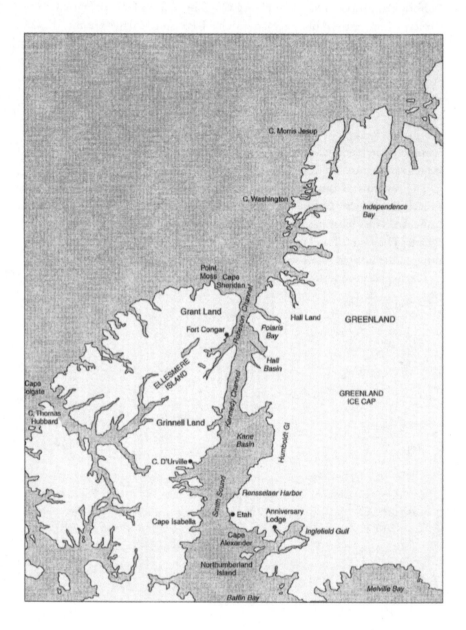

Introduction

When I was a young boy (in the late 1930s) I learned from my grandmother Mary Dunne, who raised me, that her uncle Jimmy Hand had died on an expedition to the North Pole and that the cause of his death was scurvy. Although his name was frequently mentioned in conversation at home, as a seven-year-old child its significance meant little to me, although clearly it meant a lot to my grandmother.

The Second World War broke out in 1939 and all of my uncles and aunts emigrated to England to seek employment. The name of Jim Hand faded from my mind. It was over sixty years later, in August 2004, when a cousin of mine, Jim Metcalfe drew my attention to a book written by Frank Nugent, entitled *Seek The Frozen Lands: Irish Explorers 1740-1922*. It tells the story of the contribution of Irish men to Polar exploration, and in it Frank Nugent details a doctor's report of Jim Hand's death over a period of three and a half weeks while on the expedition. Jim Metcalfe was also the custodian of Jim Hand's ships' papers. I found this information intriguing. From the book I now knew where, and when Jim Hand had died and the cause of death. But I didn't understand why he had died at the young age of twenty-eight years. Out of idle curiosity I decided to try to discover more about his background and the reason why he spent his dying days at 82°N, so close to the North Pole.

I began to read up on Arctic history and to my surprise, I began a journey, or should I say, a series of journeys, on heaving wooden sailing ships (floating ice freezers) through ferocious Arctic storms, dodging and weaving the ice-packs in unimaginable conditions, where man's mind and body were frequently stretched to the limits of endurance, and at times, beyond endurance. It was a world that I knew absolutely nothing about.

The Antarctic I knew a little about, the explorers Scott, our own Shackleton and Crean, but they all came on the polar scene many years after Jim Hand's death on the 1875-6 Expedition. I had no knowledge of the series of British expeditions to find the Northwest Passage or the North Pole, or of historic and heroic figures such as Frobisher, Baffin, Knight, Parry, and the many other British explorers too numerous to name. I knew nothing of the brave American

The view due west from River Dargle Estuary in Bray, *c.*1830.

explorers such as Dr Elisha Kent Kane, Dr Isaac Hayes, Captain Charles Francis Hall, or some of the lesser-known yet still heroic names, such as Hans Hendrik, the Eskimo hunter, Neil Petersen, the Danish guide, Captain George Tyson, and Captain Hall's dear Inuit friends Tookoolito and her husband Joe Ebeirbing. Then there was the long list of Irish explorers such as McClintock, Crozier, McClure, Kellet and others. When I began I knew virtually nothing about Greenland, of its inhabitants or its culture, or of the vastness of the Arctic tundra which is as big as Australia. I was also to learn of the 1875 George Nares Expedition, and how and why Jim Hand died.

If you enjoy adventure stories and you are not already an Arctic buff, there is a terrific range of reading material available, and I feel a twinge of guilt for naming only three books: *Seek The Frozen Lands* by Frank Nugent, *Ninety Degrees North* by Fergus Fleming, and *Life with the Esquimaux* by Captain Charles Francis Hall. *Buried in the Arctic Ice* covers a more specific period than those mentioned, but it was the most frenetic period of British and American Arctic exploration.

The Family Tree of James Hand

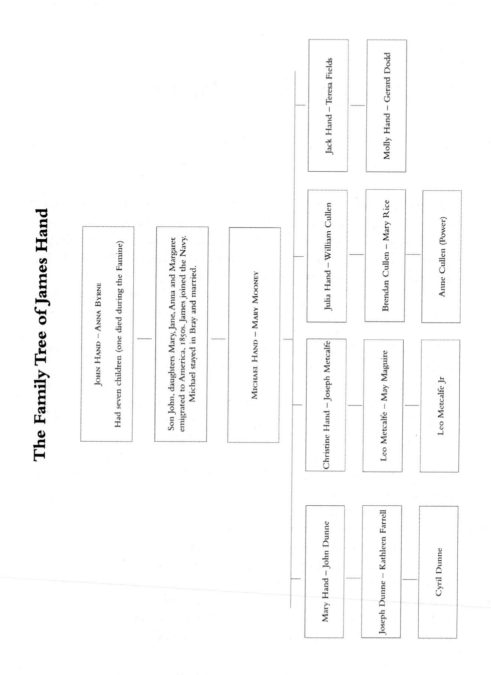

JOHN HAND – ANNA BYRNE

Had seven children (one died during the Famine)

Son John, daughters Mary, Jane, Anna and Margaret emigrated to America. 1850s James joined the Navy. Michael stayed in Bray and married.

MICHAEL HAND – MARY MOONEY

Mary Hand – John Dunne

Christine Hand – Joseph Metcalfe

Julia Hand – William Cullen

Jack Hand – Teresa Fields

Joseph Dunne – Kathleen Farrell

Leo Metcalfe – May Maguire

Brendan Cullen – Mary Rice

Molly Hand – Gerard Dodd

Cyril Dunne

Leo Metcalfe Jr

Anne Cullen (Power)

Chapter I

The Story Begins

This story begins in the town of Bray in Co. Wicklow, Ireland's garden county, in the early 1830s. The town of Bray was undeveloped. There was no harbour, no railway, no running water, no public lighting. The mud roads were deeply rutted and the paths unpaved. The population in 1831 was 2,590. Seapoint Road, as it is now known, was only a rough track through open land, which lead to Seymour Dock and the sea. The dock was one of the busiest locations in Bray at that time. Light craft unloaded cargo from offshore ships and consequently the area attracted a wide range of merchants and workers.

John and Anna Hand set up house on the Lord Meath estate on the lower Northwestern slopes of Bray Head. Anna had been raised on the nearby Powerscourt Estate, a majestic country residence in Enniskerry, one of Ireland's most picturesque villages. She was probably employed there as a servant girl, while John may have been an employee of Lord Meath. Their first child, John, was born in 1834, followed by Mary in 1837, Jane in 1839, Anna in 1841, Margaret in 1844, and James in 1847. A son was born, probably in 1848, and named Michael, but he died around January 1850. Another boy was born in the same year and he was also named Michael.

In Ireland during the eighteenth and early nineteenth centuries the vast majority of the population lived in squalid conditions. A typical peasant family resided in a dark smoky one- or two-room dwelling, with stone or mud walls, a mud floor from which dampness seeped, a thatched roof, a small front window, no toilet or running water, an open fire but no chimney. In 1841, 40 per cent of Irish homes were one-roomed cabins, while another 37 per cent had two to four rooms. Labourers lived on potatoes, buttermilk, cabbage and carrots. Those a little better off had bread, oatmeal, fish and milk. Fortunately there was one important food commodity in plentiful supply – the potato.

Inhabitants around the coasts of Ireland had for centuries profited enormously from the vast number of shipwrecks off the coasts, which tragically cost

PARISH OF BRAY.

Townlands and Occupiers.	Immediate Lessors.	Description of Tenement.	Area. (A. R. P.)			Net Annual Value. Land. (£ s. d.)	Net Annual Value. Buildings. (£ s. d.)	Net Annual Value. Total. (£ s.)
OLDCOURT—*con.*			A.	R.	P.	£ s. d.	£ s. d.	£ s.
John Grant, .	John K. Edwards, .	House, office, and land,	12	2	18	12 10 0	22 0 0	34 10
Vacant, .	John Grant, .	House, .				—	0 18 0	0 18
Michael Kelly, .	John K. Edwards, .	House, offices, and land,	11	1	14	11 15 0	9 0 0	20 15
James Connell, .	Same, .	Offices and land,	9	0	36	12 13 0	0 12 0	13 5
John Dalton, .	Same, .	Land, .	10	2	0	17 10 0	—	17 10
John Ledwidge, .	Same, .	House, office, and land,	12	2	19	21 10 0	3 0 0	24 10
James Callaghan, .	Robert Peel, .	Land, .	7	1	29	13 15 0	—	13 15
Patrick Boylan, .	Same, .	Land, .	8	3	5	15 10 0	—	15 10
Patrick Lalor, .	Same, .	Land, .	5	1	32	10 5 0	—	10 5
Ellen Weldon, .	Same, .	House, office, and land,	16	0	33	29 0 0	21 0 0	50 0
Robert Peel, .	In fee, .	House, office, and land,	17	1	17	36 5 0	28 0 0	64 5
Robert Peel, .	In fee, .	House, offices, and land,	9	2	7	19 15 0	50 0 0	69 15
VILLAGE OF NEW-TOWN VEVAY.								
Thomas Dempsey, .	John K. Edwards, .	Garden, .	0	1	38	1 5 0	—	1 5
Vacant, .	John Ferris, .	House, office, & garden,	0	0	15	0 7 0	4 8 0	4 15
Joseph Reilly, .	John K. Edwards, .	House and garden, .	0	0	10	0 5 0	1 10 0	1 15
Philip Fleming, .	Same, .	House and garden, .	0	0	7	0 3 0	1 7 0	1 10
John Murphy, .	James Cooney, .	House, .			—		1 0 0	1 0
Vacant, .	Same, .	House, .			—		1 0 0	1 0
John Redmond, .	Same, .	House, .			—		0 18 0	0 18
Vacant, .	Same, .	House, .			—		1 2 0	1 2
Vacant, .	Same, .	House, .			—		1 0 0	1 0
John Hand, .	Same, .	House, .			—		1 2 0	1 2
Daniel Carroll, .	Same, .	House, .			—		1 1 0	1 1
James Cooney, .	John K. Edwards, .	House, .			—		1 5 0	1 5
Michael Butler, .	James Cooney, .	House, .			—		1 6 0	1 6
Mary M'Adams, .	Thomas Byrne, .	House and garden, .	0	0	10	0 5 0	3 5 0	3 10
Cooke Lucas, .	William Jackson, .	House, offices, & garden,	0	0	14	0 10 0	8 10 0	9 0
William Grace, .	John K. Edwards, .	{ House, office, & garden,	0	0	9	0 5 0	10 0 0	} 11 5
		{ Office, .					1 0 0	
Rev. James Griffin, .	Same, .	{ House, office, and land,	0	0	8	0 5 0	8 0 0	} 9 5
		{ Office, .					1 0 0	
John Ferris, .	Robert Peel, .	{ Building ground & gar.	0	0	14	0 5 0	—	} 1 5
		{ Office, .					1 1 0	
Myles Byrne, .	John Ferris, .	House, .			—		1 10 0	1 10
John M'Adams, .	John K. Edwards, .	House and garden, .	0	0	14	0 6 0	1 10 0	1 16
Jane Popjoye, .	John Ferris, .	House, offices, & garden,	0	0	11	0 3 0	4 10 0	4 13
John Gibbons, .	Peter W. Jackson, .	House, offices, & garden,	0	0	10	0 5 0	3 10 0	3 15
Robert Crawley, .	William Jackson, .	House, office, & garden,	0	0	15	0 10 0	7 0 0	7 10

Primary valuation documents for the tenants of the parish of Bray, including John Hand, number ten.

many thousands of lives. The unemployed, or employed for that matter, successfully worked the beaches of Ireland. Bray would have been no different. Many shipping tragedies are recorded in local history. Seasonal storms were regarded as a blessing and provided rich reward for many a family in need.

In the year 1844, the year before the Great Famine, John and Anna had one son and four daughters all under ten years of age, living in a humble one- or two-room cabin. If the difficult living conditions and hardship described earlier were not bad enough, life for John and Anna Hand and their young family life was about to become even more arduous. Ireland was about to endure the calamity of the Great Famine of 1845–52, which would have a profound impact on every one of their lives.

The Famine was the most important event in the history of modern Ireland. It is estimated that over one million people died and almost two million more emigrated to foreign lands. The causes and the background politics have been rigorously debated down through the years. The subject is a deeply complex and an emotional one. It is not intended to re-open the debate in this narrative, but merely to give a brief outline of events leading up to it.

By the year 1800 the potato had become a staple food all the year round for the cottier (a tenant holding land as the highest bidder) and small-farm class. By 1841 there were over 500,000 cottiers, with 1,750,000 dependants. Prior to the famine, it was not unusual for a married couple to raise up to twenty children, but the mortality rate was high.

The population expanded rapidly in those parts of Ireland where cultivation was aided by access to hills (for rough grazing), to bogs (for turf) and to the seashore for seaweed, sand and seafood. For the poorest sections of society, however, the potato gradually replaced other foodstuffs and, together with skimmed milk or buttermilk, it became the main component of their daily diet. This was occasionally supplemented with fish, oatmeal, cabbage and carrots. By the 1840s, approximately two fifths of the Irish population, over three million people, were relying on the potato as their staple food.

Reports describing the appearance of a mysterious disease in the potato crops in various parts of Europe in 1845 were initially regarded with curiosity rather than alarm within Ireland. In the previous year a number of Irish newspapers had carried reports from American journals and newspapers concerning a disease that had attacked the potato crop there for the second consecutive year. In Ireland, however, there was little response to the news that the same disease had apparently spread to Europe in 1845.

No other country in Europe depended on the potato as extensively as did the people of Ireland. Apart from the vast quantities of potatoes consumed by the Irish population, potatoes were also extensively fed to pigs and farmyard fowl. During periods of scarcity, therefore, animals bore the initial brunt of the shortages.

There were reports of the appearance of the mysterious disease in the Isle of Wight and in the vicinity of Kent. *The Gardeners' Chronicle* quickly became the recognised authority on potato disease. They were unable to identify either the cause or the remedy. The disease had no name but was variously referred to as 'the disease', 'the blight', 'distemper', 'the rot', 'the murrain' or 'the blackness'. It was thought to have originated in South America from where, facilitated by improvements in sea transport, it eventually made its way to Europe.

The blight had also appeared in Scotland, Belgium and Holland. At the beginning of September 1845 sightings of the disease were also being reported in Ireland. On 16 September 1845 an official announcement was made that the potato murrain had unequivocally declared itself in Ireland. It posed the question – where will Ireland be in the event of a universal potato rot?

The answer was tragically obvious. For a population of eight million people whose staple diet was attacked by *Phytophthora infestans*, there could only be one outcome – catastrophe.

In 1845 it was estimated that one half of the Irish potato crop was unfit for consumption.

On 20 February 1846 a decision was taken to form relief committees. During the spring and summer, over 700 relief committees were established according to the instructions of the Government. In the early months of 1847 there were increasing reports of deaths by disease and starvation in all parts of Ireland. Hordes of unemployed and dispossessed people crowded into the workhouses. Orphaned children and deserted wives formed a huge percentage of the permanent poorhouse population.

The unprecedented increase in mortality, disease and emigration in 1847 was remembered in folk memory as the Famine Year or Black '47. It was known as the year of the coffin ships and it has become infamous as the worst year in Ireland's history.

It was on the last day of August of that year when Jim opened his eyes for the first time to a warm, welcoming loving family. At the time his brother John was aged thirteen, Mary ten, Jane eight, Anna six, and Margaret three. How the family survived in such dire circumstances no one will ever know. But survive they did. However, having recovered from the devastating effects of the famine, John and Anna were to experience a further tragedy with the death of their infant son Michael in 1849 or 1850. The cause of death is not certain but it was probably due to the fever epidemic which was prevalent at that time. In December of 1850 another son was born to John and Anna. They named him Michael also.

Irish people had emigrated to North America as far back as the early 1700s, a trickle at first, which grew steadily until the 1830s when the numbers increased substantially. That trickle became a torrent of humanity in the years between 1846 and 1852. It is estimated that over one million Irish people crossed the Atlantic in 5,000 dangerous, leaky, and over-crowded vessels. They sailed from Dublin, Drogheda, Newry, Belfast, Derry, Westport, Sligo, Galway, Tralee, Queenstown (Cobh), Youghal, Waterford and Wexford directly to America, arriving in Boston, New York, Baltimore, New Orleans, or Halifax, St John and Quebec in Canada. Canada was then known as British North America (Ellis Island did not become a point of entry until many years later).

The ships varied in size, safety and comfort. Needless to say safety and comfort were in short supply. Many Famine ships were tiny in size (some ships were only the length of two double-decker buses bumper to bumper), but from historical reports all were grossly overcrowded, with crew numbers in single figures.

Prior to the Irish Famine the passenger ships sailing to America and Canada from Britain and Ireland were of a reasonable and satisfactory quality in both catering and comfort, but demand soon became so great that the trade attracted unsavoury characters, crooked agents, and a new breed of ship owners who were only in the business to make a financial killing. To cope with the sudden increase in demand, unscrupulous ship owners converted ships of every shape and size to passenger ships. Ships' carpenters hastily raised bunks twenty inches wide in the holds of ships that lacked portholes or ventilation, and where twenty-four-hour darkness prevailed. These ships were totally unsuitable for the purpose of carrying passengers.

Occasionally a compassionate captain might relent and allow small numbers of passengers at a time on deck for some fresh air, otherwise they were confined below deck for days on end. There was also a choice of larger and more comfortable ships. Some shipping companies had begun to build ships specifically for the wealthier emigrant trade, as not all the travellers were of small means.

John and Anna Hand's oldest son, John, had been available for work from the age of ten or eleven. We don't know the precise date on which young John sailed to America, but the family legend is that John was among the first of those affected by the Famine to leave Ireland and sail to New York.

There was a choice of two fares to America and Canada – standard class or steerage. Standard-class passengers had berths and could walk on the deck. Steerage passengers were crowded together below decks and were not permitted to use the top deck. The cheapest single steerage ticket to New York cost £3.10 (US $10), including landing fees. This money covered the dues that might be payable by the captain at the port before any passengers were allowed to disembark.

Dishonest ships' captains contributed to the misery of the emigrants by taking on additional passengers and pocketing the money. This explains the false figures supplied by the captains and why so many ships were grossly overcrowded.

John had to sail 3,000 miles across the Atlantic to the land of opportunity, but before he reached it he and other emigrants had to undergo a voyage full of tension: fear of the punishing voyage itself, the dread of hunger and sickness, the stress of protecting a few unsecured precious personal possessions (a set of tools for instance), and the misery of seasickness. He and his fellow passengers risked their lives in terrible weather, bitter cold, storms and gales. Apart from the risk of dying from disease and the many other discomforts of the voyage, passengers on emigrant ships had to face the danger of icebergs. A large numbers of emigrants lost their lives in collisions with icebergs, either by drowning or by being crushed. The sailing ships of the mid-nineteenth century were built from wood and had no engine power to enable them to take evasive action from huge icebergs. They had only the most primitive navigational aids to assist them in an emergency (Morse code and telegraph technology had been invented in the late 1840s but was not available to ships until some time later). Wooden sailing ships in a storm were simply not equipped to avoid icebergs.

With John's departure began the first of a series of heartbreaking goodbyes for the Hand family. Throughout the famine father and son had shared great sadness. The Hand family experienced for the first time what so many heart-broken Irish families had suffered previously on the eve of the departure of a loved one. This lamentation became known as the 'American Wake'.

There were many harrowing stories of the Famine-period crossings. Some unfortunates were swindled of what little money they had by sharps and con-fidence tricksters on the waterfront or unscrupulous crewmen, who were, in most cases, indifferent to the health and comfort of the passengers. Many of those who were duped and intending to emigrate were forced to return to their homes, their plight even worse than when they started out. But passengers learned quickly; one of the measures they took was to sew their money inside their jackets or trousers.

In the earliest days of transatlantic travel, steerage passengers brought their own food store to supplement the ship's rations of bread, biscuit, flour, rice, oatmeal or potatoes. Each passenger was allowed six pints of water per day for washing, cooking, and drinking. If the journey took longer than the estimated period, the already-low water ration was further reduced causing additional hardship to the unfortunate passengers. John Hand would have had brought some food supplies of his own, mostly oatcakes – they remained fresh for longer periods than bread or potato cakes. Passengers were required to provide their own bedding which was usually made of straw, and utensils for eating and drinking. Below decks, hearths for cooking were provided. These hearths were boxes of bricks, a crude form of barbecue. No fires were allowed in rough weather on Atlantic crossings, which could easily mean no hot food or drink for days.

Mortality rates on the ships were extremely high; tens of thousands died on the journeys or soon after they disembarked, mostly from typhus. Before they even stepped aboard, many people were infected with the disease, which was rampant and spread like wildfire in the overcrowded conditions. The dead were gently slid overboard. Ashore, many a healthy doctor, nurse, priest, or policeman succumbed to the disease while trying to save the lives of the new emigrants.

Before they landed, there was one more chapter to be added to their cata-logue of horrors – the cleaning out of the holds. As each ship approached its port of entry it was the custom to throw the refuse of the voyage overboard. The ship travelled through water filled with foul-smelling straw from the makeshift beds, tattered rags and rubbish, floating broken barrels of excrement, and decomposing floating bodies (few could afford the price of a funeral on landing). With so many ships unloading this filth at the same time it was a sight and stench that remained with the new arrivals for the rest of their lives.

We know John Hand survived the journey. The next step in the procedure was to clear the medical and emigration inspection, and later he had to run the gauntlet of the rogues who were lined up on the quayside to leech off the innocent and gullible; unscrupulous confidence tricksters offering to guide the new arrivals to crooked landlords, or offering help to carry their few precious possessions which in many instances quickly disappeared.

The relief and confidence that John savoured as he made his way from the bustling wharves to the residential and commercial districts received a severe jolt when he read job advertisements accompanied by the phrase NINA – No Irish Need Apply. John and his fellow emigrants were not made welcome in some quarters; the huge numbers of newcomers were resented by the earlier European settlers and native Americans and seen as a threat to their own employment. Consequently in the early years of emigration many of the Irish were compelled to work in menial jobs for lower wages or forced to travel further afield to seek employment. They toiled on roads, railways, tunnels, bridges, and canals. Like other emigrant populations that created ghettoes, the Irish were no different, wherever they went they formed their own ghettoes. This natural clannishness of the Irish in looking after their own, in employment, commerce and politics soon became a new phenomenon in the United States.

As the Irish became integrated into the American way of life, they worked in the construction industry, joined the police forces, fire departments, and commercial enterprises. It is generally accepted that well over 150,000 Irish men fought in the American Civil War (1861–1865). They fought in both the Union and Confederate armies, while others became prominent in Government departments, trade unions, politics, and in the religious orders. The newly arrived women also played their part, becoming nurses, seamstresses, teachers and domestics. But again, like emigrants from other countries, the Irish were no different in that they also had their share of hoodlums, gangsters, and crooked politicians.

Mary and Jane Hand were next to emigrate, probably around 1855, when they were aged eighteen and sixteen respectively, it was much safer for the pair to travel together. More than likely John sent home the boat fare, as was customary at the time. John would also have made the necessary arrangements for accommodation and employment on their arrival. They settled in New York and started making preparations for the arrival of Anna and Margaret in the late 1850s or early 1860s.

Once again there was another sad parting for the remaining members of the Hand family. By now John, Mary and Jane were making life a little more comfortable for those who were still at home by sending money to their parents. But now it was Anna and Margaret's time to bid goodbye. Only Jim and his young brother Michael remained at home. It must have been a bewildering and traumatic period in all their lives.

There is every reason to believe the Hand family prospered in New York as well, if not better, than most. There were five of them to tend to one another's needs – a huge advantage – and they were young and energetic. It is known that they settled in New York because in the early years they corresponded with their parents and brother Michael in Bray, and in around the year 1900, Agnes (aged sixteen), the youngest daughter of Michael Hand decided she wanted to join her uncle John and her aunts in America. She arrived safely and apparently everything went well for a while. But things began to go awry in her personal life. Still a teenager she began a love affair with a ne'er-do-well Irishman, who was also fighting a losing battle with alcohol. Her uncle John, it seems, could not get her to see sense and wrote to her father, his brother Michael in Bray to alert him to this fact. Michael decided to take matters into his own hands and arranged to sail to America immediately to deal with the Irishman who was at the heart of the problem. By the time Michael received John's letter, which would have taken a month to arrive, and Michael spent

A copy of the birth certificate of James Hand, born 31 August 1847 and baptised on 13 September 1847 in the church of the Holy Redeemer, Bray.

Michael Hand of Bray

Michael Hand, younger brother of Jim, pictured *c.* 1910.

another month travelling to New York, Agnes had wisely broken off the relationship. Unfortunately it took Michael another two years to earn sufficient wages to send money back home to his wife Mary, and to raise the fare for his return to Ireland.

The headstrong Agnes eventually did marry, and in 1931 the Metcalfe family received a letter from a son of hers, who was a soldier in the US Army. Apart from Agnes, there is no information on the Hand family's life in America.

However, back in Bray, life went on for the four remaining members of the Hand family. Perhaps, like so many other families in Ireland, their financial situation had improved, with money arriving from the emigrant relatives in America.

In the mid-1850s, Jim was attending (or should have been attending) school on Seapoint Road overlooking Seymour Dock at the only National School for Catholic boys in Bray. As a young boy in Bray, looking in the direction of the beautiful Killiney and Dublin Bays from the top of Bray Head, and seeing a floating forest of tall masts and furled sails moving in or out of Dublin Port and Dún Laoghaire, it is easy to understand why Jim became one of those who went to sea.

He probably became friendly with ships' crews and quayside workers, and perhaps in the early stages ran errands and did odd jobs. Thus contact with foreign sailors began. He may have listened to stories of far away places and mysteries of the sea. If that is a correct supposition he would have become aware of the disappearance in 1845, of Sir John Franklin's Arctic Expedition. For sailors and seafarers around the world in the 1850s, it was the greatest mystery in maritime history up to that point.

By January of 1862, Jim was fourteen years and five months old. John, Mary, Jane, Anna, and Margaret were settled in New York. If he had intended to emigrate, America would have been the obvious choice, with a ready-made family to attend to his welfare. But he turned it down, and decided to join the British Navy instead. This decision must have caused his parents great heartache. The Royal Navy was renowned for its harsh discipline, sub-standard food, cramped living conditions, and above all, its awful pay.

Men and boys went to sea for many reasons, usually to make a living, but there were other motives as well. There is the irresistible attraction to ships and the sea in us all. The experienced seaman continued to return to sea despite it being such a hard life. Living with the terrible danger and hardship, many sailors believed they truly belonged on the decks and in the rigging of wind ships. It was the one place on earth where they felt truly at home and respected, where they could be depended upon by their shipmates to do what had to be done on-board a ship – under any conditions.

What his parents John and Anna thought about six of their seven children leaving home, perhaps never to return, will never be known, but none of the farewells can have been more emotional than John and Anna's tearful goodbyes to their fourteen-year-old son Jim, on 26 January 1862.

Having bade a sorrowful farewell to his parents and younger brother Michael, he stepped aboard his first ship, the HMS *Ajax*, a coastguard ship based in Dún Laoghaire. The *Ajax* was a wooden-hulled sailing ship armed with seventy-eight guns. The original *Ajax* sank in a collision between Bray Head and Wicklow Head in 1861. Captain Boyd lost his life in the tragedy.

When a new boy sailor arrived on-board he received boots, stockings, a trousers, a couple of rough working shirts, a jumper, a blue Navy jacket, a cap, a set of oilskins and a pair of wellington boots.

He washed and in all probability was deloused and was allocated a hammock space in the narrow confines of the cramped, overcrowded and badly ventilated lower deck. There was no dining furniture. To utilise space, tea chests were used for dining tables, seating and storage. These chests were secured to the floor and also served variety of useful purposes, for off-duty letter writing or recreational games such as cards or board games. In all probability there were many rats for company.

The food may not have been top quality. The boy, before he was much older, would become aware of the old saying among sailors, 'God sent the food, the devil sent the cooks.'

For the newcomer, the novelty of his hammock soon wore off, crowded in by rough and hardened seamen who had long ago adjusted to the rhythms of sea life. Among the first of these is sleep deprivation, but in time he would become accustomed to it. He slept in a fug of tobacco smoke in an already badly ventilated, darkened lower deck, lit only by candle light or oil lamps. To disturb his sleep there would have been the sounds of other off-duty crew members; the noises of shouting, singing, raucous laughter and men eating their meals off the tea chests.

The four-hour-on, four-hour-off routine meant that a seaman got no more than three hours rest or so at any one time. All his other activities had to be done during his off-watch; eating, washing, repairing clothing, collecting his water ration and ensuring that his oilskins and body lashings were in a good state of repair. In the event of an 'all hands on deck' order, his off-watch could be curtailed or eliminated at any time.

On 3 February 1862 Jim Hand was transferred from the *Ajax* and travelled to Southampton to serve for the next fourteen months on the HMS *Boscawen*. The HMS *Boscawen* had been launched on 3 April 1844, a triple-deck wooden-hulled sailing ship of 2,212 tons armed with seventy guns, and had served in

North America, the West Indies and the Baltic before being deployed as a training ship for boy sailors.

The *Boscawen* was named in honour of Admiral Edward Boscawen. Born in Cornwall in 1711, Boscawen joined the Navy as a young boy and received rapid promotion and distinguished himself in many battles. In 1757 he was Vice Admiral of the Red. As the Commander-in-Chief at Portsmouth, it is claimed in historical biographies that he played an important role in the trial and execution of Admiral John Byng. It would have been his duty to sign the order of execution of his fellow Admiral. Admiral John Byng had been charged with neglect of duty, a charge that fell under the Twelfth Article of War and carried an automatic death penalty. He had been ordered to relieve the French siege of St Philip's Castle in Minorca. It seems when Byng was positioning his ships in line for an attack, he was distracted and made a tactical error. Duc de Richelieu, who commanded the French Fleet, destroyed Byng's leading ships and captured Port Mahon. Byng's defence was that he had been unable to reassert control of the battle due to changing wind conditions, and he had to return to England. Admiral John Byng was arrested at Portsmouth in July 1756.

The *Boscawen* had been converted into a training ship for boy seamen and had arrived at Portlands Road in early February 1862. The basic training of a boy sailor lasted anywhere from nine to fifteen months. Jim would have been one of the first arrivals to the new training ship, arriving on 4 February. It was a swift introduction to a harsh regime, scrubbing and washing hammocks, learning to mend clothes, cleaning, washing down and painting the ship. The boys were engaged in physical drills, gymnastics and fire prevention exercises on the ship. Jim learned gunnery and ammunition instruction, and became part of a fire brigade which could be called ashore in an emergency. For this service boys were paid three pence a week pocket money. Punishment on the ship was severe, flogging for men, and birching for boys. In 1866, it is recorded that two boys each received twenty-four cuts of the birch. Boys attended Sunday Services, and in summer were granted shore leave, while dockhands joined the ship to carry out maintenance and refits.

Jim began to learn the essential skills of seamanship, and about the strange new world of heights – looking up the 200ft to the top of the main mast, aware he could be ordered to climb it regularly, perhaps in 60 knot winds, in storms, on rolling seas in pitch black darkness, without a safety net. Jim Hand learned a new nautical vocabulary: 'Loose the stops', 'Grab the leach rope', 'Pass the shank painter', 'Pull the jib downhaul', 'Clew up the topsail'.

The routine duties of catheading an anchor, fleeting its cable, securing a reef point, finding a peak halyard at clustered pin-tail, putting a long splice in a throat halyard, renewing a bolt rope on a sail, and parting a rigging lanyard in the prescribed manner would all be part and parcel of learning new sailing skills.

In the following years he served on a range of ships, on gunboats, flagships (a ship carrying an admiral), frigates (escorts to ships on the line in battle), revenue cutters (chasing smugglers), schooners, and on coastguard ships, namely the *Royal George*, based in Dún Laoghaire, for six months in 1866, all the while gaining modest promotion from boy sailor, second class, to the rank of Leading Seaman. From his papers it appears he became a very capable seaman, each ship's captain had signed his discharge as good or very good. There was one blemish however; he lost a stripe and was demoted to Able Seaman. The reason is somewhat unclear, but it appears he may have refused to transfer to another ship. Why he refused we do not know.

He learned the lessons countless sailors before him had understood: the sea is profoundly seductive, and its rhythm seeps into your very soul. The stillness of dawn on a calm sea, the rising sun, the creaking of timber, the rhythmical sound of ropes chafing together, the sound of gentle waves lapping against the hull, the sunrises and the ever-changing sunsets, the sensation of sun, wind, and spray on the face … always heading somewhere new, leaving the world and your cares behind, living in the moment, the constant awareness in a cycle and movement of nature sometimes frighteningly dangerous, and totally out of one's control, the limitless freedom, the vastness of the oceans the awesome beauty of a tropical storm. The auroras!

It is unclear from his ships' papers if he visited home. They reveal that from January 1862 when he enlisted until 9 May 1875, there was not a single day he was unattached from a ship. However, in 1866 he was serving on the *Royal George*, which replaced the *Ajax* in Dún Laoghaire, and so he was based there

HM Yacht *Royal George*.

HMS *Revenge* at
Queenstown (Cobh),
Co. Cork.

for six months. It is probable during that period he made the six-mile journey
to visit his parents, and it is possible there were other occasions during his service when his ship was in dry dock and he availed of shore leave.

Detailed extracts from Jim Hand's papers:

HMS *Ajax*
Enlisted as a Boy sailor, second class on 26 January 1862.
Served until 3 February 1862.

HMS *Boscawen*
4 February 1862–7 April 1863.

HMS *Revenge*
8 April 1863–20 May 1863.
(The *Revenge* was launched in April 1859. Wooden hull, armed with
ninety-one guns, served in the Mediterranean, North America, and the
West Indies.)

HMS *Cockatrice*
21 May 1863–8 February 1866.
(Launched 1860. Wooden hull, armed with two guns, a ships tender or lighter,
served in the Mediterranean.)

HMS *Liverpool*
9 February 1866–March 1866.
(Launched 1860. Wooden hull, thirty-nine guns. Served in North America, the
West Indies and the Channel squadron.)

James Hand's ships' papers.

HMS *Royal George*
13 March 1866–5 September 1866.
(Launched September 1827. Wooden hull, propulsion sail, 120 guns.)

HMS *Zealous*
6 September 1866–18 January 1870.
(Launched March 1864. Wooden hull, screw propulsion, central battery iron-clad, twenty guns. Served in the Pacific.)

HMS *Revenge*
19 January 1870–22 March 1870.

HMS *Excellent*
23 March 1870–2 December 1870.
(Launched 1810. Wooden hull propelled by sail, 104 guns. A gunnery training ship based in Portsmouth.)

HMS *Immortalite*
3 December 1870–12 October 1872.
(Launched 1859. Wooden hull, screw propulsion, fifty-one guns. Served in the Mediterranean, North America, and the West Indies.)

Certificate of the service of James Hand in the Royal Navy.

HMS *Excellent*

13 October 1872-21 March 1873.

HMS *Penelope*

22 March 1873-21 April 1875.

(Launched 1867. Propulsion screw, hull composite, eleven guns. Served in the Channel Fleet.)

HMS *Duncan*

22 April 1875–9 May 1875.

(Launched 1811. Propulsion sail. Wooden hull, seventy-four guns. Served as a coastguard ship.)

The Thunder Box

The HMS *Royal George* was based in Dún Laoghaire with Jim Hand on-board from 13 March 1866 to 6 September of the same year. More detailed research reveals she was launched as a three-decker sailing ship in 1827, and converted to screw in 1853. Two hundred and six feet in length, she carried a crew of 950 men and 120 guns (these old-fashioned cannon guns required up to a dozen men to operate each gun successfully and safely). The ship served as a troop carrier in 1856 during the Russian War and returned with troops to England during the Crimean campaign. (One wonders how, with a crew of 950 men, did they accommodate the troops on a ship 206 feet long?)

In 1860, six years before Jim Hand's time, she was cut down to a two-decker of eighty-nine guns. It is almost impossible to comprehend how the men coped with the sanitary conditions on-board the ship, but fortunately there was the ingenious 'thunder box' – a portable toilet. Used by seamen for centuries, it was a barrel-shaped structure, inside of which was a frame for a toilet seat with arm rests and a floor with an exit for the waste. These boxes were lashed together with strong ropes and lowered over the side, bow or stern of the ship. The need for thunder boxes is apparent when one considers the number of 950 crewmen living on the *Royal George*, and there can be little doubt that the thunder boxes helped to reduce the long queues for the toilets. Using the facility in rough seas could be a white-knuckle rollercoaster experience, but in ideal conditions the thunder box was of great practical use – and it was appropriately named.

After thirteen unbroken years of service at sea, Jim Hand had become, in the words of Conrad, writing while he was still a seaman, 'one of the rootless men whose home is always with the ship; and so is their country – the sea'.

The twenty-eight-year-old James Hand was ready for the next – and what was to be the final – voyage of his life. But to appreciate why he joined the expedition of Captain Nares to the North Pole in 1875, it is necessary to first look at what preceded that expedition, and to try to understand what drove so many men to choose terrible hardship, anxiety, and uncertainty in pursuit of the Northwest Passage and the North Pole.

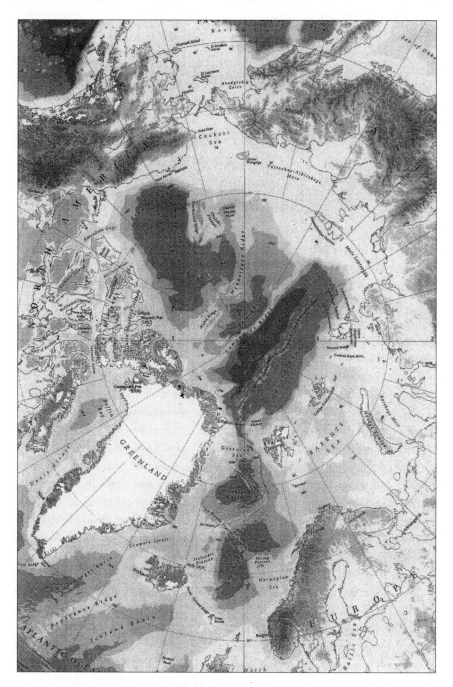

The Arctic from above.

Chapter II

Sir John Franklin

Cabot, Frobisher, Davis, and Hudson are only some of the illustrious British names in Arctic exploration; there are many others too numerous to name. At great personal sacrifice and the cost of many fatalities, these brave men charted the gulfs, bays, sounds, inlets, straits, islands, and peninsulas of the Arctic. Their names and deeds will forever retain an honoured place in their country's history. Britain considered the achievements and contributions their explorers made over the centuries entitled them to deem the Arctic waters to be their domain.

In the sixteenth century, beginning with John Cabot and continuing with Martin Frobisher, the quest for a sea route through or around America had begun. The successors of Columbus slowly realised the massive continental dimensions of the new lands across the Atlantic. Navigators had searched for a route to the lands of the Orient and their fabulous riches from the Atlantic by way of Greenland, northern Canada, Alaska and Siberia. A shorter route would eliminate the need to round the treacherous Cape Horn and allow rich merchant ships embarking from and returning to the British Isles to avoid attack from privateers or warring enemies when passing through French, Spanish and Portuguese waters. Subsequent explorers, whose names adorn the maps of North America, also searched in vain for the elusive passage. Men such as John Davis (1585), Henry Hudson (1607–11), and William Baffin (1661) explored the Canadian Arctic.

The search in a frozen wilderness for the Northwest Passage became an obsession; men and ships battling against hopeless odds to seek the most dangerous shortcut in maritime history.

In the first decades of the nineteenth century British whale-fishing off Greenland was reaching the peak of its productivity. The whalers worked in an area that might be called the Near North. Whales were eagerly sought for oil, bone and other valuable by-products. In the 1830s the industry boomed enormously, adding further to Britain's trading empire. A new fashion accessory was designed – the whalebone corset. More importantly, London's streetlights were entirely powered by whale oil before the invention of coal gas. The price for a whale rose to £2,500. It is therefore not surprising that the British Navy was constantly protecting its interests in the Near North.

One man in Britain played an outstanding role in promoting polar exploration. That man was John Barrow. As Secretary of the British Admiralty, Sir John Barrow (1764-1848) was convinced that a Northwest Passage existed. Finding it became his obsession. He was also engaged in the promotion of exploration in Africa, Canada and Australia.

In 1815 the Napoleonic Wars were drawing to a close, and with the coming of peace, many of Britain's young naval officers were made redundant. Sir John Barrow proposed Arctic exploration as the ideal means of employing these naval officers and men made idle by the ending of the wars.

In 1818 he sent an expedition to profile the Canadian Arctic. Edward Parry was second in command to Captain James Ross. The following year Captain Parry led the *Hecla* and the *Fury* and devised a method which enabled ships to overwinter in Arctic conditions. Parry attempted to reach the North Pole in 1820, equipped with boat-sledges which the crew man-hauled across the ice-pack. They reached a record north of 82°45'. They then realised that no matter how hard they tried, the icepack was drifting south faster than they could man-haul, and for that reason, in Parry's view, the North Pole was unreachable.

Royal Navy explorer James Ross led an expedition to the Arctic regions in 1840. Two other notable attempts were made. In 1853-4 Sir Hugh Willoughby of the Moscovy Company led two ships to disaster. He and his crew froze to death on the voyage to Finland from Archangelsk. William Berents, the Dutch explorer, also came to grief in the sea which now bears his name.

Sir John Barrow had overseen eight expeditions to the Arctic and considered many of the brightest officers involved in Arctic explorations his protégés; high among these were Albert Markham, Edward Parry, John Franklin, James Clark Ross, John Ross and Sherard Osborn. This elite group became famously known as 'Barrow's Boys'. Hence between the years 1817 and 1845, and thanks to Barrow's untiring energy and vision, an almost unbroken series of efforts was made by Britain to penetrate the frozen regions within the Arctic Circle. In 1843, at seventy-nine years of age Barrow knew the next expedition would be his last attempt to successfully end a 300-year search.

Sir John Franklin

The name of Franklin is now inseparably linked with the Arctic. Thanks to numerous books, newspaper articles and television documentaries, many have become aware of the failed Franklin Expedition of 1845. But what is known of his background and of his earlier naval exploits? What drove him on?

One thing is certain, John Franklin packed more adventure into the early part of his life than many men would do in ten lifetimes. He was born in a modest two-storey house in the small country town of Spilsby, Lincolnshire, on 16 April 1786, the ninth of twelve children. He was educated, but being the son of a shopkeeper his prospects were not considered great. He was attracted to a seafaring life from an early age and, against his father's wishes, joined the British Navy at the age of fourteen. Straightaway he took part in the Battle of Copenhagen in 1801 and then joined the HMS *Investigator* on an expedition to explore the largely uncharted coast of New Holland (Australia) under Captain Matthew Flinders, an uncle by marriage who taught him navigation.

In 1802-3 Flinders circumnavigated Australia but failed to complete his survey because of an outbreak of scurvy among the crew and the ship's lack of seaworthiness. The *Investigator* was abandoned in Sydney and the crew set sail for England on the *Porpoise* in August 1803, but she was wrecked on a reef after six days. The crew found refuge on a sandbank for six weeks while Flinders sailed for help in a lifeboat. Franklin eventually reached Canton (China) in a merchant ship and continued his journey to England on an East Indiaman, arriving in the summer of 1804.

Franklin returned to duty on the *Bellerophon*, which was engaged in the blockade of Brest and was later used as an escort for troop ships sailing to Malta. In October 1805 at the Battle of Trafalgar, Franklin acted as midshipman in charge of signals. He was wounded and thereafter suffered permanent deafness in one ear.

Franklin was promoted to lieutenant in 1808 and on the *Bedford* in September 1814 took part in the winter offensive against New Orleans. His meritorious record and the experience he gained under Flinders placed him at the forefront of opportunity for Arctic exploration.

Two Arctic expeditions sailed in 1818 to seek the Northwest Passage; one under the command of John Ross, the other under Commander David Buchan. Buchan attempted to cross the Arctic Ocean from Spitzbergen. Franklin captained one of the ships, the *Trent*, but the expedition ended in failure after six months of futile attempts to penetrate the pack ice.

Undaunted, back in England John Barrow despatched two more expeditions, the first under Edward Parry to continue the search for the Northwest Passage. Parry was successful in determining that Lancaster Sound opened a route towards the west.

The second expedition, to be led by John Franklin, was to set out overland from Hudson Bay to explore and chart the north coast of the American continent. The plan posed many difficulties for Franklin. The coast had been sighted by explorers only twice before – by Samuel Hearne in 1771 and by Alexander Mackenzie at the Mackenzie River delta in 1789 – and it lay hundreds of miles north of the territory explored by fur traders.

A prior arrangement had been made with British Government agents and the Hudson Bay Company at their headquarters in Fenchurch Street, London, that an escort to convey Franklin to the edge of the unknown territory would be granted. Supplies and equipment for him and his men for the coastal journey would also be provided by company representatives.

The Hudson Bay Company had been established in London in 1668 by two French traders, Pierre Esprit Radisson and Medard Des Groseilliers from Canada. They had sought financial backing from the French Secretary of State to develop trade with the American natives and the Inuit in the Hudson Bay area, but were refused. In Boston they were advised to go to England to promote their plan. The pair made their way to London to elicit support and were successful. A group of investors founded 'The Governor and Company of Adventurers of England to trade into Hudson's Bay', which became better known as Hudson Bay Company (HBC). The investors commissioned two ships, the *Nonsuch*, with Groseilliers on-board, and the *Eaglet*, with Radisson on-board, to explore the potential of the territory. On 5 June 1668, the two ships sailed from Deptford, London, but the *Eaglet* was forced back from the coast of Ireland. The *Nonsuch* continued to St James in Hudson's Bay, where contact was made with the native Indians who came from the interior to trade. When the vessel returned to England with a cargo of valuable furs and news of an abundance of beaver, the influential investors quickly realised the financial potential of the region.

On 2 May 1670 the King of England granted the HBC an exclusive right to trade in the huge territory known as Rupert's Land (so named after one of the principals of the company), now western and north Canada (roughly 1.5 million square miles). The HBC established a network of trading posts around the shores of Hudson Bay. They built the first of many forts at Albany, York and Moose. The forts were small, wooden two-storey buildings, protected by cannon guns, which stood at the mouths of the important rivers down which the native people, Cree, Chipewyans, Dene and Inuit, came in their canoes bringing skins and furs to trade. When the company began to encounter strong competition from French traders they were compelled to set up trading posts inland. Apart from the period of conflict with the French, in the decades that followed trade flourished with the natives, mostly with the Cree at first. The Cree were known as 'home Indians' because they lived near the trading posts. The Chipewyan were known as 'Northern Indians' as they inhabited lands to the north of the Cree. (The Inuit lived on lands further north.)

A Portent for John Franklin

James Knight was born in England, he joined the Hudson Bay Company in 1676 as a carpenter. He rose swiftly through the ranks was appointed Chief Factor at Fort Albany. Knight learned from the natives, through a Chipewyan woman interpreter named Thanadelthur, that there was yellow metal to be found, and also a passage through the sea many miles to the north. James Knight returned to England in 1718 with this news, and successfully persuaded the company Governor, Sir Bibye Lake, to finance an expedition. In brief, Lake ordered Knight 'to voyage to the Straits of Anian and discover gold and other commodities'. The passage that was then known as the Anian Straits, is now known as the Northwest Passage.

On 5 June 1719, James Knight's Expedition set sail from Gravesend on the Thames Estuary. It comprised of two small vessels, the *Albany* of 100 tons, and the sloop *Discovery* of 40 tons. They reached St James Bay in the south of Hudson Bay before continuing their voyage, but neither the ships nor their crews were ever seen again. It seemed they vanished off the face of the earth. Ken McGoogan's *Ancient Mariner* discusses the mysterious fates of the ships, explaining that traces were found to the north-west of Hudson Bay. He surmises that the ships were trapped or wrecked in the ice and that the crew probably attempted to cross the strait, either on foot or by rowing, in 1720.

Franklin's Expedition

To Franklin's great disappointment the HBC contacts were only established as far as the Northwest Territories, and the supply lines were tenuous to say the least. The Company's representatives were busy expanding their own trade and considered Franklin's Expedition a low priority, which did little to help his cause.

Franklin had just three months to prepare for an expedition that had few precedents in the history of exploration. Communications were almost non-existent, advice was scarce and often misleading or excessively optimistic, and he had received assurances of greater assistance from the HBC than they could actually provide.

The party selected to accompany him consisted of George Back (a surgeon and a naturalist), John Richardson, seaman John Hepburn, and midshipman Hood. The party set out on the HBC supply ship *Prince of Wales* on 23 May 1819 and wintered at York Factory, a fort in Manitoba. The small party then made its way to Fort Chipewyan, Alberta, where Franklin recruited Indian guides and hunters. The group then continued along the Yellowknife River into unexplored territory, and built winter quarters which they named Fort Enterprise.

There Franklin encountered further problems, arising mainly from the acute shortage of essential supplies. Frustrated, he began to respond with tactless and entirely uncharacteristic displays of aggression. His manner served only to diminish his authority over the Indians and voyagers and deprived him of much of the goodwill shown earlier by the fur traders. His demands to the HBC and the Indians for supplies, accompanied by high-handed threats and accusations, met a cold, resentful response. George Back, on a winter journey to Fort Chipewyan, did manage to recover enough of the supplies left at York Factory to secure the expedition's immediate future. The party, consisting of twenty men and two Indian canoes, set out down the Coppermine River for the coast in early July 1821, with critically limited food and ammunition. Franklin's hopes rested on the co-operation of the Inuit. But his approach to them was less than diplomatic and they fled.

By 18 August they had only reached Kent Peninsula, where unrest among the men was turning into rebellion. Their supplies being almost exhausted, Franklin decided to turn back. The canoes were too badly damaged to permit a return by sea, so they set off with one canoe up the Hood River. They were soon reduced to travelling on foot and the journey quickly became a terrible ordeal. Frequently they had only lichen to eat; cold and exhaustion further weakened them.

Nine men died of starvation and exposure; one of the party was later suspected of cannibalism. The accused shot Hood and was executed by Richardson. Further distress awaited the survivors when they reached Fort Enterprise, for the Indians had not stocked it with food as expected, and they lived for three more weeks on a broth of discarded deer skins, bones, and lichen. Their horrific experience ended on 7 November with the arrival of Indians located by George Back, who took them to Fort Providence.

They spent one more winter in the north and returned to England in the autumn of 1822. The expedition had been a failure in many respects, involving much suffering and loss of life in return for limited geographical achievements. It also posed some questions about Franklin's leadership qualities, though there could be little doubt about his courage, which he had shown in large measure in the face of great hardship and deprivation. Despite this, Franklin quickly won fame and respect and established himself permanently as a British hero. He was promoted post-captain on 22 November 1822 (having been made a commander in his absence on 1 January 1821). He was also elected a fellow of the Royal Geographical Society.

It is said by polar explorers that the beauty and the danger of the Arctic can be addictive and it may well be true; how else do we explain why, time and time again, explorers who had suffered some of the most unimaginable, terrifying, and death-defying experiences wanted to return to it for more punishment.

Evidently John Franklin was afflicted by it, because on his return to England he began to draw up a plan for another expedition, this time to extend the exploration of the Arctic coast by travelling east and west from the Mackenzie Delta. This was accepted by the Admiralty in the autumn of 1823. However, this new plan showed considerable changes from his first expedition. Franklin had learned some hard lessons and would plan well in advance, strive for self-sufficiency, and reduce his dependence on outsiders, whether they be fur trappers, recruits, Indians, Inuit or hunters. He would place his greatest trust only in British seamen and British equipment, and he would deal with the Hudson Bay Trading Company for conveyance and supplies, but only when it suited him. In the meantime, he and his fellow explorers would enjoy some well-earned leave in London.

The early 1820s marked the entry of Arctic officers into polite society. Officers experienced in Arctic conditions entered new social worlds, those of London society, the literary scene and the kind of clubs and salons to which a Navy man might not be admitted. Indeed this was quite a change for Naval officers, as up until then their company was not always acceptable in Victorian drawing rooms. This new and welcome departure was brought about by the publication of the narratives of their brave exploits in prestigious newspapers.

In Britain, organised sport, amateur or professional, as we understand it today, was in its infancy. Franklin and his fellow adventurers became the heroes and new celebrities of the day. John Franklin, who was not the greatest of personalities in his own right, was soon warmly embraced by London's golden circle of socialites. People from the world of the arts began to take notice of the media coverage of Arctic exploration. The nobility began to visit the officers on their ships, and a whole new topic of conversation began at social events among the aristocracy. This was the period of Charles Dickens, Byron, the Brontë sisters, Shelley and Poe.

The Northwest Passage and the attainment of a farthest North was a great topic for debate. It was while preparing for his next voyage there that Lieutenant Franklin met Eleanor Anne Porden and later, her friend Jane Griffin.

Eleanor Porden

Eleanor Porden was born in London on 14 July 1795, the younger surviving daughter of William Porden and his wife Mary Plowman. William Porden was a successful, wealthy and talented architect, who was awarded contracts by the Royal household. The family lived at 55 Devonshire Street, London. Eleanor's mother Mary was an invalid, and after her older sister's marriage, Eleanor nursed her mother from 1809 until her death in 1819.

Eleanor, who was educated privately at home, was interested in arts and science but her forte was poetry. She was described by a biographer of Sir John Franklin as short, dark, pretty, witty and possessing a lively enquiring mind. Her first major work, *The Veils; or the Triumph of Constancy*, was published in 1815 when she was just twenty – although she had written it at the age of sixteen. The success of this poem resulted in her election to the prestigious Institut de Paris.

On a sightseeing tour of the Trent at Deptford Dock, in London, prior to its departure to chart the North Canadian coast in 1818, Eleanor, the young romantic poet met the gallant naval Lieutenant John Franklin for the first time. While he was away on the voyage Eleanor composed a long poem called 'The Arctic Expeditions'. The following are the opening lines:

> Sail, sail, adventurous Barks! Go fearless forth,
> Storm on his glacier-seat the misty North,
> Give to mankind the inhospitable zone,
> And Britain's trident plant in seas unknown.

Young ladies of Eleanor's social standing did not work for a living, instead they were well tutored in deportment and the social graces. The young lady would be taught good English, some French and Latin. She would be expected to have good fashion sense, learn horseback riding, have the skill to play board games and cards, while an ability to play piano or a stringed instrument would be considered a definite plus. A woman's place was deemed to be in the home. She ought never to work, or even acquire the means of working. The most important career for a lady was marriage.

Jane Griffin

Jane Griffin was born in London on 4 December 1791, the middle daughter of three. The family could trace its roots to the Huguenots. Jane Griffin's father was a prominent figure in the British gold and silk trade. He was an extremely wealthy and influential man who became Governor of the Goldsmiths' Company in London. Jane's mother Mary Guillemard came from a wealthy family which was also in the gold trade. Mary died before she reached the age of thirty, when Jane was only three years old.

John Griffin doted on his motherless daughters, especially on Jane, who was considered the clever one. Mary was the youngest, and Frances, the eldest, was known as Fanny. Jane was educated at an exclusive Chelsea boarding school and from an early age she meticulously wrote and retained diaries and journals of her extensive travels, a habit she adhered to throughout her life (she would in time become arguably the best-travelled woman of her generation). Jane was described as petite, dark, and blue-eyed, and highly intelligent – a woman ahead of her time. As teenagers their father John indulged his daughters, and Jane in particular travelled extensively throughout England and Europe.

In 1805, when Jane was fourteen, the Griffin family moved to a five-storey terraced house at 21 Bedford Place in Russell Square, a most desirable address. Their neighbours were prominent in the professions, one of them, Isaac Disraeli – a writer and the father of one of England's greatest prime ministers – was a close friend.

In 1814, Jane's twenty-year-old younger sister Mary, married John Francis (Frank) Simpkinson, an Oxford graduate, and in the same year, at the age of twenty-three, Jane travelled to Europe, where she spent the next two years and two months travelling with her father John and sister Fanny. Jane excelled at mountain climbing and on one occasion she climbed Montenegro (15,781 feet), one of the Mont Blanc range. By the time she was twenty-five Jane had rejected several offers of marriage, as she considered the suitors unsuitable. She continued her reading, writing and travelling, and of course engaged fully in the social events of London Society.

In 1818, when Jane was twenty-seven she began to take an interest in exploration. She learned from her friend Sarah Disraeli of a brilliant young poetess named Eleanor Porden. Soon after, Jane visited Deptford Dock, where a four-vessel Arctic expedition was fitting out to seek the Northwest Passage. She was introduced to Captain John Ross, leader of the expedition, and learned that John Franklin was one of the officers.

In February 1819 Jane met Eleanor Porden on the social scene for the first time and they became close friends. Eleanor was not in robust health. During Franklin's absence Eleanor researched and wrote a historical epic poem *Coeur de Lion, or The Third Crusade*, a poem of over 50,000 words, in sixteen books. She also wrote several more successful poems, which further enhanced her ever-growing reputation.

John Franklin's new book *Narrative of a Journey to the Shores of the Polar Sea*, the story of his Arctic expedition, was published and became a minor sensation. Jane met Lieutenant John Franklin and his fellow explorers on the social circuit on a regular basis.

In 1822, Eleanor Porden's father died, and her health was further affected. Soon after, Lieutenant John Franklin was promoted to Captain and he and Eleanor became engaged in May of 1823. London Society was puzzled at the engagement and considered them a curious couple; the sophisticated Eleanor eleven years younger than her fiancé and a star of the Bohemian set, while John, although a heroic figure, came from a small country town in Lincolnshire.

The engagement was a stormy one. Eleanor was of independent means. She also had a substantial financial inheritance bequeathed by her deceased father. In March 1823 John Franklin announced that he would find it improper for a woman to become the wife of an explorer or for anyone connected to him – for example by marriage – to have work appearing in public print. In effect Franklin was asking her to abandon her writing, deeming it an unfit profession for a woman. John was a strict Sabbatarian by upbringing and did not want his wife to have an occupation.

Eleanor was shocked at John's demand and made it more than plain to him she was ready to call off the engagement if she were not permitted to continue her writing career. John backed down and the two were married in August 1823 at Marleybone church in London. To the surprise of many, Jane Griffin did not attend the wedding.

In the following spring Eleanor was pregnant. On 27 March 1824, the Franklins organised a most important dinner party to honour the leading figures of Arctic exploration. Among the guests were Jane Griffin, and her father John, Isaac Disraeli and his daughter Sarah, John Barrow, Royal Navy Captains Edward Parry, George Lyon and Frederick Beechey.

In June 1824 Eleanor gave birth to a baby girl, who was christened Eleanor Isabella Franklin. The baby was described as fat, fair and funny. Eleanor did not recover full health following the birth of her baby and was eventually diagnosed with recurrent tuberculosis. In January 1825 Eleanor's condition became grave. Her husband John was under orders to sail for northern Canada in February. In the meantime he was being feted at dinners and other social occasions arranged in his honour, while he prepared for the expedition. In public and in private, there were unfavourable comments on his plans to leave his stricken wife Eleanor at such a critical time.

In his defence, Franklin claimed he had been fully aware of Eleanor's weak condition, and that he had offered to postpone his journey but that she had insisted that he fulfil his duty and sail on the expedition. She had also vowed to regain her full health for the sake of Little Ella.

In preparation for the forthcoming expedition, Franklin despatched the first load of provisions, together with three specially constructed boats, and a party of seamen was sent ahead through York Factory, Canada, in 1824, to ensure their safe arrival. Captain Franklin sailed from Liverpool for New York on 16 February 1825, cheered on by thousands of supporters on the quayside. He was accompanied once more by John Richardson and George Back.

But less than a week after Franklin's departure, the twenty-nine-year-old brilliant poetess Eleanor was dead. The funeral took place at St John's Wood Chapel, and in John Franklin's absence, his sister Mrs Booth cared for little Ella.

On-board his ship John anxiously waited for news of Eleanor's well being, but for the duration of his voyage communication was impossible. On his arrival in the US Franklin was shocked to learn that his beloved Eleanor had died on 22 February, a mere six days after his departure. John Franklin was intensely worried, wondering who was caring for his infant daughter Eleanor and not knowing if or when he would return safely to her.

But he deemed it his duty to continue with the expedition. He and his party travelled along the fur-trading routes far into the north, catching up with the advance party of seamen and boats. Early in August they reached Fort Norman in the North West Territories (NWT). Franklin and Kendall travelled the Mackenzie River to the sea. The rest of the party went on to the Great Bear Lake, where they constructed their winter quarters. They named this base Fort Franklin.

After a comfortable winter they left for the coast on 26 June 1826. All of Franklin's explorations and the chartings by his teams achieved their goals, apart from one skirmish with some Inuit who pillaged their boats. Having been impeded by ice and fog, the party returned to Fort Franklin, where they spent a second winter adding to their store of knowledge. They sailed for England in early 1827 and reached Liverpool on 26 September 1827. John Franklin was once again acclaimed a hero, and was considered a certainty for a knighthood when the next honours list was announced.

Meanwhile Jane Griffin's thirty-sixth birthday was looming and she still hadn't found a husband. Perhaps she had no desire to be married, as she was wealthy, and so had her independence and a most enviable life style. John Franklin, on his return to England arranged for his sister Isabella to care for baby Eleanor. He returned to London where he visited the Griffin family on a regular basis and made clear to her father John, of his intentions to marry Jane.

Jane also knew a proposal of marriage was in the offing but she was uneasy about the serious financial implications the marriage would have for the wealthy

Griffin family. John Franklin was not bringing many positives to the marriage. He did not have much money and was poorly paid in comparison with Jane's social set, although there would be royalties from his book sales. Also he was a man of short stature, overweight (he weighed fifteen stone), was deaf in one ear and was inarticulate compared to Jane and her social circle. He also had an impish, almost three-year-old daughter. On the plus side, he was a national hero and a celebrity, and he would soon become Sir John. If he remarried, his new wife would receive an aristocratic title.

Jane discussed her dilemma with her father, and proposed an agreement for John Franklin to sign which would safeguard the family's wealth and property, because, according to the Married Women's Property Act, unless written provisions stipulated otherwise, on marriage, a woman's property automatically became her husband's. John Griffin would not hear of such a document and told Jane so. He judged her husband to be an honourable man. If he did not consider him so, he would not have agreed to the marriage in the first place.

Jane was aware of idle gossip about herself and John Franklin, who had been deemed callous when he left his wife Eleanor on her deathbed while he sailed to north America. But the courtship continued, and on 5 November 1828, they were married and sailed for France on their honeymoon. Little Ella was left behind.

When they returned to England the second of Franklin's successful narratives was published. He again received formal honours and won the gold medal of the Société de Géographie de Paris. Along with W.E. Parry, he was knighted on 29 April 1829 and also received an Honorary Doctorate of Laws from the University of Oxford in July. But amid all the celebrations there was a serious problem, Sir John Franklin did not have a ship to command, and certainly not one bound for the Arctic, which was what he was hoping for.

He was offered a well-paid civilian job in Australia, but he declined, preferring to bide his time at home with Little Ella and Lady Jane. In 1830, he was given command of the frigate *Rainbow* for duty in the Middle East, mainly playing a peacekeeping role along the coast of Greece during that country's war of independence. The ship was based in Malta. From the first time she had visited Europe as a teenager, Lady Jane had fallen in love with the climate and adored the Mediterranean. Subsequently at every possible opportunity she escaped from the London cold, fog, dampness and smoke. There now arose another heaven-sent opportunity to go abroad.

In 1831 Lady Jane arranged to spend the winter in Corfu, where the British Navy had a presence, and Sir John would join her there. She took two servants with her; her maid and her man servant. Little Ella remained in the care of John's sister Isabella Cracroft, since Lady Jane declared it would be unsafe to bring a six-year-old child to a risky war zone.

In March 1832 Sir John returned to duty at sea, but Lady Jane still craved adventure and arranged a grand tour of the Holy Land, Egypt, Athens, Petras, Turkey and Syria with the servants. She returned to Corfu in the spring of 1833, but did not stay long, as she had promised some friends she would sail up the River Nile with them.

By this time Sir John had finished his tour of duty and returned to London. He was paid off and left twiddling his thumbs, waiting for his wife's return. He was also waiting for another command and living on half pay. For his sound diplomacy in the Mediterranean he later received the Order of the Redeemer of Greece and the Royal Hanoverian Order.

Lady Jane did not return to London until 19 October 1834. She had been abroad for almost three years, but had only spent three months of that time with her husband.

She had difficulty settling down after the exhilarating holiday, and her disposition became even more upset when she heard that Naval Lieutenant George Back was to lead a rescue mission to the Arctic to search for John Ross and his nephew James Clark Ross. Jane looked upon the Arctic as Sir John's territory. However, it was a false alarm and the pair turned up safely. But to the annoyance of Lady Jane, George Back, a former subordinate of Sir John's, was feted when he returned to London.

George Back was despatched to complete the mapping of the northern coast of Canada, while Sir John was offered a posting to Antigua, as Lieutenant Governor. Lady Jane considered the offer an insult and it was refused. She then began to lobby for a better posting and eventually her efforts paid off. Sir John was offered the Governorship of Van Diemen's Land (Tasmania), a young colony with a population of 24,000 colonial settlers and almost 18,000 transported convicts. His salary was £2,500 per annum.

On 26 August 1836, Sir John, Lady Jane, Eleanor (who was now aged twelve), and John's niece Sophy Cracroft (who was the daughter of his sister Isabella, and would go on to become a lifelong companion and confidante of Lady Jane), plus an entourage of servants, sailed on the *Fairlie*.

On 6 January 1837 they arrived in Hobart, the main anchorage for Royal Navy ships bound for Australia. Sir John and Lady Jane welcomed the visiting naval officers from Britain into their home with open arms, many of the them they already knew. Sophy Cracroft, now in her early twenties, was described as fascinating, a young lady of beauty and fortune. The young officers found her very attractive and she soon earned the reputation of being an outrageous flirt.

Sir John's Governorship of Van Diemen's Land was not considered to be a happy one, as it was deemed too liberal and there were many problems. Influential people in Tasmania considered Franklin's tenure of office a failure, mainly because he and Lady Jane did not always obey their wishes. He supported the introduction of a representative assembly on an island he was obliged to maintain as a penal colony. This decision was not welcomed by the Colonial Office. It was also alleged Lady Jane interfered too much in Government business (though she excelled as hostess at the Government Mansion). The viceregal couple's preoccupations, notably in education and the welfare of female convicts, served to create tensions with the Colonial Office, though their approach won the affection of many convicts and settlers.

In 1843 Sir John was dismissed. In some disgrace, the Franklin party departed from Hobart on 3 November 1843, arriving back in England in June 1844. Sir John was in very low spirits – and badly wanted to restore his reputation.

Chapter III

Franklin's Expedition of 1845

In the James Hand story there are many references and links to previous major polar expeditions, notably the search for the Northwest Passage, the disappearance of Sir John Franklin, and the searches for Franklin and his expedition by Leopold McClintock and the American explorers De Haven, Dr Elisha Kane, Dr Isaac Hayes and Charles Francis Hall, among others. The background outlining the reason for the British Naval Expedition of 1875 is central to our understanding of why Jim Hand volunteered to join the Navy and ultimately, the British Naval Expedition of 1875, under Captain Nares.

In 1839, two famous Hudson Bay explorers Peter Warren Dease and Thomas Simpson had discovered that the Simpson Strait opened up a new approach to the Pacific, and all that was needed was to discover a north–south channel linking Barrow Strait, accessible from the Atlantic, and the new Simpson Strait, which should make it easy to achieve the Passage.

The British Admiralty received permission from Prime Minister Peel to organise an expedition to discover a Northwest Passage. It was decided that this ought to precede any attempt to reach the North Pole. The successful expedition leader would receive a reward of £10,000.

The Admiralty was asked to appoint a commander. The most obvious choice was George Back, but he was unable to accept due to ill health. James Clark Ross, then headed the list, recently knighted and only newly wed he declined, which left Edward Parry, Francis Crozier, Sir John Franklin and James Fitzjames. Fitzjames was Sir John Barrow's choice.

Lady Jane Franklin was aware that her husband Sir John was considered low in the pecking order for this prestigious post because he was now fifty-eight years old, and also because of his recent enforced absence from contact with the upper echelons of the Admiralty and its decision makers. Lady Jane wanted the appointment for Sir John. He himself was at a low ebb and facing an uncertain future. Needless to say he was desperate to obtain the prestigious honour at this late stage in his career. Jane, being a most formidable woman, began to exert her influence in high places.

For a variety of reasons, the most experienced Arctic candidates, Edward Parry and Francis Crozier, would not, or could not, take command of the expedition, so the field was narrowed down to two: Franklin and a young unknown naval commander James Fitzjames, who was only thirty-three years old. Franklin, in an interview, agreed he was too old for the task if the expedition was overland, but it was not, it was a sailing expedition, and there was no one with more experience than himself. There was a great deal of political manoeuvring done behind the scenes as to who should lead the expedition, but ultimately Lady Jane's efforts were successful. Among those she had lobbied was Sir James Clark Ross, who had been the Admiralty's first choice. Ross gave his backing to Franklin, and it was sufficient to sway the seven-man board: Sir John Franklin was appointed Commander.

George Back made it known to anyone who would listen that he considered Sir John Franklin far too old for such a demanding expedition, and it was with a heavy heart that Sir John Barrow opposed the appointment. He also considered Sir John Franklin (one of his original 'Boys') too old to cope with the rigorous demands on mind and body that a three-year expedition in an ice-strewn Arctic would entail. Barrow considered Franklin's best years in the Arctic behind him; distinguished and inspirational as his heroic deeds may have been to young seamen in the past, Barrow was conscious of the demands made on the commander of an Arctic expedition; the ordeal of being on duty for days and nights at a stretch, possibly beset in the ice for months on end, compelled to duck and weave among ice floes in the stormy and freezing Arctic waters. Sir John Barrow was not alone in his misgivings. But despite Admiralty reservations and because of the lack of experienced alternatives available in the time permitted, there appeared to be no one with superior experience. Sir John was appointed leader of the expedition, and Captain Francis Crozier was appointed his second in command.

Francis Rawdon Moira Crozier had been born in Banbridge, Co. Down, Ireland, one of thirteen children. His father George was a wealthy solicitor. Shortly before his fourteenth birthday young Francis Crozier joined the British Navy and was soon in action in the Napoleonic Wars. In 1821 he became another of those officers destined for Arctic exploration, and in 1827 was a crew member of Captain Edward Parry's unsuccessful attempt to reach the North Pole, where they were defeated by the tidal drift. Crozier rose through the ranks and served with distinction on voyages to the Arctic and Antarctic.

Crozier was not altogether happy with Franklin's appointment as commander of the expedition. It has been claimed he volunteered for the expedition in order to impress Lady Jane's niece Sophy Cracroft, with whom he was in love. Sadly, his love was unrequited. Sophy refused to be a sea captain's wife, and Crozier sailed a sad and lonely man filled with anxiety, his letters to loved ones back home illustrating his concerns regarding Franklin's leadership.

Franklin captained the *Erebus*, Crozier captained the *Terror*. The expedition departed the Thames on 19 May 1845 with 133 officers and men (soon reduced to 129 as four were sent back to England from southern Greenland, deemed useless for the task) on two of the Royal Navy's finest ice sailing ships. These vessels were furnished with steam power, albeit to a limited extent. Their personnel comprised the flower of the British naval service.

Soon after the ships departed, Lady Jane planned another escape from London's winter chill, this time her destination was the West Indies. She took Eleanor, now twenty-one, and Sophy, twenty-nine, plus the usual retinue of servants. Her first stop was the beautiful island of Madeira, then on to the West Indies, Mexico, and finally to the United States, where Lady Jane welcomed the opportunity to do some mountain climbing. The party returned to London in November 1846.

In early 1847 Lady Jane began to worry. Sir John should have reached the Pacific by then. But nevertheless she began to get itchy feet once more and arranged to go to southern Italy for four or five months, taking Eleanor, Sophy and the servants with her. They returned in August of 1847, but there was still no news of Sir John.

Sir John Franklin and his companions, like so many who preceded them, would have been aware of the many difficulties the task faced. However, they had set sail with what still seemed a fair probability that their mission would be successful. They had two stout ships (the best ever built for the purpose) and a crew to match for a voyage through the Arctic to the Pacific. Sir John Franklin and his officers were well prepared for the challenge. The expedition had food and supplies for several years, silver cutlery and a library of one thousand books. Nothing could possibly go wrong, it had been claimed.

Franklin and Crozier had anchored at Upernavik (which means 'spring square') off the coast of Greenland on 19 July 1845. The last recorded sighting of *Erebus* and the *Terror* was by the crew of the whaling ship *Prince of Wales* on 26 July 1845, in latitude 74°48'N, longitude 66°12'W.

Between Greenland and the Canadian Arctic lies the body of water known as Baffin Bay. From Baffin Bay three possible sea routes lead into the Arctic; Smith Sound to the north; Jones Sound to the west, and south of Smith Sound, Lancaster Sound. It was into Lancaster Sound Franklin had sailed in 1845, travelling west until he reached Cornwallis Island, at which point he had turned south down Peel Sound and there, off King William Island his ships had become icebound.

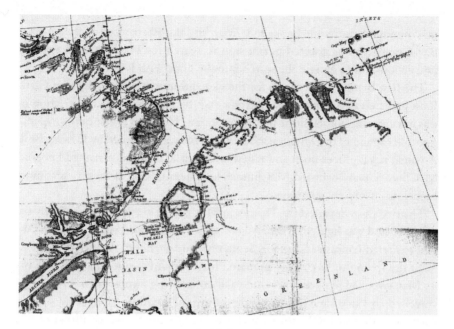

Smith Sound.

Prior to the expedition's departure for a voyage of three years' duration, Sir John Franklin and the British Admiralty failed to make any arrangements for communication or rescue in the event of an emergency. This decision would prove to be a tragic miscalculation and was quite surprising in the light of what was to happen.

In 1848, three years after the departure of the expedition, grave concern and widespread alarm was expressed regarding its whereabouts, not only in Britain but also in the United States. The story quickly became front-page news in the world press. What had happened? What could have become of Franklin and his crews? Where could Franklin be?

The Admiralty knew where he should be. Franklin's orders had been to sail as far west as possible and then to strike south. Among those who were greatly concerned was one Dr Richard King, a proponent of land-based exploration who had travelled down the Great Fish River (Northern Canada) in 1833. He urged the Admiralty to send a relief party on an overland search towards the mouth of that river. The Admiralty sought the advice of Sir James Clark Ross, who rebutted Dr King's persistent concern. Ross harboured the view that to search the Great Fish River would be pointless.

On 9 February 1847 John Ross offered to attempt a rescue but the Admiralty Board politely turned down his offer. When in 1848 there was still no communication from *Erebus* and *Terror*, Sir John Richardson of the Hudson Bay Company was granted permission to search for Franklin with explicit instructions not to extend the search into the Great Fish River.

The first British Navy search for the expedition was organised. James Clark Ross prepared two ships – the *Enterprise* and the *Investigator*. The motivation in this instance was not scientific but humanitarian. Ross was leader of the expedition and captain of the *Investigator*. The *Enterprise* was captained by Edward Bird. A young naval officer born and raised in Dundalk, Co. Louth, named Leopold McClintock was on-board. McClintock later became one of the Britain's most highly decorated polar explorers.

The two ships departed the Thames in May 1848. On 7 June the southerly tip of Greenland was sighted. On 20 August they reached open water at Baffin Bay. They entered Lancaster Sound in September and anchored for the winter.

In the spring of 1849 they prepared for overland sledge journeys and on 15 May two sledge parties set out, each comprising twelve men. One party travelled to Fury Beach to ascertain if any of Franklin's men had visited there. Ross and McClintock journeyed to the north-west following the coastline, turned south and reached the furthest point on 6 June. The return journey was of extreme hardship. Constant exposure and insufficient food caused four men to break down and one had to be carried on the sledge. They had completed the longest sledge journey made to that time, 500 miles in thirty-nine days.

McClintock noted everything and learned a number of lessons from the experience: inadequate meat – the stipulated pound of meat per day in their diet contained too much bone, overly heavy loads on the sledges, insufficient spirit stoves resulting in cold food.

Meanwhile two smaller sledge parties had set out on 31 May. They also failed to find a trace of Franklin. The lack of fresh meat resulted in an outbreak of scurvy (now known as 'the curse of the Arctic regions'). Further searches were hampered by bad weather, which prevented them from carrying out their planned itinerary. They were beset in ice for weeks. Drifting with the flow into Baffin Bay from Lancaster Sound, Ross decided to sail for home but was unable to get through the ice of Melville Bay and was forced to winter on the Greenland coast. They did break out the following summer and arrived in Scarborough on 5 November, 1849. The crews had hoped to hear that Franklin had returned safely ahead of them, but there was no news, Franklin's fate was still shrouded in mystery.

In Dublin's Christchurch Cathedral the officers of the Arctic expedition composed of *Enterprise* and *Investigator* erected a marble memorial to Henry Mathias, assistant surgeon of HMS *Enterprise*, who departed this life on 5 June 1849 in his twenty-eighth year at Port Leopold lat. 74°N. This fine sculpture was an apt memorial to the first volunteer who gave his life in the noble quest for Franklin. It can be viewed in the crypt by visitors to this day.

Slowly but surely, as each search proved fruitless, the awful realisation that Franklin and his 129 officers and men must all be dead began to register in the public consciousness. There was an immediate increase in the public's demand for a new search. The Government was forced to put adequate resources into the operation at a time when it was clear to many that it was too late. The *Enterprise* and *Investigator* were re-commissioned to go by way of the Pacific to the Bering Strait, under overall command of Captain Richard Collinson on *Enterprise*, with Robert McClure in his first captaincy in charge of *Investigator*. In support was the supply ship, HMS *Plover* under the command of Commander T.E.L. Moore, supported by Captain Henry Kellett aboard HMS *Herald*. The *Herald* left Panama on 9 May 1848, reaching Alaska on 14 September. Two weeks later, when *Plover* failed to show, Kellett returned south to winter in Hawaii.

It had been intended that *Plover*, a depot ship, should be stationed near Cape Barrow to wait with supplies for Franklin. Sailing from Hawaii in August, *Plover* made a long slow voyage to the Bering Strait, not reaching its intended rendez-vous point with Herald until mid-October, a month after Kellett had left. Moore overwintered at Providence Bay. There were a number of Irishmen among the crews on both the *Plover* and *Herald*. Among the men listed in the muster books are names associated with Co. Cork and Munster in general. Many of them are listed as recipients of the Arctic Medal, awarded to all who participated in the search for the Northwest Passage and the search for Franklin. Among them were Patrick Fitzgerald, John McCarthy, William McCarthy, Patrick McSweeny and Peter McSweeny.

In 1850 a squadron was assembled under Horatio J. Austin to search from the Atlantic. Two barque-rigged vessels, *Resolute* and *Assistance* sailed with the screw steamers *Pioneer* and *Intrepid*. Accompanying the expedition were the brigs *Lady Franklin* and *Sophia* under whaling Captain Penny.

Robert McClintock was promoted to first Lieutenant under Captain Ommaney on the *Assistance*, as was Sherard Osborn. Another Irishman, George Meecham from Cobh, Co. Cork, was second Lieutenant.

On 15 April 1850 the tiny fleet crossed the Atlantic and Cape Farewell was sighted. Whalefish Islands were reached on 15 June and the transfer of supplies took a week to complete. The steam-powered vessels *Pioneer* and *Intrepid* were engaged with the Melville Bay ice. Taking forty-five days to break through, the ice was cut with saws, charged at by the vessels and blasted with gunpowder before Cape York was reached. In Melville Bay they encountered a little eighty-nine-ton schooner *Prince Albert*, captained by the highly regarded William Kennedy (second in command was the distinguished young French Arctic explorer Joseph Rene Bellot). The *Prince Albert* had been fitted out and financed by Lady Franklin to search Prince Regent Inlet. Having reached that point the captain returned without probing the place that Lady Jane had intuitively selected for a search.

In all, twelve ships were searching for Franklin and his men in 1850. The remains of a camp, suggesting that a party of Franklin's men had wintered in the vicinity, was all that was found. McClintock favoured a thorough search, but the sight of open water convinced Captain Ommaney to proceed for home. The search of Beechey Island was left to *Pioneer*, *Resolute* and the American ships. Search parties from these ships discovered the graves of three sailors at Beechey Island – one from the *Terror* and two from *Erebus* – and identified the base of a magnetic observations station. They also found many empty food tins and other signs of Franklin's winter quarters, but no official records. Still not knowing the cause of the disappearance, they had no clue as to where to target further searches.

When ice prevented further progress, Austin's squadron set up winter quarters at Griffith Island and Cornwallis Island. McClintock's first innovation was to stockpile a supply depot thirty miles from their base. On-board the squadron's ships, winter was a much more comfortable affair than in the previous year, with an adequate supply of food, organised exercise, lectures, theatre and other entertainments to relieve the boredom of the long Arctic nights.

Captain Austin now had 220 men to select from. With the return of the sun, he sent out search parties in seven different directions. They covered 1,225 miles of new territory. Frederick Meecham was away for twenty-eight days and travelled 236 miles. McClintock and his party were away for eighty days and covered 770 miles, dragging the sledge at a daily rate of 10.5 miles.

On the return journey, the summer sledging proved more difficult. The ice crust occasionally collapsed under their weight, sinking them into pools of ice-cold water, or they were trapped on top of floes surrounded by melted water, which often had to be waded through.

The sledge parties searched Prince of Wales Island, Bathurst Island, Cornwallis Island and Melville Island, among others. There was one death from frostbite and three cases of toe amputations. Despite their gallant efforts, none of the search parties found any sign or evidence of Franklin's passing. Despite the fact that one of the sledge parties had searched down the east coast of Prince of Wales Island, and that they appeared to have been in the vicinity, or to at least have travelled parallel to the direction in which it is now believed the two ships had sailed, no traces of Franklin's Expedition was found.

To access open water in the next navigable season, they had to cut and blast lanes for the ships. This they accomplished on 11 August. They proceeded to search Jones Sound with the *Pioneer* and *Intrepid*, while the *Assistance* checked out the Cary Islands in Baffin Bay without success. The squadron returned to England on 4 October 1850.

Chapter IV

The Search Continues

In Sir John Franklin's absence Lady Jane had become a heroine in the eyes of the British public and donned the mantle of one of the first ladies of the land, basking in her husbands reflected glory, she thrived on the adulation. But five years had passed and she was sick with worry. The most difficult part of the sorry saga was the uncertainty. What had caused the ships' abrupt disappearance? Were they trapped in the ice? Lost in an Arctic storm? Sunk due to a fatal collision with an iceberg? Was it possible they been rescued by Eskimo and were all still alive?

This was the decade in which spiritualism reached Britain from America: a time of seers, mediums, clairvoyants, and charlatans. Lady Jane was prepared to reach out to Sir John and in desperation she visited spiritualists, but all to no avail. The winter of 1852-53 revealed nothing of Franklin's whereabouts. It seemed as if he had vanished from the face of the earth.

Lady Jane had made it known both publicly and privately that she would stop at nothing nor spare any financial expense in the search for Sir John. Her father John Griffin, her sister Mary, and Mary's husband Frank Simpkinson, were all very unhappy with this stance, and considered it to be both mistaken and possibly financially ruinous. The family advised her to let the Admiralty continue the search. They had the expertise and the means, and there was no need for Lady Jane to finance hugely expensive private expeditions, or to offer large financial rewards for the rescue of Sir John with her own money. The feisty Lady Jane refused to heed the advice. Eventually matters came to a head; so serious was the row with her father that she moved out of 51 Bedford Place and arranged to stay at an apartment at the Admiralty buildings. It was around that same time that Eleanor Franklin announced she was going to be married.

In 1849, the expedition had been missing for four years. Eleanor was twenty-five and living in the Porden home on her own. It is quite clear from correspondence that Lady Jane and her stepdaughter Eleanor were not very close. Eleanor was also regarded as an outsider by her aunts, Sophy and Mary. Eleanor may very well have felt excluded, as, apart from the period spent in Van Diemen's Land with her father and Lady Jane, she had spent most of her young life living with her aunt Isabella in Lincolnshire. Now Eleanor had fallen in love with John Philip Gell. The couple had met in Van Diemen's Land, and John followed Eleanor back to England.

John P. Gell (1816–1898) was born on 10 March 1816, in Matlock, Derbyshire, England. He was a young Anglican minister and on a tiny income. If the couple married, John would have great difficulty in keeping Eleanor in the lifestyle to which she had become accustomed – and they both knew it. A review of the financial situation of Sir John Franklin and Eleanor is pure guesswork, but it possible to reconstruct a likely scenario. Sir John was the beneficiary of his first wife Eleanor's will. He had his Navy salary, the royalties from the sales of his books, and he also had a legal right to Lady Jane's finances and property. Eleanor was only seven months old when her mother died and it is possible that she had not made provision in her will for her young daughter, relying on her husband to take good financial care of her. If that were the case, then the unfortunate young Eleanor was in dire straits. The daughter of a titled couple could not be expected to work or have an occupation, and therefore Eleanor had no finances of her own. She did have the Porden family home, and in all likelihood Sir John had arranged a monthly income for her which would have been adequate under normal circumstances. Neither Eleanor's decision to marry nor her father's four-year absence (presumed dead by many) had been foreseen. It meant that her father was not available to provide her with the additional financial support she needed for her wedding, or with a dowry. Eleanor discussed the problem with her stepmother, Lady Jane, who proposed to provide her with an income of £300 per annum (a significant sum in 1848). John Gell's income was roughly £200 per annum. Eleanor, who could have anticipated a considerable inheritance in the event of Sir John's death, was clearly unhappy with Lady Jane's response.

Sir John had granted Lady Jane power of attorney over all his resources, so while there was no proof of his death, Jane could spend his money on as many fruitless searches for him and the expedition as she wished. But if Sir John were deemed to be dead, it would alter the situation completely. The remainder of the Porden estate would go to his daughter Eleanor, and she would probably receive Sir John's estate, which would amount to a substantial sum of money.

Eleanor fixed the date for her wedding – 7 June 1849. Lady Jane, meanwhile continued to invest heavily in unsuccessful searches for Sir John. The family squabble continued to simmer, both privately and publicly, with letters to the *London Times* from family members. It was Eleanor and her husband John against the rest, and Eleanor declared publicly that Lady Jane was squandering money that rightly belonged to her.

Lady Jane's father John Griffin was now in his nineties and was probably fed up with the whole unseemly affair, because on 11 March 1851, the unthinkable happened. John Griffin cut his beloved daughter Lady Jane out of his will and left his entire estate to his favourite grandson Francis Guillemard Simpkinson. Lady Jane was stunned, but shortly afterwards she organised yet another search for Sir John.

This time she engaged the services of William Kennedy, the son of the Hudson Bay Company Chief Factor Alexander Kennedy and his Cree wife Aggathas. Kennedy was a remarkable man. He worked for the Hudson Bay Company and was a fur trader, sailor and explorer. Second in command of the search was Joseph Rene Bellot. He had been born in Paris in 1826, and was a gallant young Frenchman who had earned a high reputation. Before the age of twenty he had received the cross of the Legion of Honor for distinguished conduct. Bellot appeared to have a glittering career ahead of him.

They sailed on the *Prince Albert*, a ninety-ton pilot boat. On the voyage they discovered a new channel, Bellot Strait, but overall, apart from that important find, the search was unsuccessful.

From Britain, Europe, the US, Van Diemen's Land and Australia, the news had spread about the searches for the missing Franklin Expedition. Lady Jane had now become a well-recognised figure across the globe through newspaper coverage, and soon donations of money began to flow into the search fund in substantial amounts, in particular from an admirer, the American philanthropist Henry Grinnell in America. Henry was fascinated by the Franklin mystery and wrote to Lady Jane frequently on the progress of the various searches.

In 1851 two American vessels had also joined the search, the *Rescue* and the *Advance*. In 1852, Lady Jane financed another search, this time in the Wellington Channel – the Edward Inglefield rescue mission of 1852–53. Lady Jane acquired the *Isabel*, a 150-ton steam schooner. She again chose as second in command the brilliant young explorer Joseph Bellot. In August 1853 Joseph Bellot, with four other crew members, set out on foot in difficult conditions from the *Isabel* in an attempt to reach Sir Edward Belcher with despatches. Belcher at the time was leading a five-ship search. Bellot, walking ahead of the party fell into a crack in the ice and although his companions rushed to his aid they were too late to save him from drowning. Joseph Bellot died at the age of twenty-seven. A memorial grave was built on nearby Beechey Island by his shipmates.

Lady Jane had met Joseph Bellot many times and liked the young man immensely. She formed a committee in London to raise funds to erect a suitable memorial to his memory. Money flowed in and an obelisk was unveiled in 1855. It stands on the Thames riverside in front of Greenwich Hospital in London.

Lady Jane and her father had apparently agreed to disagree, and she moved back to the family home, but shortly afterwards, in May 1852, her father, John Griffin died. William Kennedy was commissioned by Lady Jane to take the *Isabel* for another search, this time from the Pacific route, but again to no avail.

By 1854, nine years after the disappearance of Sir John, Lady Jane still refused to believe her husband was dead and continued to pester the Naval Chiefs at the Admiralty to instigate more searches for him. The Crimean War (1854–56) was now taking up most of the Royal Navy's resources. The Admiralty considered this campaign their top priority; ships were needed to ferry troops, ammunitions, the cavalry and hospital ships to the Black Sea. The Admiralty deemed enough time and money had been expended over the previous ten years on the search for the Franklin Expedition and even Lady Jane's close friends in the Admiralty had grown tired of the relentless pressure.

By the year 1855 the British Admiralty, much to Lady Jane's consternation, struck the names of Sir John and the ships' crews off the Navy register, all presumed dead. She refused to accept the Navy's decision until evidence was available to prove conclusively that Sir John was dead. But his will and testament could now be administered. Sir John's assets were divided; peace reigned among the interested parties and the bitter war of words ended. Eleanor, now aged thirty-one, with several very young children, was still a young woman. It is presumed she was satisfied with her new financial security and decided to get on with her life. But sadly, that was not to be. Eleanor died five short years later, in 1860, from scarlet fever. She was buried in Monmouthshire in Wales. Lady Jane and Sophy were unable to attend the funeral as they were on their way to South America.

Chapter V

Dr Elisha Kane

Americans had been aware of Franklin's disappearance and had participated in the unsuccessful rescue attempts. One young American medical doctor, named Elisha Kent Kane, became interested in Arctic exploration. Kane was born on 28 February 1820 into an upper-class Philadelphia family. He was not in robust health and consequently was an unlikely polar explorer. As a child he had been of delicate health with a suspected heart condition brought on by a debilitating bout of rheumatic fever. Despite his weakness, Kane lived an active life. Having studied medicine he graduated from the University of Pennsylvania in 1842, earned a commission as a naval surgeon, and embarked on a succession of exciting voyages to China, the Philippines, and West Africa, and took part in the Mexican-American War.

Elisha Kane craved adventure, and the perfect opportunity presented itself, when in 1852, he volunteered as medical officer on one of the missions to find the lost Franklin Expedition. Under Captain De Haven, the ship *Rescue* was sponsored by Henry Grinnell.

Henry Grinnell was born in 1799. The New York philanthropist was a hugely successful businessman, a founder member of the American Geographical and Statistical Society, its president in 1862-3 and had played a unique roll in Arctic discovery, financing some of America's most important Arctic expeditions. Grinnell Land (or Peninsula) in Canada's Northwest Territories, and a genus of red algae (Grinnellia) are named after him.

Hitherto the Arctic waters had been the preserve of British explorers. The fledgling United States Navy began to take an interest in Arctic affairs and in a very short time so did the American public. This activity did not go unnoticed by the British Establishment as many of its influential figures considered it to be 'their patch'.

Elisha Kane was a brilliant self-publicist and was deemed by the opposite sex to be a man of great charm and eloquence. He was also gifted with an imaginative mind, which helped to make him a successful writer. After De Haven's search for Franklin, although it was unsuccessful, the captain and crew were given a heroes' reception in New York on their return. Kane wrote and lectured extensively on his Arctic experiences and soon captured the imagination of the American public. Kane lectured to thousands and captivated his audiences with his insights and descriptions of life in the frozen north. His growing reputation enabled him to demand (and get) five-figure sums for a single lecture. He became known as 'Dr Kane of the Arctic Seas'. He also led a tumultuous love life.

Henry Grinnell sponsored Kane for a second attempt to rescue Franklin. The ship chosen was the 114-ton *Advance* with Kane in command. Lady Jane Franklin was a great admirer of Dr Kane and an avid reader of his descriptions of life in the Arctic. The pair corresponded, and Kane learned that Captain Edward Inglefield was setting out in one of England's best steam-powered ships to follow the rescue path which De Haven and he had pursued in 1850–51. (What Kane did not know was that Inglefield was only joining Sir Edward Belcher's ships in the search for Franklin around Beechey Island.) Disturbed to hear this news, Kane adopted a more aggressive approach. Before setting out on his journey he altered his route, but in doing so recognised that by taking this new course he would also risk being frozen into an ice floe for the winter. He decided to take the risk. This decision would prove to be a grave error. Kane stored a two-year supply of food for what he hoped would be a one-year journey.

Kane reckoned on being able to procure provisions in Greenland and on catching enough fish and shooting sufficient wildlife to keep the expedition healthy. Dr Isaac Hayes was the Medical Officer, and joined what eventually became a seventeen-strong crew.

Kane sailed from New York on 31 May 1853. On 20 July the *Advance* reached the tiny village of Upernavik, the northernmost European settlement in Greenland. Two further crew members were signed on by Kane at Upernavik. The first of these was Neil Carl Petersen, a Danish guide fluent in Inuktitut, who had previously worked for British expeditions. (Some explorers called him Carl, but he is referred to here as Neil.) The other man was Hans Hendrik (also known as Hans Heindrich to some explorers, his native name was Suersaq). Hans was a cheerful Eskimo. He was a hunter and dog-handler, aged nineteen. He was born in 1834, in Fiskenaesset, Greenland. In 1853 Jim Hand was only a small boy, but later in his life he would meet and get to know these two men, who became icons in Arctic exploration.

Kane also purchased a team of forty-six huskies. With Petersen and Hendrik to guide him, he hoped to lead these dogs on sled journeys the following spring.

Kane soon had reason to worry; there was no fish to be bought, the cod season being late that year. He was not unduly concerned.

By early August, with the entrance of Smith Sound in sight, Kane deposited provisions and a lifeboat in the event of an emergency and pushed northwards. Facing lashing gales and blizzards in the ice-clogged waters, they made slow progress. At times the men were compelled to don harnesses and man-haul the ship free of the ice. By late August, the *Advance* had travelled further north than any other expedition, but there were rumblings of discontent among the crew at the unrelenting hardship. On 10 September Kane was forced to anchor for the winter. The crew prepared for their winter ordeal, building a wooden shelter to secure their supplies on shore and a rough shelter for the dogs.

By mid-October the sun had disappeared completely and would not be visible again until early March. The crew was confined below deck for weeks on end and quickly became bored. Of primary importance was their well-being. Previously experienced Arctic commanders had instituted rigorous discipline to keep the men not only busy, but amused and entertained. Apparently Kane did not consider the monotony to be a serious problem. His men simply idled and sat around waiting for spring. Inactivity and the sunless polar winter sapped morale.

By the end of February, with no fish or game available, Kane's supplies were running low. Outside the temperature was between -98° and -82° and the dogs were dying off one by one. From then onwards any sledges would have to be man-hauled. The *Advance* was beset in ice in a body of water later to be named Kane Basin. It was clearly evident that she might never reach open sea again. The expedition's prospects of survival were grim.

In mid-March, despite protests from the crew that conditions were too awful for travelling, Kane despatched eight men to attempt to reach the Humboldt Glacier and beyond. Within a week three of the men staggered back to the ship, the other five were ill and freezing. These five men had to be rescued. On the return journey the rescue party met some Eskimo from Etah. Petersen's interpreting skills were invaluable and Kane, fully aware of their parlous state, was much relieved to know there was an Eskimo settlement within seventy miles of his stricken ship.

On 3 June 1854 Kane despatched Hans Hendrik and William Morton on land to search for a route to the sea. Others were despatched to climb the Humboldt Glacier to seek alternatives. Both parties failed, although Hendrik and Morton, travelling north, reached an all-time record of 81°22'N before being unable to travel any further. They also discovered an unbroken stretch of water as far as the eye could see, which they believed to be the Open Polar Sea (in this they were mistaken).

They described how they climbed a cape almost 500ft high and saw nothing but open water. Kane was elated to hear of the existence of the Open Polar Sea; he had achieved one of his goals, but now he had to figure out a way to get the *Advance* clear of the ice and out to open water.

On 8 August Kane again tried to blast the ship free with gunpowder but to no avail. The *Advance*'s position was now utterly hopeless. Kane accepted the ship was trapped and was faced with the hideous prospect of spending another Arctic winter on-board. At a meeting to discuss their predicament, disagreements arose amongst Kane and his crew. Some crew members wanted to take the whaleboat and drag it towards the open sea. Kane made it clear that he was staying. An agreed group decided they would seek help by making for the open sea in an effort to reach Upernavik. Kane was very unhappy at this turn of events, as they were leaving without his blessing. Kane insisted that the deserters sign documents attesting Kane was no longer responsible for them. Kane suppressed his anger as they departed for Upernavik, assuring them, however, that should they decide to return, they would be welcome. Those leaving did not consider they were deserting the ship. The ship was about to break up. Where did Kane intend to sail to? The crew was available to sail whenever Kane would give the order.

Neil Petersen was elected leader by the breakaways. Accompanied by Dr Isaac Hayes and seven or eight other crew members, they set out with the whaleboat on sledges for the open sea.

Kane had learnt lessons from the previous winter. He insulated the ship to make it igloo-like. Regarding the matter of food supplies, Kane was confident a mutual arrangement could be reached with the Eskimo at Etah. But he was wrong.

Meanwhile the deserters were enduring great hardship, day followed day of slow progress and unmitigated misery on the ice until they began to realise the utter hopelessness of their plight, and it dawned on them they may have made a big mistake in striking out on their own. 'What shall we do?' Hayes despairingly asked.

The *Advance*'s prospects of survival were no better. Illness and falling temperatures, together with the strain on food stores, added to their misery and led to flaring tempers. The food shortage was the most critical issue and Kane's plan of leaning on the Eskimo for food were dashed when he learned that the atrocious weather was playing havoc with their own hunting season and that they were also hungry. The Eskimo realised Kane's desperate predicament and were prepared to take full advantage of it, bartering poor quality food for valuable equipment. Kane soon realised that if he and his crew died, the Eskimo had much to gain. His ship and its equipment was more valuable to the Eskimo than its weight in gold. Soon relationships had hit rock bottom.

By 5 December the men were afflicted with scurvy. The fuel for heating purposes was desperately low and they were reduced to burning non-vital wooden sections of the ship for heating. Kane prayed that the ship's timbers, if used sparingly for firewood would be sufficient to last until spring. On 7 December 1854, much to Kane's astonishment, Petersen arrived back to the *Advance*.

The whaleboat group had not reached the open sea as they had hoped. Since Morton's and Hendrik's report, the sea had frozen over and it was impossible to remain where they were with no sea in sight. The other option was to drag the sledge and boat over the ice to Upernavik, an impossible task. It was decided to return to the *Advance*.

Petersen was to proceed ahead with crew member Bonsal. They set out on 28 November. Hayes and the remainder of the whaleboat party reached the ship on 12 December in a most distressed condition. One crew member required amputation of a number of toes. The party also received a very frosty reception from an angry Elisha Kane, who realised the remaining food supplies would have to be shared with the deserters.

Needless to say with the uncertainty of survival, and with the combination of frayed nerves and tempers of the crew, it was a most unhappy ship through the winter of 1854-55.

By the month of April, however, the walruses and seals reappeared, the men began to eat well, and the scorbutic crew members began to recover their strength. Hayes made a final attempt to blast a channel with gunpowder to free the ship, but without success.

In desperation Kane decided to abandon ship and prepared the crew for another attempt to reach the open sea. They took three boats, and every item of practical use was gathered and loaded on the sledges for the journey. On 20 May 1855 Kane abandoned the *Advance*. He and his crew began pulling their boats over the ice. Working in stages it took them a month to reach open water. It was a terrible journey. Scurvy struck down the original invalids. The starving and famished crew in the small open boats were pitched violently in the ice-filled waters.

By mid-June they had reached Etah. One man had died but the worst was yet to come. On 19 June they took to their boats once more and headed for Cape Alexander. Before them was one thousand miles of sea. Their spirits and morale were low, their food supplies were depleted and many were in failing health. For forty-nine days of sheer hell they rowed and sometimes hauled their boats across the ice through Smith Sound and Baffin Bay, surviving on fish, and by burning oars and any timber they could burn to melt ice for drinking water.

On 3 August, the crew was rescued. Neil Petersen spotted a Danish whaler in the fog, captained by his friend Carlie Mossyn. Taken on-board, the famished survivors devoured their first full meal for months. On 6 August 1855 they reached Upernavik after a journey of eighty-four days in the open. They were picked up by an American ship that had been sent to their rescue.

Kane and crew arrived in New York on 11 October 1855 after an absence of two and a half years and he was once again accorded a hero's welcome.

The New York Times filled its whole front page with the news of his return. Britain's Royal Geographical Society awarded him its Gold Medal. Kane's status in the United States had never been higher. He was feted on the American social scene, and needless to say his love life took a turn for the better. Kane published his book on the expedition, *Arctic Explorations*, which sold thousands. He was enjoying his well-earned rest, until he learned that Lady Jane Franklin was determined that he head another expedition to rescue her husband Sir John. Kane was honoured by Lady Jane's request and felt obliged to lead the new rescue mission.

In early October he set off for England for a series of engagements culminating in a breakfast with Queen Victoria, but he arrived an ill man. His health was failing and his busy schedule was taking its toll. On 29 October 1856, Kane collapsed and was advised to seek a warmer climate immediately to convalesce. He chose Cuba, where, shortly after his arrival, he suffered a stroke. After a brief rally he died on 16 February 1857 at the age of thirty-seven. Kane of the Arctic Seas was dead.

The American people gave him a send off of which he would have been proud. The obsequies that embellished the transportation of his body (which took a month) by ship, riverboat, and locomotive from Havana to New Orleans through Ohio and Cincinnati to Philadelphia, can be compared only to those that were observed at the death of Abraham Lincoln, before Elisha Kent Kane's remains were laid to rest at Laurel Hill Cemetery.

But Sir John Franklin, his ships and crews had yet to be found.

Chapter VI

Leopold McClintock's Voyage in the *Fox*

The earliest evidence of Franklin's fate was discovered by Dr John Rae. Rae was born on 30 September 1813 near Stromness on the windswept Orkney Islands. In 1833 he graduated in surgery at the University of Edinburgh, becoming a chief factor of the Hudson Bay Company in Canada. Working as both a doctor and a trader for the Company, Rae was unusual. Clearly he wished to broaden his horizons and did this by choosing to leave Scotland to begin a life of adventure, living with, and learning the survival skills of, the Eskimo. Rae was vastly experienced. In 1848 he accompanied Sir John Ross in a search for the missing Franklin Expedition. In 1851 he was again unsuccessful in his search. But after a mapping expedition in the Arctic in 1853-4, Rae returned to London with the first solid evidence from Eskimo sources of the fate of Franklin and his crew.

Rae outlined his findings. While completing a survey of the west of Boothia on King William Land, which Rae discovered to be an island, he met Eskimo in Pelly Bay who told him of forty white men (Kablounans) dragging a boat on a sledge in the direction of Great Fish River. The party of white men had perished from want of food some distance to the westward and not far beyond a large river, containing many falls and rapids, in the spring of four winters past (1850).

According to the Eskimo the men were thin. The bodies of thirty persons were discovered on the continent and five others on an island. Rae's Eskimo informants claimed to have walked among the scattered bodies and the abandoned equipment of the expedition. Rae goes on:

> ...one of those found on the island was assumed to be an officer, as he had a telescope strapped across his shoulders, and his double barrelled gun lay underneath him. From the mutilated state of many of the corpses, and the content of the kettles, it is evident that our wretched countrymen had been driven to the last resource – cannibalism – as a means of prolonging existence. Could the officer with the telescope be Captain Crozier?

Rae observed in the possession of the Eskimo many personal items that had belonged to the crews, such as watches, silver spoons, forks, compasses, telescopes and guns. Among the items he recovered was a bone-handled knife made by Millikin of London and inscribed C. Hickey. This was from the kit of the young caulker's mate born in Limerick. Rae also saw a silver tablespoon made by Isaiah Law of Dublin, inscribed with Captain Crozier's crest and initials. One of Sir John Franklin's magnificent medals presented to him in 1836 was also in the possession of the Eskimo.

Lady Jane was incandescent with rage at Rae's charges of cannibalism levelled at the men led by her husband, as were many others. Highly indignant articles and letters were published in the press refuting Rae's implications of this alleged moral collapse of Sir John and his crews. Charles Dickens replied to Dr Rae in the pages of *Household Words* (Dickens had set up this weekly magazine in 1850):

> In weighing the probabilities and improbabilities of the 'last resource', the foremost question is – not the nature of the extremity – but the nature of the men. We submit that the memory of the lost Arctic voyagers is placed, by reason and experience, high above the taint of this so-easily allowed connection; and that the noble conduct and example of such men, and of their own great leader himself, under similar endurances, belies it, and outweighs by the weight of the whole universe the chatter of a gross handful of uncivilised people, with a domesticity of blood and blubber.

But Dickens was just warming up, clearly the Inuit did not rate highly in his estimation. He wrote of the injustice and much more, of charges against men who, due to their absence, were unable to defend themselves. Rae was hard pressed to defend the character of his Eskimo informants from Charles Dickens and many other influential and eloquent figures of Victorian Society. Indeed Rae did have a real problem defending his claims. He himself had not seen any of the kettles of human flesh with his own eyes, but was relying on the integrity of his Eskimo friends, whom he trusted implicitly. The British public, and Lady Jane in particular, were deeply shocked and refused to believe in the scale of the moral collapse implied by Rae. The British population was accustomed to reading glowing reports in the books and diaries written by returning Naval Arctic explorers. The texts of such books usually combined retrospective narrative and descriptions with supposed actual quotations from on-the-spot journals. The quotations from the journals, however, had usually been carefully edited by both the author and the publisher before they saw print. In the case of British Naval Officers, their writings had also been pre-censored. Officers knew their superiors would scrutinise their journals at the conclusion of an expedition.

Eskimo were looked down upon and in the eyes of many had no place in the stories of British expeditions or Arctic conquests. They had no interest in exploration or reaching geographical landmarks on the world map. To the Eskimo, a land objective was meaningless unless it encompassed their seasonal food cycle and did not impinge on their hunt for seal, bears, caribou, fish or game. Considered a primitive people by the explorers of the seventeenth, eighteenth and nineteenth centuries, they were studied, described and marvelled over as a strange little people. Information was available on their customs and habits; Eskimo rub noses instead of kissing, they eat raw flesh, swap wives and live in houses built of blocks of ice. Eskimo and 'white men' differed in many ways. There is little evidence of them to be found in the paintings of the period, as it would appear that the Inuit contribution to polar exploration was being airbrushed out of history by British society. Clearly there was a giant chasm between the two cultures, which does explain the British public's difficulty with Dr Rae's allegations.

The controversy developed into a smear campaign against Rae and the Eskimo. Rae's implicit challenge to Franklin and his officers' competence rankled, despite Rae's undoubted knowledge and experience. The onslaught on Rae became nasty. A *Times* editorial said 'All savages are liars.' Extracts from the seventh edition of the *Encylopaedia Britannica* were circulated, which gave a composite report on igloo manners in 1842. The following is an extract:

> In their domestic economy, however, they are uniformly filthy and disgusting in the extreme. The Greenlanders, says Egede, in their manners and their common way of life, are very slovenly, nasty and filthy. They seldom wash themselves, will eat out of plates and bowls after their dogs without cleaning them and what is most nauseous to behold, eat lice and such like vermin which they find upon themselves and others. They will scrape the sweat off their faces with a knife and lick it up.

It continues in that vein and finishes up with the following, 'Details similar to the above are given by others who have visited these countries, but they are too disgusting to be quoted here.'

Dr Rae had no answer to this tirade of abuse and the thrashing of his character. His honesty cost him his chance of a Knighthood. His consolation however was to collect the £10,000 reward for conclusive information on the expedition. Rae's Eskimo interpreter Ouligbuck received £210 as his share of the reward. And the Eskimo? They were temporarily relegated to the lower division of England's favourite natives.

The unfortunate Dr John Rae became *persona non grata* to Lady Jane and her friends. He was given little credit for his findings and charted discoveries. Nevertheless, Lady Jane was anxious to show that if Rae's claim about Franklin's men having reached Back's Great Fish River were true, credit would be due to her husband for having completed the first Northwest Passage to the Canadian coast from Lancaster Sound. Lady Jane refused to accept the evidence that Sir John was dead. It was not in her interest to do so. If he was dead she would not retain her heroic status and would be relegated to normal widowhood. She continued to keep the image intact, and did so with great determination.

Dr Richard King had been quite right all along about the likely route Franklin's crews would follow if they were forced to abandon their ships in the ice. Ross, who had vetoed Dr King's suggestion and claimed the Great Fish River would yield nothing, jeopardised his future prospects of promotion. Lady Jane refused to allow Dr Rae to assist McClintock in his search for Franklin on his voyage on the *Fox*. Dr Rae spent the later years of his life in London where he died on 22 July 1893 at the age of eighty.

Public interest was reawakened by Dr Rae's news, but the Government and Admiralty were still fighting the war with the Russians in the Crimea, and were not prepared to send any more expeditions on what they considered to be fruitless searches. If somebody wanted to be reckless and needlessly risk their lives, they could do so on their own ships and at their own expense.

Lady Franklin had always vigorously supported the searching of Boothia toward the Great Fish River, and so she decided to finance and fit out another expedition. She was determined to finally establish the truth or otherwise of the shocking allegations of cannibalism. If Sir John could not be rescued, she at least wanted to preserve his good name and fine reputation so that his sacrifice was not in vain. In 1857 her good friend Dickens mounted the spectacular pro-Franklin play *The Frozen Deep* at Tavistock House.

With Dr Elisha Kent Kane seriously ill, Lady Jane turned to Leopold McClintock and offered him command of a new expedition, having in mind the ship *Fox*. McClintock's response in part was, 'how could I do otherwise than devote myself to save at least the record of faithful service even unto death of my brother officers and seamen?' He applied from Dublin (he then lived at 2 Gardiner Place) to the Admiralty for leave of absence to complete the Franklin search. On 23 April 1857, he received at Dublin a communication from Lady Franklin; 'Your leave is granted, the *Fox* is mine, the refit will commence immediately.'

He surveyed the *Fox*, a screw yacht of 177 tons which was sent to Aberdeen for refitting. Eighteen of her crew were polar veterans including Neil Petersen, the Eskimo interpreter who had been with Dr Elisha Kent Kane. Provisions for twenty-eight months were embarked including 6,682 pounds of pemmican provided by the Admiralty. (Pemmican is preserved in tins; it is made of beef cut in thin slices and dried, then either cut up fine or, as some firms prepare it, ground up and mixed with an equal quantity of fat. It is considered very nourishing and some people like it. But among the Americans and Europeans it was not popular.) On the evening planned for departure – 30 June – Lady Jane came on-board to bid farewell.

The *Fox* sailed north but it was a very bad ice year and the small ship was soon beset in the drifting ice of Baffin Bay. It was trapped, not to be released again for 242 days. During this time the ship drifted over one thousand miles before finally exiting in the Davis Channel. They had many anxious days and nights during the Arctic winter, culminating the following April in a two-day nerve-wracking exit through the drifting blocks of ice in high winds and waves over 13ft high.

When eventually released from the pack in April 1858, McClintock steered back north again to refresh the crew and to hunt caribou. In September he began to plan for spring 1859. There would be three search parties. Each would comprise a leader and four men and be provided with a dog sled and driver. The first party would be led by McClintock himself, with whom Neil Petersen would travel as dog-sled driver. They would search the Great Fish River Estuary, on the shores of King William Land. Lt Hobson would lead the second party to the magnetic pole area and to the west coast of Boothia in autumn, and from Gateshead westward in spring. The third search party was led by Allen Young, a Merchant Navy captain. His party would search Prince of Wales Land. Allen Young was a close friend of the Franklins, and he not only refused a salary for the duration of the search, he also contributed £500 to the costs of the mission.

The journeys were planned to start on 29 March 1859, and would involve sixty to seventy days of travelling, but first, during the autumn of 1858 they had to lay out depots and meet the native Boothians, the local Inuit who lived south of Bellot Strait. In the process McClintock would train his dog teams in preparation for the spring search programme.

On 17 February 1859, Young and McClintock set out. McClintock was looking for the Boothians. On 1 March they stopped to build their evening hut close to the magnetic North Pole. When they turned around, behind them stood four Inuit men who had been hunting. They had started out for their village when darkness descended upon them and were about to build a shelter.

McClintock traded a sewing needle with each of the Inuit in exchange for them to build him an Inuit hut there and then. They completed it in one hour and both parties slept in it together. McClintock observed that the records of architecture do not mention another instance of a house being built so quickly or so cheaply.

One of the Inuit had a naval button on his dress. Upon enquiry it was learned that it came from some of the white people who were starved on an island where there are salmon – this implied a river and that the iron from which their knives were made came from that place also. One of the men said he had been there for wood and iron but none of them had seen the white men.

The next morning they travelled ten miles closer to Cape Victoria. The Inuit here built a commodious hut that, despite the gale outside, kept them all warm. McClintock showed the articles brought for barter – knives, files, sewing needles, scissors and beads, and expressed through Petersen their desire to barter for anything the Inuit had picked up that had belonged to the white men. Despite the cold, two of the Inuit took off their outer coats and traded them for a knife. The following morning forty-five Inuit arrived, the entire population of the village. Silver spoons and forks, a silver medal (property of Mr A. McDonald, the assistant surgeon), part of a gold chain, buttons, knives made out of iron, and wood from the wrecks (*Erebus* and *Terror*) were produced and successfully traded. The Boothians remembered another explorer, Ross and his ship the *Victory*. When McClintock enquired after a man to whom they had supplied a wooden leg, his daughter was pointed out. Petersen interpreted this to mean that the man had died, as the Inuit did not like to refer directly to the dead.

None of the Eskimo had seen the white men, though one man said he had seen their bones on the island where they had died, and that only some were buried. With this intelligence, McClintock returned to the ship, reaching it on 14 March. The journey of 420 miles completed the discovery of the coast of continental America and added 120 miles to the existing charts.

On 2 April 1859 the main sledge journeys commenced. Hobson was directed to search the west coast of King William Island while McClintock headed south across the pack and established a depot for their return. With thirty days' supplies he was trying to locate some local Inuit in their residences who, he thought, might lead them to the remains of Franklin's crews. He described the empty huts he found as being 12ft in diameter, 7ft high and mostly constructed in pairs, with a common entrance passage. A small hut served as a receptacle for items of food intended to be kept frozen.

On 7 May an inhabited snow village was found further south on King William Island. Here they purchased six pieces of tableware bearing the crest and initials of Franklin, Crozier, Fairholme and McDonald, together with tunic buttons and uniforms. The silver spoons and forks were exchanged for four sewing needles each. The Inuit told them that it was a five-day trip to the wreck, that it was accessible, and that most of it had already been carried away by the local Inuit. When asked about the condition of the masts, they were told they were down – felled it seemed by burning their bases close to the deck. The Inuit said the last person from their group to visit the wreck did so during the winter of 1857–58. A woman said that many of the white men dropped on the way as they went to the Great Fish River. Some were buried and some were not. The Inuit had passed their fallen bodies the following winter.

McClintock's team reached Great Fish River. Two days of gales forced them to stay put. After the storm they marched onwards. On 25 May McClintock came across skeletal remains on a ridge between the beach and the island, lying face downwards and partly exposed. The tattered remains of clothing indicated a steward or officer's servant, a clothes brush and comb were also found – an indication that the natives had not discovered this corpse. McClintock carried on for twelve miles until he found a small, recently built cairn. It was erected by Lt Hobson's party and contained a note from Hobson reporting that he had not seen anything of the wreck or of the natives, but they had found a record – the record so ardently sought to tell the fate of the Franklin Expedition. He had found it at Cape Victory on the north-west coast of King William Land. The note was written on a standard printed form of a type usually supplied to discovery ships. These notes would be enclosed in a bottle and thrown overboard at sea in order to ascertain currents, with blank spaces left for the date and position. Any person finding one of these records was asked to forward it to the Secretary of the Admiralty.

The message read as follows:

28th of May 1847. HMS ships *Erebus* and *Terror* wintered in the ice in lat. 70°5'N long. 98°23'W. Having wintered in the ice in lat. 74°43'28", long 91°39'15"W after having ascended Wellington Channel to lat. 77°N and returned by the west side of Cornwallis Island, Sir John Franklin commanding the expedition. All well. Party consisting of two officers and six men left the ships on Monday 24th 1847. G.M. Gore Lt Chas. F. Des Voeux Mate.

This brief message meant that Franklin, in the first ice season, had followed orders and had discovered new lands on both sides of the Wellington Channel, the entry of which discovered in 1819. They went north for 150 miles and reached lat. 77°N. They had then overwintered. That winter appears to have passed without any serious loss of life and when, in spring, Lt Gore left the ship with a party, all was well and Franklin was still in command. However, a second message, written on the margins of the document reads as follows:

25th April, 1848: HM ships *Terror* and *Erebus* were deserted on 22nd of April. Five leagues NNW of this, having been beset since 12th of September, 1846. The Officers and crews consisting of 105 souls – under the command of Captain F.R.M. Crozier landed here in lat. 69°37'42" long. 98°41'.

This paper was found under the cairn presumed to have been built by Sir James Ross in 1831, four miles to the north, where it had been deposited by the late Commander Gore in June of 1847.

Sir John Franklin died on 11of June 1847, and the total loss by deaths in the expedition has been to this date nine officers and fifteen men. (Signed) James Fitzjames. Captain Crozier ordered abandon ships, which were hopelessly beset in ice with no possibility of assistance and seek sanctuary elsewhere.

F.R.M. Crozier Captain and Senior Officer, start on tomorrow 27th for Backs Fish River.

The crews of both *Erebus* and *Terror* had then attempted to march south to the Canadian mainland and had perished from a combination of scurvy and starvation. McClintock described how the record was 'indeed a sad and touching relic of lost friends'. The first message told of the success of the expedition in its first navigation season (1845–46). The second message told how in the second season (1846–47) they navigated into Peel Strait and what is now known as Franklin Strait, where the ships became beset in pack ice. They drifted and were crushed. In the final statement, the leaders Crozier and Fitzjames demonstrated their lofty sense of duty and calmness, having made the decision to struggle for life rather than perish without effort on-board their ships, for we know that *Erebus* and *Terror* were only provisioned up to July 1848.

Hobson's note told McClintock that he had found a large quantity of clothing and articles of all kinds about the cairn, as if the men were fully aware they were retreating for their lives and had abandoned everything they considered superfluous. Hobson's last observation was that he had experienced bad weather, gales and fog, and feared he might have passed the wreck without seeing her. He hoped to be more successful on the return journey.

McClintock and his party travelled west. On 30 May they camped alongside a large wooden board which was another relic found by Hobson – but there was no written record. Regarding the vast quantity of tattered clothing, no article bore the name of its owner. On examination they discovered that the boat had been built with a view to lightness, but the sledge on which she travelled was unusually heavy. Made of oak planks, it was 23ft long, and given the direction in which the boat was pointed, he surmised it was on its way back to the ships, which he calculated were sixty miles to the north-east. Two skeletons were also found in the boat, one of a slight young person and the other of a large, strongly built middle-aged person. McClintock's opinion was that wolves had probably destroyed much of one of the skeletons; he thought this might have been an officer. They also found a staggering array of items, including two rolls of lead sheeting, nails, saws, files, boots, shoes and silver cutlery, which cumulatively amounted to a considerable deadweight. In the opinion of McClintock, this was a load likely to break down the strength of any sledge crew.

They continued to follow the coast until mid-June, when McClintock was forced to abandon the sledges, and the footsore and exhausted dogs (he intended returning to recover the dogs). They walked over the remaining hills and valleys, until, on 19 June 1859, after an absence of seventy-eight days they sighted *Fox*. Hobson, who had arrived a week earlier, was still unable to walk from the effects of scurvy; he had been brought back on the sledge.

Thomas Blackwell, the ship's steward, who had been sick with scurvy on McClintock's departure, was dead on his return, bringing to three the death toll for the expedition.

McClintock and his crew celebrated their achievements (which included recovering his dog team). They had found written records – the only tangible evidence of the Franklin disaster – and the remains of some of his men. McClintock had also discovered the first practical route by way of the Rae Strait that would lead eventually to the first water navigation of the Northwest Passage forty-five years later by the Norwegian Roald Amundsen.

McClintock and his crew busied themselves by preparing for the journey home. On 9 August the ice was cleared and the *Fox* steamed to Disko Bay and from there back to London's Blackwell Docks, arriving on 23 September 1859.

Leopold McClintock received a knighthood from Queen Victoria and the freedom of the City of London. The Royal Geographical Society presented him with its Patrons' Gold Medal. To this day a polar bear shot by Sir Leopold McClintock can be seen in the Natural History Museum in Merrion Street, Dublin.

A committee was established to erect a suitable memorial to the memory of Captain Crozier and a fine monument was erected in his honour in 1862 at Bridge Street, Banbridge, Co. Down.

McClintock's revelation that Sir John Franklin had died on 11 June 1847, two years before the crews did or did not cannibalise each other, exonerated him, as he clearly could not have been involved in those events. The expedition was deemed to have reached the threshold of the Northwest Passage.

Permission was given to memorial artists for busts and statues identifying Sir John as the Discoverer of the Northwest Passage. The Royal Geographical Society presented its founders' Gold Medal to Lady Jane Franklin in recognition of her noble and self-sacrificing perseverance.

Lady Jane Franklin was happy in the knowledge that she had played a huge part in clearing her husband's name. She did not remarry, and spent much of her remaining life travelling the world accompanied by her niece Sophy Cracroft. Lady Jane's last project was the completion of a monument to her husband's memory in Westminster Abbey. On it was an epitaph by Tennyson:

Not here! the white North has thy bones; and thou
Heroic sailor soul,
Art passing on thine happier voyage now.
Toward no earthly pole.

Time is a great healer, and in her twilight years Lady Jane welcomed the visits of Eleanor's husband John Gell and his toddling grandchildren. She died, aged eighty-four, on 18 July 1875, roughly six weeks after the George S. Nares North Pole Expedition set out, and two weeks before the unveiling of Sir John's cenotaph. She was buried in a vault in Kensal Green cemetery in London. Sophy Cracroft died on 20 June 1892, at the age of seventy-six. She had never married.

The personal papers of Sir John and Lady Franklin, including Franklin's journals, letter-books, etc., are in the Scott Polar Research Institute in Cambridge. Portraits of Franklin are in the collections of the National Portrait Gallery, London. There is a monument to Sir John Franklin erected in his home town Spilsby in Lincolnshire, and another one in Hobart, Tasmania.

McClintock's findings answered many of the questions regarding the fate of Franklin. But very little is known of the detail or chronology of events surrounding the expedition's demise. Franklin and Crozier's contemporaries were baffled by the absence of messages left by the crews of *Erebus* and *Terror*, and had difficulty in understanding why no apparent effort was made to establish a food cache to which they could retreat in the event of either or both ships becoming beset in ice. The reports lacked clarity on the sequence of events.

The intention in sending two ships together was so that each could support the other in the event of one ship having a mishap or sinking. That both ships became beset in the main pack ice in the same place undermined the logic of this tactic and was incomprehensible to experienced Arctic explorers. This may be a trifle harsh, however. The tactic was sound, but in the Arctic it could be thwarted, as the ships were in the midst of enormous masses of floating ice, in a vast uncharted area, without communication, and in one of the largest archipelagos on the planet.

Arctic experts questioned Crozier's reasons for retreating toward the Great Fish River with the entire complement of both ships. They also asked why he did not at least send one sledge party eastward, where they could have perhaps met with whalers or left messages at Beechey Island or Fury Beach indicating their whereabouts or intentions, and why not a single crew member from either ship survived, and not a single page from a journal of one of the officers has been found.

That such a prestigious Royal Navy Expedition led by the high-profile Sir John Franklin should end in a debacle was hugely embarrassing for the British Admiralty and also a huge disappointment for the British Government. It would be a long time before they got over it.

Leopold McClintock's reports and conclusions on the expedition raised many awkward questions regarding Sir John Franklin's performance as Commander. Experienced Arctic explorers including Captain Nares and Clements Markham were extremely puzzled at a succession of strange decisions. The following is an extract from *Narrative of a voyage to the Polar Sea during 1875-6 in H.M. ships Alert and Discovery* (1878) by George S. Nares. The introduction to the book was written by George Henry Richards and in it he presents his analytical summary of the Franklin Expedition:

The decade of rescue missions laid bare a mystery that is still being examined today. It also revealed a futility of trying to find a profitable seaway through the ice-choked archipelago of the north.

Looking back with our present knowledge it may well seem unaccountable that the idea of succour becoming necessary never entered into the minds of Franklin, or the most experienced of his contemporaries, and that no single precaution for relief was ever contemplated before the expedition sailed. We now, indeed, know that if it had been arranged that in the summer of 1847 an expedition should proceed to some appointed rendezvous in Barrow Strait, there to remain until the autumn of 1848, it is certain that most if not all the surviving crew would have been rescued; we know this now because we know where the ships were abandoned, and that the spot was within reach of such succour; but had they penetrated a hundred miles further westward it would have taken them out of such reach; all attempts however at rescue, at whatever time undertaken, would have been in vain, unless pre-arranged with Franklin.

This is the fatal mistake which experience has taught us, and which can never be repeated; but had it been recognised as a necessity to send a second expedition one or two years after the departure of the first, to secure its safety, would the two ships it may be asked, have sailed at all? Would not the question have arisen, 'Is expedition to follow expedition while a ship remains absent?' And there could probably have been but one reply. Much has been written by theorists, after the event, to prove that the long and fruitless search was made in the wrong direction, and that where Franklin was ordered to go, he should have been sought. But what are the facts; instructions to the leaders of such expeditions can be considered as advice to be followed under certain assumed conditions; but in the uncertainties of Arctic navigation, circumstances are almost certain to occur which may render it impossible to act upon instructions, however ably conceived.

Franklin was indeed ordered to go to the south-west in the direction of Cape Walker, but none knew what was beyond that Cape. If unsuccessful there he was to try the Wellington Channel, only sixty miles to the eastward, which had been seen and pronounced a promising channel by Parry, and which being nearer the open sea is probably always free from ice before the more sheltered inlets to the westward.

In all probability the south-west was tried and found closed; it is certain as we know now, that he did ascend the Wellington Channel to 77°N. and finding the outlet westward sealed returned, wintered at Beechey Island, and later on in the year 1846 succeeded in penetrating to the SW beyond Cape Walker; but a ship's keel leaves no track behind, and no scrap of paper was ever found, or probably ever left, to indicate the course taken by the *Erebus* and *Terror* until the fatal one discovered by McClintock's parties on King William's Land, which recorded the abandonment of the ships and thus revealed the sad story that all must probably have perished ten years before.

The only clue ever found by the searching ships previous to this – the three graves on Beechey Island at the entrance to Wellington Channel – a significant clue indeed, probably led those who followed in a direction at once in the track of the lost expedition, and at the same time hopelessly astray. Be this as it may, it must be confessed, and perhaps with humiliation, that the united wisdom and judgment of the most experienced Arctic navigators, and the energy and perseverance of the most able leaders, were alike at fault, so that it was left for the solitary little *Fox* equipped by Lady Franklin and her friends, and commanded by McClintock, to solve the mystery which had previously baffled so many able commanders (himself among the number) with means and resources unlimited. His success however, complete as it was, detracts in no way from the credit of those who went before. Working in the dark, so to speak, they did all that undaunted perseverance and devotion could accomplish, in the face of difficulties and hardships which have rarely been equalled.

The shock and the disappointment of failing to navigate the Northwest Passage after more than ten weary years of effort since 1845 and an enormous expenditure of money, made it evident to all the that the Northwest Passage was in no way viable. Thus the fields of discovery narrowed to the other point of interest and a more direct approach – the North Pole.

Some conclusions were reached based on the reports of the searchers. A coastline or a frozen sea that neither a ship nor boat could approach, could only be accomplished by manual labour, with men dragging heavily laden sledges for weeks or months together.

As much as 400 miles in a direct line on an outward journey had been accomplished by these means (each man dragging 200–300 pounds in weight, and being absent from the frozen-in ships for often 90–100 days), which opened up the possibility of the pursuit of geographical discovery.

These findings made a strong argument for those urging upon the British Government the expediency of further explorations. Their efforts, however, were to no immediate avail and a long struggle over many years would ensue. After the abandonment of the Franklin search, the British Admiralty's attitude towards Arctic discovery was to let sleeping dogs lie. But that was not the response in the public consciousness.

The sensational revelations of the Franklin Expedition and the successful charting of the Northwest Passage put the Arctic and North Pole firmly back on the table for debate both in Europe and the United States. The conundrum was, apart from it being a geographical point on the world map, what kind of place was the North Pole, and did anyone live there?

In 1866 the Government erected a statue in memory of Sir John Franklin at Waterloo Place in London, and on its plinth it bears the inscription:

Franklin,
To the great navigator
and his brave companions
who sacrificed their lives in
completing the discovery of
The Northwest Passage.

To say the least, the inscription is inaccurate. The Franklin Expedition sailed no further than Peel Sound in the centre of the Archipelago, 200 miles away from the Pacific and the completion of the Passage.

How much had the ten-year search for the Franklin Expedition cost? It would be impossible to put a figure on the costs expended on what was up to then the biggest and longest manhunt in history. Estimates vary; some experts estimate that from 1845–55, between public subscription, Lady Jane's own money and the searches by the British and American Navies, a figure equivalent to €100 million today would be a modest estimate.

Lady Jane had also corresponded with Charles Francis Hall, the famous American Arctic explorer, and learned of his conversations with the Inuit. On 15 August 1870, during Lady Jane's and Sophy Cracroft's last visit to the United States, Lady Jane visited Charles Francis Hall in his hometown of Cincinnati, to learn about his Arctic experiences when he was writing his book *Life with the Esquimaux.*

Chapter VII

Dr Isaac Hayes

Dr Isaac Hayes, who had served on Dr Elisha Kane's Expedition on the *Advance*, was born in Chester County, Pennsylvania, in 1832. After finishing medical training he joined Captain De Haven's unsuccessful search for Franklin. Hayes then enlisted on Dr Kane's ill-fated 1853-5 Grinnell-sponsored Expedition. While the *Advance* was iced in, Hayes set out on explorations by sledge from the northern part of Ellesmere Island and was convinced he could see open water, the Open Polar Sea.

His name was added to the list of explorers who were convinced there was an navigable sea to the North Pole, alongside Elisha Kane, Sir Hugh Willoughby, William Barents, Sir John Barrow and Captain Inglefield. Had Hayes become afflicted with the Arctic addiction? Having narrowly escaped death he was prepared to risk his life once again to reach the Pole. He embarked on a new fundraising campaign to finance the expedition. He lectured at the American Philosophical Society, the Academy of Natural Sciences of Philadelphia, the Boston Society of Natural History, the New York Lyceum of Natural History, and the Smithsonian Institute. Aided by some financial assistance from Henry Grinnell, he had secured sufficient funds for his next trip to the Arctic. In 1860 Hayes purchased the 133-ton schooner *Spring Hill*. He had the ship rebuilt in Boston, reinforced and adapted for Arctic exploration. Learning from the *Advance* disaster, he laid particular emphasis on ice-strengthening. He renamed her the *United States*, and remembering Kane's many shortcomings, he took aboard a vast amount of food and equipment.

The *United States* left Boston on 10 July 1860 with a fifteen-man crew led by Hayes (second in command was August Sontag, an astronomer, and the experienced Gibson Carruthers was Boatswain). The weather that year was unusually good and as they sailed up Baffin Bay, Hayes waxed lyrical in his journals about the beauty and colours of the countless icebergs, some the size of cathedrals. He marvelled at how the sky glowed in crimson, gold and purple, colours he or the crew had never seen before, adding to reflections of rainbows on the pristine ice and clear sea. He noted how the elements had sculpted and shaped the bergs, and the ear-splitting crash, as collisions between icebergs being blown in the wind caused giant eruptions, these eruptions completely changing the formations and scenery as huge segments were smashed off and massive new creations were formed, which only nature could fashion.

They reached Upernavik on 12 August but while the achievement should have been a cause of celebration, it was marred by the sudden death of Gibson Carruthers, found dead in his bunk. He was buried the next day.

In Upernavik Hayes renewed his friendship with Neil Petersen and engaged him, and bought some dogs for the expedition. Hayes sailed further up the coast to Cape York to seek Hans Hendrik, the Eskimo hunter who had proved so helpful on Kane's voyage. Hans was more than happy to join the expedition, but only on condition that his wife Merket and their child could come with him.

At the beginning of September, Hayes found winter harbour at Port Foulke, north of Cape Alexander. There was then a sudden and most dramatic deterioration in the conditions. For days on end snow blizzards and hurricane winds lashed the small ship.

'The imagination cannot conceive of a scene so wild', Hayes wrote in his journal. 'It is impossible for me to convey to this page a picture of that vast volume of foam which flutters over the sea.' In the storm they lost a lifeboat, a jib boom and two masts. The severity of the weather became a serious worry for Hayes as the ship became trapped on the coast of Greenland. It had been his intention to overwinter at the eightieth parallel or beyond, but that was now impossible and Hayes was faced with the prospect of his expedition ending in a fiasco and his voyage being no more successful than Kane's.

Hayes made the ship ready for winter. He and five others set off in mid-October to seek the Open Polar Sea. They travelled seventy miles inland and reached a height of 5,000ft above sea level where they faced a stupendous expanse of immeasurable ice. The temperature was -34° and the winds so fierce that unless they walked backwards their faces became frostbitten within seconds. With two men already ill, Hayes did not dare continue. The party barely had the strength to wrap the tent onto the sledge. 'We ran to save our lives,' Hayes recorded.

During the winter an epidemic broke out among the dogs. Needing additional dogs, August Sontag and Hans Hendrik were despatched to purchase replacements at Cape York. Tragedy struck once more. August Sontag perished on the sea ice from cold and exhaustion. Hans Hendrik's efforts to save him were in vain.

The weather in November continued to be atrocious and at one point there was nineteen inches of snow. Hayes was fortunate that game could still be hunted and during lulls in the bad weather the crew were able to collect a stock of fresh meat to see them through the winter. Added to the ship's provisions, they were well equipped. They settled down to a monotony of daily chores, which was not helped in any way by the twenty-four-hour Arctic night. The days passed silently and gloomily, 'Each hour of darkness growing a little longer, and soaking a little more colour from the blood and taking a little elasticity from the step.' Hayes wrote, 'The first sledge party attempted to reach the Open Polar Sea via Greenland's coast – and they failed. The ice rose in endless hummocks and icebergs. If a thousand Lisbons were crowded together and tumbled to pieces by the shock of an earthquake the scene could hardly have been more rugged.' On 6 April they abandoned the boat. It would have taken 100 men, in Hayes's estimation, to drag it across Smith Sound. By 24 April they were thiry miles into Smith Sound. One of the sledges had broken. Four men were seriously ill and the others were exhausted. The chances of ever reaching the west coast with this party looked almost hopeless, Hayes admitted. Two days later he was even more pessimistic, 'The men are completely used up, broken down, dejected to the last degree. Human nature cannot stand it. There is no let up to it.' As one of them told him, he 'might as well try to cross New York by rooftops as tackle this tangle of ice'.

On 27 April Hayes gave up. It was agreed they would return to the ship. Everything had changed since Hayes had last been there. There was no sign of Kane's abandoned *Advance*. The cold was killing, at one point sinking to −100°F. Hayes headed back to the ship where he put in motion his long-anticipated thrust towards Grinnell Land.

A northern-most point had been reached, Lady Franklin Bay at 81°35'N. From there Hayes looked out over the Kennedy Channel, which apparently led out directly into the polar sea. Hayes estimated that the seaway to the North Pole could be navigated in the period from July to September, which he would attempt if they had the good fortune to sail through Smith Sound.

When Hayes returned from Lady Franklin Sound he found the ship had suffered damage when released from the grip of the ice and he was forced to change his plans. He would quickly leave for the United States and, with a more robust steamship, return the following summer to make the break through to the North Pole. Hayes experienced many travails before arriving back in the United States.

On 12 August they reached Upernavik, where a Danish vendor came aboard. Hayes asked for the news of the outside world. He was stunned by the reply. There was plenty of news, he said, the Southern States were fighting the

Northern States in America. When Hayes received his mail from Copenhagen the awful news of a Civil War in his homeland was confirmed.

They reached Boston in October 1861 after a stopover at Halifax. Hayes offered his services to the Union Army and was accepted, eventually rising to the rank of Colonel. He still planned to go to the Arctic again, as he explained in the last pages of his journal, but when the war ended, he was too exhausted to continue his quest for the non-existent Open Polar Sea.

Dr Isaac Hayes, however, had still not conquered his Arctic addiction and in 1869 he travelled to north Greenland, this time to live among the Eskimo population. Hayes's Arctic journals and books are still available and make great reading. He later settled in New York, became a politician and died in 1886, maintaining to the last that the Open Polar Sea was within reach. But after all his trials, valiant attempts, and punishing ordeals, he had not even beaten Morton's and Hendrik's farthest north on Kane's ship *Advance*.

Chapter VIII

Hall's Search for Franklin, 1860

The publication of Kane's and Hayes's journals in the United States had created a huge interest in the Arctic. The proprietors of *The New York Times* and *Tribune* newspapers in particular gave great coverage to their exploits. National magazines and periodicals became alert to this new-found Arctic patriotic fervour. Among them was a man named Charles Francis Hall, the owner and editor of the *Cincinnati Occasional* and the *Daily Penny Press* newspapers. In terms of circulation, they were miniscule in comparison to the New York dailies. Nevertheless, Hall spoke for the nation in his editorials by proclaiming that Americans could and would find the answer to the Franklin mystery.

Charles Francis Hall was a remarkable man in many ways. In appearance he was short and thickset with broad shoulders and a curly beard. He was not a highly educated man, having worked as a blacksmith and an engraver before becoming editor of his publications.

Hall was born in the State of Vermont in 1821. His family moved to Rochester, New Hampshire, where he spent his boyhood. In the 1840s he married and drifted to Ohio, arriving in Cincinnati in 1849. Single-minded, determined, but naïve, there was nothing to suggest that this obscure man from the American mid-west would become one of the country's most famous Arctic explorers.

Charles Francis Hall had become fascinated by Dr Kane's journals and the disappearance of the Franklin Expedition. Having read the journals, he then read everything else available on the subject, notably the accounts of Captain Martin Frobisher's three Arctic expeditions. Hall was particularly impressed with Leopold McClintock's mercy mission to rescue Franklin and came to two conclusions: the Franklin Expedition had disappeared but the crew could be alive and awaiting rescue, and the Eskimo were the key to Polar success.

Hall's theory was that the key to Arctic survival lay in the adoption of

Eskimo clothing and Eskimo diet. Hall thought to himself, 'If I know it, Franklin must know it.' Hall was confident he possessed the necessary know-how to find Sir John Franklin despite the fact that he lacked every skill required for an Arctic rescue, he had no experience of navigation, of ice, or the Arctic, and he had ever commanded a ship. Isaac Hayes's recent lectures had whetted Hall's appetite even more and were the final clincher in making his decision.

At the age of thirty-nine the naïve Charles Francis Hall began to make his preparations. 'Courage and resolution were all that I needed', he wrote in an editorial. He felt as if God was backing him, 'it seemeth to me as if I had been called'. Hall sold his newspaper interests, left his pregnant wife Mary and young daughter, and caught a train to New York. His mission was to acquire the ways and means to sail into the Arctic to find Franklin.

Leopold McClintock's findings proved unequivocally that many of Franklin's crew were dead. When the news broke, Hall was unconcerned. He would go to the Arctic and attempt to link up with Sir Leopold McClintock and find the remaining survivors still unaccounted for. In his view the searches had not been extensive or thorough enough and were constrained mainly because the searchers were unable to understand the language of the Inuit. Hall's writings include the following extract:

> Yes, a document was discovered which proved the ships had been abandoned. It is believed by many that they are all dead and Britain has discarded all idea of farther search though the truth could now so easily be obtained.
>
> Why could not their true fate be ascertained? Why should not attempts be made again and again, until the whole facts were properly known?
>
> Other persons that I called upon for assistance in New London were Captains Sisson, Tyson, Quayle and S.O. Budington, with whom afterward I embarked on my voyage.

Hall purchased the *George Henry*. Its dimensions were as follows: length, 28ft; beam, 7ft; depth, 29½ inches; thickness of her planking, 7/8 inches, drawing only 8 inches of water when loaded with stores, and a crew of six persons. She had one mast, on which a jib and main-sail could be carried, a heavy awning to shelter the crew at night or at rest, and the lockers for stores at each end were sufficiently large that a man could, if need be, comfortably sleep in either of them.

Hall engaged a five-man crew. Among them were Captain Sidney Budington and navigator George Tyson, both of whom would play hugely significant roles later on. Before his departure Hall went to great lengths praising the generous deeds of Henry Grinnell (his chief benefactor) and emphasised Grinnell's support, his financial generosity and encouragement to the other American explorers who had searched for Franklin.

On 29 May 1860, Charles Francis Hall set sail. He was a courageous man, travelling to the Arctic in a 28ft boat through iceberg strewn waters. He described this most unpleasant experience:

As I write my head is like a mountain of solid rock. Our small boat was tossed about like a cork on waves and in troughs, rising to the crest of a wave and then crashing to the bottom, heave to the top, crash to the bottom, heave and crash day after day, night after night. More miserable days than these past few have been to me it would be hard to imagine. And why? Because of seasickness. And what is seasickness? Can any one tell unless they have experienced it? Especially after eating or trying to eat a meal. I imagine not; nor perhaps, can many describe it who have come under its affliction. I know that I cannot do so. I have found myself swung, tumbled, jammed, knocked, struck, rocked, turned, skewed, slewed, warped, pitched forward and backward, tossed up and down, down and up, this way and that way, round and round, crossways and kit-a-cornered, in every possible manner. On the ocean, fresh from civilised life, this may be called seasickness, but elsewhere I should term it next to a torturous death! No more terrible experience can a man have of life upon the

'A floe-berg aground.' (*Illustrated London News*, 11 November 1876.)

broad waters than his first few days at sea when thus attacked.

It was 9 June in calmer seas before Hall recovered from his health-weakening ordeal and reached Greenland where he and his five-man crew met Governor Elberg of the Holsteinborg region. Hall was impressed by his visit and went on to say:

The early history of Greenland is generally well known yet a brief 'resume' may not be uninteresting to the reader. In many respects it borders upon romance, well-attested facts state nearly as follows: about the middle of the tenth century, one Gunbiorn, an inhabitant of the previously settled Iceland, discovered land to the west, and on returning made a report of what he had seen. Soon afterwards in the year 983, a person known as 'Eric the Red' was sentenced by the Icelanders to banishment for the crime of manslaughter, and he determined to visit the country Gunbiorn had discovered. He arrived at a point now known as Cape Farewell. He finally returned to Iceland, where he gave such a report of 'Greenland'.

In 1576 Martin Frobisher visited Friesland, now known to be Greenland, on his voyage of discovery to the Northwest, but brought to light no particulars concerning the original colonists. Other voyagers touched upon the shores; but not until 1721, when the brave and good, and truly Christian man, Hans Egede, conceived the project of himself going to Greenland, to spread religion among its natives, was anything permanently affected. Then Greenland soon came into notice and at various times, colonies and missionary establishments, under the Danish flag, were formed along its coasts. The most northern official settlement is Upernavik in latitude 73° north. The only European who has penetrated far to the eastward is Kielsen in 1830.

I now proceed with my personal narrative.

Among the numerous visitors that greeted us on our arrival, I was astonished to find myriads of mosquitoes. Little did we expect so warm a reception in the Arctic regions. Talk about mosquitoes in the States as being numerous and troublesome! Why, no man who has not visited the Arctic shores in the months of July and August can have a good idea of these Lilliputian elephants. In the States the very hum of a mosquito is enough to set any one upon his guard. How many a poor soul has been kept in a state of torment all night by the presence of only two or three mosquitoes! But here, in the north, it is a common every-hour affair to have thousands at one time around you, some buzzing, some drawing the very life-blood from face, hands, arms, and legs, until one is driven to a state approaching madness. Even the clothes worn in the States are no protection here against the huge proboscis with which each lady mosquito is armed.

On 17 December, Hall describes the splendid displays of the aurora:

Again at six o'clock, the heavens are beaming with aurora. The aurora shoots up in beams scattered over the whole canopy, all tending to meet at zenith. How multitudinous are the scenes presented in one hour of the aurora! Casting the eye in one direction, I view the instantaneous flash of the aurora shooting up and spreading out its beautiful rays, gliding this way, then returning, swinging to and fro like the pendulum of a mighty clock. I close my eyes for a moment; the scene has changed for another of seemingly greater beauty. Who but God could conceive such infinite scenes of glory; Who, but God execute them painting the heavens in such gorgeous display?

Hall fell into the Eskimo way of life with the same lack of inhibition that categorised everything he did. He slept in Inuit snow houses, he adopted their clothes and, above all, he ate their food and so progressive was his attitude that he called the Eskimo what they called themselves – Inuit, 'the people'. He wrote:

Eating meat raw or cooked is entirely a matter of education, polar bear meat was passable with a taste akin to lamp oil, but yet on the whole good. Whale gum could be sliced like mature cheese; its taste was like unripe chestnuts and its appearance like cocoa-nut meat. Raw venison was better than the best of beefsteaks so tender that it fell to pieces when I lifted it to my mouth; its fat was sweeter than the golden of butter; and the paunch was delightful in its flavour, a kind of sorrel acid; it had an ambrosial taste. Of raw seal it is ambrosia and nectar! Seal spine was excellent and slices of whale vertebrae looked just like turkey breast, whale skin was very palatable with a bit of vinegar, and nice enough with-out. A smoking bowl of seal blood was delicious. I drank mothers milk from the stomach of a baby seal – a great delicacy, and when I ate a stew of seal brains and entrails I knew I had arrived: I was one of them – welcomed like a brother – one of the honoured few!

On one of my visits to Joe Ebeirbing and Tookoolito's snow house I met their adorable little boy Tukerliktu. Tookoolito's pet name for him was Johny. [To British whalers the couple were known as Joe and Hannah. Hall was startled to hear Tookoolito and Joe speaking very good English. The captain of a British whaler in the early 1850s had taken them to England where they remained for some time and were even invited to an audience with Queen Victoria. They had dined with Prince Albert, and Tookoolito in particular had developed a good command of English.]

On May 10th Ebierbing's grandmother named Ookijoxy Ninoo arrived with him from Grinnell Bay I was anxious for a conversation with her, as she could give me much information from native traditions and personal observations, about the Frobisher Expeditions of 1576–8. Joe Ebeirbing interpreted.

Extracts from the translation of their conversation relate how areas of Greenland are rich in open seam coal deposits. Ninoo explained how she and her children friends played with the black stones. Placing before her his sketch charts, she pointed out where she had spent most of her life, and the place where the Kablounas (white men) landed at Niountelik, an island near Oopungnewing.

Asked her if she knew how many ships had come there, her reply was they came every year; first two, then three, then a great many ships. Five Inuit were also killed by the Kablounas.

Hall immediately took the only book he had on the subject, Barrow's *Chronological History of Arctic Discovery*. Written history tells that Frobisher made three voyages to the Arctic: the first voyage in 1576, with two vessels; the second in 1577, with three vessels, and in 1578, with fifteen vessels. The old lady informed him that frequently in her lifetime, she had seen wood, chips, coal, bricks and large pieces of very heavy stone, on the island of Niountelik. This puzzled him. What could she mean? Again she repeated, no Inuit had ever seen such kind of stones before. This at once led Hall to conclude that the heavy stones were iron (anvils used by Frobisher's blacksmiths). Hall determined that as soon as he could he would visit Niountelik and ascertain all about the matter. After eliciting all the information he then could from the old woman, he left with great astonishment at her powers of memory, and the remarkable way in which this strange people of the icy North, who have no written language, can correctly preserve history from one generation to another.

On 29 May 1861 Hall and his Eskimo friends set out for Niountelik and eventually reached the location of Frobisher's anchorage as directed by Ninoo. It was there they found the sea coal of Frobisher's Expedition of 1578.

On 10 October 1861, Hall prepared to depart for home; but ice had begun to form around the boat. He had left it too late, the *George Henry* could not break free and Hall and his crew were forced to spend another winter with their Inuit friends. Charles Francis Hall was content; the delay allowed him more time to search for relics from Frobisher's Expedition. Hall made no reference to the crew in his writings or how they felt about having to endure another winter in the Arctic. In the spring of 1862, Hall discovered very clear evidence of the existence of a blacksmith's forge or furnace. He collected 136 separate parcels of relics, which on his return he sent to the British Government, through the Royal Geographical Society. They were deposited in the Greenwich Hospital Museum in London.

Hall recorded that the Eskimo language had words of more than fifty letters. For instance there was a significant difference between Eskimo place names and European place names. Eskimo language would describe an intended journey thus: travel half a day, look for a hill or rock. European names were more practical, they oriented ships in relation to longitude and latitude and named a feature as outlined above.

Hall also discovered that the Eskimo oral tradition was flawlessly accurate: centuries after the event, they recounted exactly how many ships Frobisher had on each of his three visits to the area, what he had done and what he had left behind. Hall's towering achievement, however, was to prove that white men could survive in the Arctic without recourse to Western methods.

Charles Francis Hall gave a masterful account of his time living with the Eskimo, he covered every facet of their lives and culture. A very limited selection from his narrative includes the information that Eskimo are called 'In-nu-it', 'the people'. 'In-nu' in the singular number signifies man; in the plural, 'Innuit', 'our people', to distinguish from foreigners.

In Chipeway 'ush-ke' means raw. In the same language 'um-way' signifies 'he eats'. From these elements we readily form the word 'ush-ke-um-wau', 'raw he eats', and a noun derived from this verb, as a national denomination, must be some such form as 'Aish-ke-um-oog', 'raw flesh eaters'; use has softened this name pronounced 'Es-ke-moog'.

According to Inuit mythology the first man was imperfect, though made by the Great Being; therefore he was cast aside and called 'kob-lu-na' or 'kod-lu-na' as pronounced by the modern Innuits, which means 'white man'. A second attempt of the Great Being resulted in the formation of a perfect man, 'In-nu'.

Because there is no written language, pronunciation varied from settlement to settlement and the Inuit had difficulty communicating with each other. The Inuit Hall was acquainted with could only count in words as far as ten. By signs and throwing open the fingers Inuit everywhere can and do count much larger numbers.

Hall goes on to describe their dress and how they constructed their winter dwellings. He also described their marriage rites, and how their children are reared.

After spending two winters living with the natives, Hall found the charm of Eskimo life had worn thin and was anxious to return to the United States. His adventure was deemed a great achievement. He had charted one thousand miles of new coastline and had named many features.

Naming practices varied from expedition to expedition and from commander to commander. By custom it was both the commander's duty and prerogative to name the newly charted features. Some were named in tribute to the great, the learned, and the powerful. There were names given in honour of men actually on-board ship who had distinguished themselves in the affection or estimation of their shipmates. There were private family compliments, there were names recalling specific incidents that had befallen expeditions (more often grim than happy ones hence the names Starvation or Desperation). There were also purely descriptive names, conveying the look or colour of a feature.

Hall made preparations for the voyage home. He invited Joe Ebeirbing, Tookoolito and their infant son to return with him to the United States. This would appear to have been an unusual decision, but the reason why becomes clearer later. By the summer of 1862, the ice had disappeared and the vessel moved out into the open sea. On 23 August 1862, near St John's in Newfoundland, a pilot came on-board and informed Captain Budington that there was a war in the United States. Hall exclaimed, 'What – war in the United States, and among ourselves?'

They arrived in New London on Saturday morning 13 September 1862, after two and a half years in and about the Arctic seas. On his return home, Hall, who was as stubborn as ever, stated he hoped to raise funds to finance another expedition. He was still convinced he could solve the mystery of the disappearance of the Franklin Expedition. If the Eskimo of Baffin could remember Frobisher, they could remember Franklin. So ended Hall's first journey to the Arctic on the *George Henry*.

Like Hayes's, Hall's homecoming was as disrupted by the American Civil War. As the conflict dragged on Hall's hoped-for sponsorship for another expedition to King William Island and Boothia took a nosedive. Henry Grinnell's fortune had deteriorated dramatically. The turbulent wartime conditions gave American society more important matters to think about than Arctic exploration.

The $20,000 that Hall needed for his next expedition would not be easily found. Hall forgot all about the war and embarked on a series of fundraising lectures. He did not lack eloquence but did not have the charisma and crowd-pleasing personality of Kane or Hayes. 'Lecturing is a curse on my soul', he wrote to Henry Grinnell. At last, however, the money materialised; a bit from Grinnell and some from Grinnell's friends, together with contributions from unlikely and unexpected sources, much to Hall's great delight and relief.

On 1 July he left for the Arctic again aboard the whaler *Morticello*. He would spend the next five years looking for Franklin or his remains. He did eventually reach King William Island from which he returned with fascinating oral testimony interpreted by Tookoolito regarding Franklin's men. In every other respect, however his second mission was just a protracted version of his first. Also, he began to suffer ill health; the Eskimo diet was taking its toll.

By this time Arctic exploration had become his obsession and he was reluctant to give up. 'Give me the means', he declared in March 1865, 'and I will not only discover the North Pole but survey all the land I might find between Kane's farthest North and it, and have my whole soul in the work.'

He returned to America in the autumn of 1869. The undiscovered Pole, he wrote, was a great sad blot upon the present age that ought to be wiped out, and he was the man to do it.

Chapter IX

Hall's Voyage on the *Polaris*

Promoting his latest and most ambitious expedition to reach the North Pole, in late 1869 and early 1870 Charles Francis Hall began to seek sponsors. He sought support from wherever and from whomever he could, but with limited success. Hall then decided to go right to the top; he would solicit support from the President of the United States no less.

He felt that what he needed was the right ship, enough money for supplies and manpower and, with a little luck, man could stand on the North Pole, the top of the world. Charles Francis Hall considered himself the leading candidate. As one newspaper claimed, the solution of the Northern mystery would be the event of the nineteenth century. And in a heroic age, the discoverer would be a hero on the world stage.

A consummate letter writer, Hall contacted well-connected friends in Washington and New York who arranged for him to meet the American President, Ulysses S. Grant, the popular army general, who at the age of forty-six had won the 1868 election in a landslide, becoming the youngest American President to date.

Grant showed a genuine interest in Hall's bold plan for reaching the Pole. Hall, in his own inimitable way presented the route details to Grant, spoke about the determination that would be required for the mission, and the physical deprivation that would be faced. In Hall, Grant saw someone of vision who was worth backing and the President never wavered in his support either publicly or privately, for the man who regaled him with his fascinating stories of life in the Arctic.

Hall was invited to lecture on his Arctic experiences at Lincoln Hall in the nation's capital. President Grant and Vice-President Schuyler Colfax sat in the front row, smiling and nodding with approval throughout Hall's animated talk. Hall was at heart a sincere and modest man. He clearly lacked the flamboyancy of Dr Kane but he spoke from great experience of Eskimo facts and folklore.

Then it became clear why he brought the Eskimo family to America; in a dramatic moment Hall presented the Eskimo couple Tookoolito and Joe to the audience. Both of them, sweating profusely in their seal-skin outfits, mesmerised the packed house simply by their appearance. Barnum (the great American showman) would have been proud of Hall's theatrical flourish. Tookoolito and Joe, short, chestnut-brown people of the Far North, were a great oddity at the time. They brought with them authentic bows and arrows, fish spears, dog harnesses and other articles of Eskimo paraphernalia. The house erupted in applause. It was a spellbinding performance.

Sadly their young son Tukerliktu had died while Hall was away on a lecture tour. He was buried at Groton, Connecticut. Tookoolito was inconsolable. (On returning to the Arctic Tookoolito conceived another son named King William, but tragically this child also died. Tookoolito and Joe then adopted an Eskimo baby girl named Puney. Puney is a mispronunciation of the Inukitut word 'Panik', which means daughter.)

On 8 March 1870 the US Senate authorised the President to provide a voyage of exploration and discovery under the authority and for the benefit of the United States. It authorised the President to provide a naval or other steamer and, if necessary, a supply tender for a voyage into the Arctic regions under the control of Captain C.F. Hall. Never having served in the Navy or commanded a vessel of any type, Hall had no claim to the title Captain. Though honorary at best, the title stuck and overnight the former engraver became known as Captain Hall.

His plans to reach the North Pole impressed the commercial interests, the whaling industry, and other business offshoots, but Hall had sacrificed too much for far too long to take the financial interests of others into account. Charles Francis Hall's only driving ambition was to raise the Stars and Stripes on the North Pole for Uncle Sam.

Unexpectedly, another candidate was seeking US backing for a strike at the Pole – none other than Dr Isaac Hayes. Hayes appeared before the Foreign Relations Committee to put forward his claim that he was more entitled to the Government's backing than Hall. (Hall and Hayes had previously fallen out and had become bitter rivals.) There followed a long and lengthy debate for the hearts and minds of the key political figures. Hayes's case was based on his scientific ability and his experience on the well-publicised expedition in his search for the Open Polar Sea. Hall, while admitting that he was not a scientific man, pointed out that, apart from Dr Hayes, Arctic discoverers had not been scientific men. Neither Sir John Franklin nor Sir Edward Parry were of this class, and yet they loved science and did much to enlarge her fruitful fields. Frobisher, Davis, Baffin, Bellot, Hudson, Fox, Kane, Back,

McClintock, Osborn, Dease, Simpson, Rae, Ross and a host of other Arctic explorers had not been scientific men. The debate was finally and dramatically settled in the Senate by the casting vote of Vice-President Colfax after a tie. The House agreed to finance Hall to the tune of $50,000 with full Navy support.

The jubilant Captain Hall was allocated the SS *Periwinkle*, a 140ft gunboat of 387 tons, which had done duty in the American Civil War. Hall renamed it *Polaris* after the North Star and reinforced it for the Arctic combat at a cost of $50,000 dollars.

On July 29 1871, the *Polaris* departed for the Pole. 'Glorious is the prospect of the future', with these words Charles Francis Hall signed off his last letter to the shore before *Polaris* sailed from New London, Connecticut.

The doomed *Polaris* Expedition of 1871 stands out amongst the great epic journeys to either the North or South Pole. There was death – or was it murder? – grief, sorrow, starvation, deprivation, utter despair, unimaginable suffering, squalor, but also unlimited and undiminished determination; in short, every gamut of human emotion.

The crew of the *Polaris* was as follows:
Captain Charles Francis Hall, Commander
Sidney O. Budington, Sailing and Ice Master
George E. Tyson, Assistant Navigator
H.C. Chester, First Mate
William Morton, Second Mate
Emil Shuman, Chief Engineer
Alvin A. Odell, Assistant Engineer
Walter Cambell, Fireman
John Herron, Steward
William Jackson, Cook
Nathan Coffin, Carpenter

Seamen:
Herman Sieman
Frederick Anthing
J.W.C. Kruger
Henry Holby
William Lindemann
Joseph B. Mauch
G.W. Lindquist
Peter Johnson

Frederick Jamka
Noah Hayes

Scientific Corps:
Emil Bessels, Surgeon and Chief of Scientific Corp
R.W.D. Bryan, Chaplain and Astronomer
Frederick Meyer, Meteorologist

Eskimo:
Joe Ebeirbing, his wife Tookoolito and their adopted daughter Puney
Hans Hendrik, his wife Merkut and three children Augustina, Tobias,
    and Succi

The United States' Naval Department was not a charity organisation. It had
invested a great deal of time and money in the venture and would expect results
and also demand the highest standards of accountability of those involved in the
mission. It was both unusual and surprising for the United States Government
and the Navy to become involved in a private individual's expedition. Part of
the contract required Captain Hall to keep a daily journal; records must be
transparent, no erasures with a rubber or knife should be made. When an entry
required correction, the figures or words should merely be crossed by a line,
and the correct figures written above. The ship's log was to be maintained as
thoroughly as possible. The United States Government insisted that a scientific
corps must accompany Hall. The chief scientific officer was Dr Emil Bessels,
a highly regarded graduate from Germany, a zoologist, entomologist and surgeon. Frederick Meyer, also German, was a meteorologist. R.W.D. Bryan was
the Astronomer and Chaplain. Relationships among the party were quiet early
on in the voyage, but various groupings did form.

Captain Hall was leader of the expedition, in command of a twenty-three-
man crew plus the Eskimo hired hands, a role for which Hall had neither the
training or experience. His objective was the North Pole, and to sail as quickly
and as far as possible through the Arctic before the winter freeze set in. Captain
Sidney Budington, the ice master, was assisted by navigator George Tyson.
They were responsible for the safety of ship and passengers. The objective of
the scientists led by Emil Bessels was scientific observation and geographic
discovery, and they did not intend to be hurried as they carried out their
specific orders.

Hall, Bessels, and Budington frequently clashed. These confrontations were
mostly caused by a lack of demarcation, and because the objectives of the
groups were not prioritised before the expedition began. A long series of bitter

arguments and acrimonious exchanges ensued between the three men and their loyal supporters. This friction did not bode well for the for the success of the mission.

Hall, who had been a successful explorer in his own unorthodox fashion and always had unfettered control on his past expeditions resented this new discipline, or perhaps he was suffering from an inferiority complex as a result of having scientists on his ship. He most certainly feared that there would be too much time spent on scientific work, which would not only hamper his progress but could jeopardise the entire project. Bessels, meanwhile, considered Hall to be an ill-educated, unprofessional buffoon, notwithstanding the fact that Hall already knew more about the Arctic than Bessels would ever know.

The scientific team had orders to take four astronomical observations a day, repeated three times to prevent mistakes: to observe the aurora borealis; to make pendulum experiments to determine the force and gravity in different latitudes; to record the variation and dip of the needles; to measure the tides, currents, soundings, bottom dredging and density of sea water, and to register temperature, air pressure, humidity, wind velocity, rainfall, the form and weight of hailstones, the character of snow, the speed of glaciers, the frequency of meteors, the presence of ozone, and electricity in all its multiform developments. When putting their observations on paper, the scientific team was to do so with complete transparency. The evidence of the genuineness of the observation brought back should be of the most irrefutable character, orders stated. For the rest of the voyage the crew and Eskimo passengers of *Polaris* would be split asunder.

On 4 August *Polaris* arrived at Disko Island on the west coast of Greenland. Captain Hall describes his arrival:

> There are over 20 houses here. I have since ascertained that the Danes who come out here reside in the governors suite, and others who visit the country for commercial purposes, and stop any length of time – especially those who intend to make it their home – not infrequently marry native women; so that at some of the settlements you may see a family where the children have the light flaxen hair of the Dane, and the dark bronzed cheek of the native. This mixture makes a curious physiognomy.

Hall had hired Hans Hendrik at a salary of $300 a year. Hall was taken aback by the Eskimo hunter Hans Hendrik's pleas to bring along his wife Merkut and their children but quickly agreed. Tookoolito, her husband Joe, and daughter Puney were already on-board.

To the surprise of the crew, on 12 August 1872 Hans's wife Merkut gave birth to a baby boy on-board the ship (her heavy furs had concealed her pregnancy). To the hardened seafarers, the birth of a baby boy was a nostalgic event. The baby was christened Charley Polaris. The child was special. He had been born further north than any other child in recorded history.

The *Polaris* swept through Smith Sound and passed Cape Alexander and by 27 August it reached Kane's old quarters off the coast of Grinnell Land. At 81°35'N. they were now past Kane's farthest point north and in uncharted territory. These new territories entered the charts as Grant Land and Hall Land. The body of water between them was christened Robeson Channel in honour of the US Naval Secretary.

On 2 September *Polaris*, reached 82°16'N 61°44'W, their farthest point north. However, arguments developed. Some members of the expedition accused Budington of drunkenness. But Budington himself was worried, he felt the anchorage was too far north and the risk of becoming frozen-in was too risky. Tyson and Chester wanted to press onwards. While they argued, the current carried them down Hall Land for fifty miles. Thus at 81°38'N they settled down in Hall Land Bay, which measured twelve miles long by nine wide. The insecure Captain Hall named it Thank God Harbour, possibly with the relief at having overcome the rancour among the crew and the distinct possibility of mutiny.

Hall was pleased with their rate of progress. They had come farther than any previous expedition through Smith Sound. They had charted the area with absolute precision. Hall congratulated all on their fine achievements. He and his crew built a wooden structure in which to keep and protect their stores and spare equipment. This shelter became known as Polaris Bay Depot.

While the scientists were carrying out their duties, Hall took Hendrik and Chester to explore the surrounding terrain in atrocious conditions. This was an ill-advised decision.

Charles Francis Hall was not a healthy man. Before the journey he had complained of pains, symptoms which may have indicated a minor stroke. When this occurs the sufferer can be oblivious of any mental aberrations, such as paranoia or absent-mindedness.

Hall and his sledges departed on 10 October. He returned to the ship on 24 October, pleased with his findings and confident he could reach the North Pole from the Greenland Coast in 1872. He drank some coffee and complained it was too sweet and foul tasting. Then almost immediately he became weak and violently sick. He complained that someone was trying to poison him. Unfortunately he was no better the following morning – if anything he felt worse. Dr Bessels's diagnosis was that Hall had suffered a mild stroke.

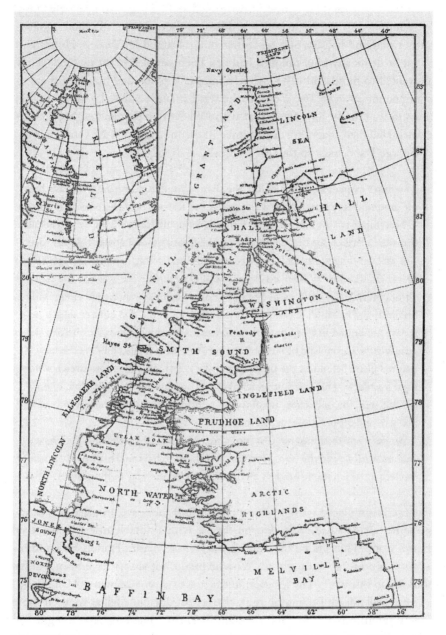

Map of the Smith Sound route to the North Polar Sea. (*Illustrated London News*, 29 May 1875.)

As the days passed his condition worsened and he began to rave deliriously. He continued to claim the coffee had been poisoned – it had tasted unpleasantly sweet and had burned his stomach. He blamed Dr Bessels. He refused to eat or drink anything unless it had first been sampled in his presence. They all wanted to murder him, he raved. In moments of lucidity he urged them to continue the struggle. Two days later he was partially paralysed. They took it in turns to watch over him. Bessels sat with him for two days and nights. Charles Francis Hall died at about half past three in the morning of 8 November 1871.

George Tyson takes up the story:

The ship's carpenter made a coffin, the men assisted in preparing the grave but the ground was so frozen even with picks it was scarcely possible to break it up.

November 11th. At half past eleven this morning by lantern light we placed all that was mortal of our late commander in the frozen ground. It was a gloomy day and well befitting the event. The place is rugged and desolate in the extreme. The mourners were led by Richard Bryan the ship's chaplain (he was also the ship's astronomer). Hall's body, shrouded in the American flag was buried along with his dreams of North Pole conquest. Away off, as far as the dim light enables us to see we are bound in by huge masses of slate rock, which stand like a barricade, guarding the barren land of the interior; between these rugged hills lies the snow-covered plain; behind us the frozen waters of Polaris Bay, the shore strewn with great ice blocks. The little hut which they call an observatory bears aloft, upon a tall flag-staff, the only cheering object in sight; and that is sad enough today, for the Stars and Stripes droop at half mast.

As we went to the grave this morning, the coffin hauled on a sledge, the Esquimaux followed the crew. There is a weird sort of light in the air, partly boreal or electric, which shone brightly at 11a.m. while on our way to the grave.

George Tyson placed a large stone at the foot of the grave. In place of a headstone he buried a half cabin door in the ice with a suitable inscription carved in the wood. Thus ended the courageous life of Charles Francis Hall and his ambitious projects. Tyson wrote, 'Wise he might not always have been, but his soul was in this work.' The location of the grave became known as Hall's Rest.

After Hall's death Budington took charge, but discipline fell apart; there were renewed tensions, friction and constant bickering. The long Arctic night had only begun, and for most it would end in abject terror and indescribable misery.

Polaris was encased in the ice till the spring of 1872 when it was agreed to return home. But the crew, despite mighty efforts, was unable free the ship from the ice. Eventually, on 12 August the Polaris escaped into the Robeson Channel, but made slow progress through the fields of ice.

On 15 October at 6p.m. in temperatures of −60°F, a violent snowstorm struck, causing a mighty iceberg to crash, cracking the ice all around and squeezing the ship. The vessel was nipped in the ice. Most of the crew were already on deck. The ice around the ship was very heavy and the ship creaked and groaned under the pressure. Shuman, the engineer, shouted that the vessel has started a leak aft and the water was gaining on the pumps. Budington reacted by shouting at them to throw everything on to the ice. Fearing a break-up the crew began to throw overboard boats and various provisions. Most of the important items had previously been placed on deck in anticipation of such an emergency. There was total confusion. Superhuman efforts were made by the men and by the Eskimo women and children, heaving food, clothing, coal and bedding on to the ice in indiscriminate haste.

So bad was the snow and sleet that one could not look windward. All hands worked through the night to prevent the further loss of precious possessions. Individuals performed gigantic feats of strength as the blizzard continued unabated. The ship was rising and falling, some of the men got on to the ice floe to move whatever supplies they could away from the heaving ship, but were unable to prevent the goods being crushed or lost, and unfortunately much of the valuable cargo was washed back into the raging sea and under the ship.

High seas were striking the ship itself and the air was filled with frozen spray – more like shotgun pellets than hail. It was impossible to see whether the provisions were on the ice or in the water, or to show the direction in which the great icebergs were being blown. Without exception everyone that could move worked until they almost dropped.

Captain Tyson, who was working on the ice floe, was puzzled. The surrounding icebergs seemed to have stabilised and the *Polaris* was no lower in the water than when the disaster began. Tyson began to think it was a false alarm; he went on-board and discovered he was correct. He asked Budington how much water the vessel was making. Budington said he feared now that he had been mistaken. The vessel, it seemed, was mostly sound, but when the ice nipped her, she had heeled, and the little water in the hold was thrown over, which made a rush that suggested to Shuman that a new leak had sprung.

Tyson and Budington had gone below deck to double check and found the ship was making no more water. As suspected, the water in the hold had shifted; there was no hole, and the pumps were coping perfectly well. Furious and frustrated, Tyson returned to the ice floe to try to save the remaining provisions. While the men, women and children on the ice were toiling to rescue the supplies, the ice floe began cracking. Budington ordered them to get everything back as far as possible from the ship. In the confusion no one knew who was on the floe or who was on the *Polaris*. Tyson continued:

I knew some of the children were on the ice and I noticed a heap of musk-oxen skins, lying across a crack in the ice, and as I pulled the skins to retrieve them I saw two or three of Hans' children safely rolled up in a ball in the skins.

Moments later the ice floe seemed to explode under their feet, fracturing all around them. The stern anchor broke loose. John Herron tried in vain to grab the hawser, the ship's cables snapped. Herron called out 'good-bye *Polaris!*' The ship, blown by the snowstorm, drifted into the darkness. Some of the men ran after it on the ice, but they were too late.

No lives were lost but most of the provisions disappeared in the ice floe's break-up. The survivors were gathered together on firm ice, but were unable to determine the size of the floe due to the lack of visibility in the blizzard.

Fortunately two whaleboats, fire arms and ammunition were also saved, but the survivors were horrified to discover the rudder of one of the whaleboats had been lost in the evacuation, as had some of the oars. They now had only one boat with a rudder and sufficient oars. Four-hour watches were arranged and a roster of the crew organised.

During the nerve-wracking night that followed, the frozen and terrified survivors huddled together for warmth and protection from the crashing icebergs, terrified the ice floe would splinter, not knowing if or when they would be upended into the broiling sea and certain death. After that night, the memory of which all involved would carry to their graves, the storm abated, but then the true reality of their predicament became clear.

The factual account of this part of the story is widely known, and is available from the American Naval investigation, the evidence of survivors and other witnesses, and from Captain George E. Tyson's *Arctic Experiences*. Tyson's book, when published, sold in tens of thousands, but one should exercise caution when reading Tyson's one-sided narrative. The hostilities from a section of the crew, mostly German, which Captain Hall had previously had to endure, were rekindled. The Germans, led by Frederick Meyer, wanted total control and resented Tyson's leadership just as they had resented Captain Hall's. Tyson recorded:

I took first watch at 3.00a.m. By the light of a full moon, I could see we were marooned on a circular cake of ice roughly four miles in circumference, not level, some mounds and hills but that didn't matter. Budington would soon pick us up and we would not have to endure this awful misery for much longer, the *Polaris* would return to our rescue.

But it didn't.

After their rest in the Arctic darkness they took stock. The castaways were: Eskimo Hans Hendrik and his wife Merkut and her four children Augustina, Tobias, Succi, and the newborn infant Charley; Eskimo Joe and his wife Tookoolito with her daughter Puney; the Germans Frederic Meyer, Ronald Kruger, William Lindermann, Fred Jamka and Matthias Anthing; Soren Madsen, Danish; Gus Lundquist, Swedish; John Herron, English; William Jackson, the American cook, and Captain George Tyson who was now in command. They possessed two seal-skin kayaks, two whaleboats, fourteen forty-five–pound tins of pemmican, eleven bags of biscuits (bread), one can of dried apples, fourteen canned hams, and six Eskimo dogs, named Sambo, Poodle, Chink, Spike, Gumbo and Bear. On-board *Polaris* were Captain Budington, Bessels, first mate Chester, and the rest of the crew.

When the survivors awoke, still exhausted after their night of terror, they were frozen, wet, and hungry. They built a fire of some broken gaff poles retrieved from the whaleboats. They had only flat tins to cook in, and they fried some tinned meat.

After a discussion among the survivors, it was decided to try to get off the ice floe and make for land in the whaleboat. When on watch Tyson had seen an escape through open water and through the icepack. He also feared the *Polaris* might have foundered in the storm during the night as there was no visible sign of the ship. They got the boats away, taking as much as they could, intending to return for the remaining provisions and equipment, but they had gone hardly any distance to the shore when the leads closed in, forcing them back onto the ice floe.

Within minutes, to their huge relief, they saw the *Polaris* as she came around a point eight or ten miles distant. But she did not make in the direction of the castaways. The survivors set up a flag and watched through a spyglass, noticing she was under steam and sail. Instead of steaming towards them, she disappeared behind Littleton Island.

Tyson was perplexed. Why couldn't the crew men on the *Polaris* see those who were stranded? After all, their signals were dark on a background of white ice. Tyson ordered the men to lighten the boats. They would row to *Polaris*. He thought the ship must be disabled and could not come to their assistance … or perhaps Budington intended to leave them on the ice.

Tyson knew that while he and Budington certainly had had their differences, as friends they went back a long way together quite apart from the three years with Hall on the *George Henry*. Besides, Budington thought too much of Tookoolito, Joe and Puney to leave them to their fate. To Joe Erbeirbing and Tookoolito the possibility that Captain Budington would deliberately abandon them was just unthinkable. Sidney Budington and his wife Sarah had taken them into their home for long periods while Captain Hall was on his lecture tours and fundraising campaigns. When Tookoolito's little son Johnny died, Sarah Budington had been a great source of comfort to her, especially on the day of the funeral. Sarah had become attached to the little Eskimo woman and her beautiful manners.

Tyson considered the consequences. What could he do without a vessel, shelter or sufficient food for the women and children through an Arctic winter? Another storm gathered, with mountainous seas and Arctic winds. The men considered conditions too dangerous and were too afraid to venture out in the stormy sea in a boat with no rudder and insufficient oars. They were compelled to haul the boat back on to the ice floe and leave it where it was, as everyone was too tired to drag it back. One of the kayaks was saved. These little boats are invaluable to the Esquimeax, who are accustomed to managing them; but they are extremely difficult for anyone else to handle with safety.

That day in twenty-hour darkness, the marooned group could see the outline of the *Polaris* anchored in the distance. The castaways shouted till they were hoarse, screamed until their lungs almost burst, fired guns, and finally in despair they sobbed their hearts out. But when the squall ended, the *Polaris* was nowhere to be seen and their ice floe began drifting south into Baffin Bay.

Another night was spent in the saturated and frozen animal skins on the ice floe. They were awakened by shouting and dogs barking. The ice floe had split, separating them from the boat and from their cache, which they had intended recovering the next day. Their cache consisted of six bags of biscuit (500lbs) along with Tyson's compass and chronometer. The Eskimo began to utilise the survival skills that they had honed over the centuries; snow houses were built, supervised by Joe Ebeirbing and Hans Hendrik and assisted by the crew. They had to work in the minus temperatures and fading light. If it rained or snowed there was no daylight at all. They built one small house for the officers Tyson and Meyer, a house for Joe, Tookoolito and Puney, a house for the crewmen, store huts for provisions and equipment and a cook-house, all united by arched alley-ways built of snow. There was one main entrance and smaller ones branching off to the huts. Latrines were dug out. Hans built his family hut nearby. By the time the houses had been completed, the sun had disappeared completely, and would not be visible for another four months. The castaways dined on their rations of pemmican and bread. The bread, of course, is simply biscuit; it is bread on-board ship and biscuit to landsmen.

After a week, the survivors gave up all hope of *Polaris* coming to their rescue. The piece of ice they stood on was no larger than 150 yards in length and breadth. They would have to seek a larger ice floe. Tyson ordered an evacuation. They loaded the boat, harnessed the dogs and sledged all the supplies to the largest ice floe in sight.

Tyson describes the rationing allocation:

The food ration was reduced to two meals a day, which was weighed out by Meyer's cartridges and shot used for the weights. The allowance was 11 ounces for each adult, half ration for children, barely enough to keep body and soul together, already there were signs of weakness and suffering. Hans had killed and skinned two of the dogs, Sambo and Poodle to feed his family and Merkut had the unenviable task of cooking them,

All the children are crying with hunger. Our remaining dogs are very thin and poor, and unless we get more food they will have to be killed. It is a great pity. May the great and good God have mercy on us, and send us seals or I fear we must perish. Hans Hendrik has found it difficult to change the habits of a lifetime. Eskimo only worry about the next day's meal when the time comes and for the same reason he found short rations hard to accept. Water is collected in whatever will hold it. Names were found for the various features on the floe. The highest point was named Mount Hall.

Tyson may have given up hope of rescue but in his heart he prayed for a miracle. A couple of days later, driven by hunger, three of the four remaining dogs were also killed, this time by the crew, and the food was shared among the survivors. The last of the six dogs was Spike. His intuition alerted him and he evaded capture. He was last seen scampering across the floe, never to be seen again.

The loss of the daylight, added to the lack of food, caused much despondency. In freezing temperatures the castaways were slowly starving to death. Their estimated position was 77 N - 30, and so far west of Greenland that there was no chance of reaching the shore. Tyson prayed, 'May the one authority that none can challenge continue to watch and help us all.'

The men chopped up the rudderless and oar-less whaleboat for firewood leaving them with only one whaleboat. Tyson describes conditions on the ice floe:

November 21st. I am down sick, hardly able to hold a pencil. Today the natives brought in two seals, a cause of much rejoicing, without them we would have no fire. The remaining whaleboat must be preserved at all costs. As for Captain Hall's writing desk which is all we have left of him, I asked Joe to keep it safe. For the first time since separating from the ship I have fed heartily on seal, yes, and drank its blood, and eaten its blubber, and even its skin and hair. The seal's blood is very savoury.

If only we had two small chairs or stools to go with the writing desk, then we could sit properly, and also I could write there. I am determined to protect it, as is Tookoolito. Puney at least derives some amusement from it, making a truckle-bed for her doll in the larger ink drawer. We are now living on as little as the human frame can endure without succumbing, and suffer much from the cold. When the body is ill-fed the cold seems to penetrate to the very marrow. God guide us. He is our only hope.

To satisfy my hunger – fierce hunger – I was compelled to eat frozen seal's entrails, and lastly sealskin, hair and all, just warmed over a lamp, and frozen blubber which tastes sweet to a man as hungry as I was. If only we can get enough of such food as this as this we can live, with the aid of our small stores, with economy, until April. No doubt many who read this will exclaim I would rather die than eat such stuff! You think so, no doubt; but people can't die when they want to; when one is still in full life and vigour, albeit as hungry as we are, he or she doesn't want to die. Neither would you. The ration scales are two pemmican tins yoked together by a fulcrum of gaff wood, cartridges are the counterweights. The stomach is gnawing. It is almost impossible to fix the mind clearly, for any length of time, upon anything else. The scenes that have passed before my eyes during the past weeks were many of them worthy of the best efforts of the most accomplished artist and of description by a poet's pen, but I have not the heart to enjoy or record them, for the disgust at the way in which I have to live.

Poor Puney, the child is so famished, that while eating, she entirely forgets to feed her dolly Elisapee too, as she usually does.

December 7th. It is over a month since we lost sight of all land. Hans is sick, only Joe goes out sealing these days but without luck. I do not write every day it would take too much paper. Our daily ration is five ounces of biscuit, six ounces of canned meat, and one and a half ounces of ham. These ingredients are mixed with brackish water to season them and heated over a lamp. With the return of migrating game, things can only get better.

Divine providence then took a hand. One night when all were asleep a lost hungry polar bear scented food, and approached the encampment. As soon as the animal was in range it was shot, and a great feast was enjoyed by all. Tyson continued his narrative:

December 22nd. We have turned the darkest point of our tedious night, and it is somewhat cheering to think that the sun, instead of going away from us, is coming towards us. I am thankful perhaps the worst may be averted.

Christmas dinner, two biscuits, a small piece of frozen ham a few morsels of dried apple, and half a cup of seal's blood. It is eaten in minutes.

A happy new year for all the world, but us cold, half starved wretches; though today we will eat well. Joe shot a seal. Now it has sometimes happened that when the Esquimaux have been tramping about for hours on the hunt for seals and at last get one, they are by that time famished. When they bring it into the camp, they know they will get no more than those who have been home all day. They sometimes open the seal, and eat the entrails, kidneys and heart, and perhaps a piece of liver, and who could blame them? They must do it to keep life in them. Yet the men complain of this and say they do not get their share, so unreasonable and unreasoning they are.

January 9th. The west land still in sight about 80 miles off. Temperature between -20° to -36°.

January 19th. Joe and Hans hunting. Five miles from the huts they found water, and saw a number of seals, but it was blowing heavy, and very cold. Joe says he tried to shoot, but that he shook so with the cold that he could not hold the gun steady, and that his fingers could not feel the trigger of the gun, and so the seal escaped.

It is not easy to find the seal in winter; they live principally under the ice, and can only be seen when the ice cracks; an inexperienced person would never catch one. Being warm blooded animals, they cannot always remain under the ice without breathing; and in consequence they make air-holes through the ice, through which to breathe; but at the surface these holes are so small, not much more than two and a half inches across, that they are not easily distinguished, especially in the dim and uncertain light which we now have. They are very shy, too, and seem to know when they are being watched. A native will sometimes remain watching a seal-hole for 36 or 48 hours before getting a chance to strike, and if the first stroke is not accurate the game is gone for ever.

Tyson reduced his writings, knowing that if he survived and their story were to be made public he would have to expand his notes at a later date.

Joe Ebeirbing and Hans continued their ceaseless search for seals and caught just about enough to keep us all alive. Were it not for little Joe, Esquimau though he be, many if not all of this party must have perished by now.

January 20th. The filth in the huts is truly incredible. I cannot allow myself to dwell on it for long. The inhabitants appear sadly to lack the inclination or perhaps simply the strength to keep them as they once did. But then, these days, I feel little more than the rawest of savages myself.

January 24th. Today is our one hundred and second day on the ice, one of the most wretched I have ever known. The mercury is frozen. The men are seldom seen out of their huts. The monotony is fearfully wearisome; if I could get out and exercise, or hunt, it would help to relieve the tedium; but while this wind and severe cold lasts, it is not to be thought of. The glass tells 45° below zero, large pieces have broken off the sides of our floe and soon we may have to rebuild our huts further inland.

January 28th. For those accustomed to action and averse to sloth, I think Hell will be a place not of everlasting toil but of eternal inactivity. Sitting long in a chair is irksome enough, but it is far more wearisome when there is no proper place to sit. No books either, no Bible, no prayer-book, no magazines or newspapers.

Newspapers I have learned to live without, having been to sea most of my life, where it is impossible to get them; but some sort of reading I always had before, and it is now one hundred and six days since I have seen printed words! This engenders a kind of hunger, too, and one which the reader of these lines will be sore pressed to imagine. If this life on the ice should last much longer, we shall forget that we have brains and souls, and remember only that we have stomachs. Still I believe God is watching over us, unworthy though we be and that He will guide us into safety. For although I am overcome sometimes with certain thoughts, as I think of loved ones at home, I am not without hope. God, in creating man, gave him hope. What a blessing! Without that we should long since have ceased to make any effort to sustain life.

February 1st. The north wind still continuing to blow with violence. The children are crying that chronic hunger whine. We are all permeated with dirt, I have not had these clothes off for over a hundred days, and it sickens me to think of them, saturated as they are with all the vile odours of the hut, of seals entrails and greasy blubber and smoky lamp oil. A streak of luck today, or rather, I should say a Providential gift. Joe has brought home a seal. There will not be hide or hair of him left, or anything inside or out, but the bone and the gall that we throw away. All else is consumed.

February 7th. We are all rejoicing, Hans shot a seal at noon. Hans, if he gets a seal – which is very seldom – wishes to appropriate it all to his family's use, without considering that he and his family get their daily allowance of biscuit and pemmican with all the rest. Of course he must not be allowed to have more than an equal share. We ate it partly raw and partly cooked. Latterly we cooked the skin and drank the greasy water. Joe says any thing is good that don't poison you and repulsive though it be, it is astonishing how this warm greasy water, with a little seal's blood in it, stimulates the flagging energies. We save the blood by letting it freeze in hollows made in the ice. Temperature today is minus 26°. There are now many openings in the ice and numbers of narwhales going north. Joe and Hans shot two this morning but could not get them, they both sank. These narwhales are sometimes called sea-unicorns, or monodons, on account of the long horn – six to eight foot long – which projects from the upper jaw. In reality however, this appendage is not a horn, but an elongated tooth, including the rudiment of a second tooth. This formidable weapon is quite straight, tapering from base to point, and has a spiral twist from left to right. The animal (for it is not a fish) is 15 or 16 feet long. On the back, instead of a dorsal fin, there is a low fatty ridge, extending for between two or three feet. They are harpooned for their oil and ivory, and also by Greenlanders for their flesh. The flesh is highly relished by them. The oil is excellent; the ivory is both hard and white, and takes a good polish. The Danes and natives work it up into many articles of domestic use.

February 21st. This morning, land became visible to the west, perhaps 60 miles distant. This should be more heartening; but considering our weakness and the condition of the ice, it might as well have been a thousand miles.

February 22nd. God help me. I have never felt so tired! If men (or women) ever suffered on earth the torments of wretched souls condemned to the ice-hell of the poet Dante, I think I have felt it here; living in filth, like an animal. Sometimes I feel almost tempted to end my misery at once, but thoughts of divine restriction hold me back. I think there would be one wretched being less in this world. The men are frightened; they seem to see Death staring them in the face and saying 'In a little while you are mine.' Joe is frightened too. He feels if he and his family were alone on the shore, without this company of men to feed, he could catch game enough for his own use until it was more abundant; but to catch a living for 18 discourages him.

February 25th. I have explained to the crew that I hope soon to get to the ground of the bladder-nose seal, which in March comes onto the ice, not far from where we are now, to breed. I have told them how little biscuit and pemmican we have left.

February 27th. Clear and cold. The mercury has gone down again to minus 38°. Such a set of skeletons as we would have had a poor chance camping out on such a night without the shelter of our huts.

March 7th. I received a severe shaking last night several times, these noises startled me from my sleep. Each time I thought our ice was breaking in fragments. I begin to have some idea of how people in earthquake countries must feel when the ground is trembling and shaking beneath their feet, especially in a dark night, when one cannot see a foot before him, and knows not which way lies danger and which safety, if indeed there is safety anywhere. It is impossible to describe, so that, without the actual experience, the sounds of breaking ice floes and bergs can be realised.

Their force and human helplessness compared, make one realise that there are yet elements in nature which man's ingenuity can never control.

5p.m. Our Joe has shot a giant oogjook! – a large kind of seal – the largest I have ever seen. The warm blood of the seal was scooped up in tin cans and relished like new milk. How we rejoiced over the death of the oogjook it would be impossible to describe. Just on the verge of destitution along comes this monster seal, the fellow must weigh six or seven hundred pounds, and will furnish, I should think, 30 gallons of oil. Praise the Lord for all his mercies!

We eat no biscuit to-day, oogjook is the only dish. We had oogjook sausages for breakfast, the intestines being stuffed with blubber and tied into links. He measured fully nine feet and seven inches long! What a Godsend.

'They are coming sir.' Tookoolito saw the flock of dovekeys first, these little speckled birds only weigh only four ounces, they have a very plaintive cry, as they paddle about in the icy water. The crew with guns loaded at the ready braced themselves, the men open fire, it is hard to miss, food of life, raining down on the ice.

March 10th. These storms seem endless, and continue to eat away at our raft, which is now only perhaps a quarter of its original dimensions. There is precious little room left. We had to stay alert all through the night – and with such feelings as I leave the reader to imagine.

George Tyson then goes into great detail on the effects the conditions had on the various members of the party, and other serious problems. For instance the food store was frequently pilfered but conditions were so atrocious Tyson could not bring himself to post a sentry. Relationships with the German contingent deteriorated to such an extent that the Germans set up a separate camp and only arrived to collect their food rations. The narrative is edited, but retains the most important elements:

The gale still blows this morning, and there are some rough seas under the ice We have never before felt it move up and down like this; but then our raft is only a fraction of its original size. But a kind and merciful God has thus far guided and protected us, and will, I trust, yet deliver us. With the winds more moderate, we recommenced shooting. Game is plentiful, seals are scarce. We got another oogjook to-day though not as large as our first kill. Our floe is so diminished that it is only 40 paces to the water. And so it seems that one danger – that of starvation – may be receding even while another, more urgent one, closes in.

March 28th. The bladder-noses are here! I thought they could not be far off. Shot nine seals to-day. Our whole company feel cheered and encouraged, knowing we have now got to the promised seal grounds, where plenty can be obtained. We are now in the strong tides off the mouth of the Hudson Strait; but no land to be seen. Huge bergs – and I do not exaggerate when I say hundreds in number but our little ice-craft is making its way through the sea without any other guide than the Great Being above. February and March have been dreadful months, blowing and snowing almost continuously.

March 30th. Hans shot a young seal. When the young of the seal can be secured without shooting, it is customary to press them to death by putting the foot down heavily upon them, as by this means not only all the blood is saved, but the milk in the stomach; and among the Esquimaux this milk is highly relished. The men put some of the milk in their blood-soup. These bladder noses, when attacked, often show considerable fight if approached with spears or clubs. But they can do nothing against bullets but get out of the way.

April 1st. We have been the fools of fortune now for five months and a half. Last night there was a heavy sea, water all around us and scarcely any ice to be seen. We got launched towing the kayak behind us. The boat was laden very heavy, and was, of course low in the water, with 19 souls aboard, instead of the six or eight it was intended for, and also ammunition, guns, skins, and several hundred pounds of seal-meat; so the sea began to break over us, the men became frightened, some of them exclaiming that the boat is sinking. Meanwhile our home of some five months receded behind us, the huts where we had lived so long soon resembling at a distance, mere hummocks or slabs of raftered ice. The seas were such that for a while our island came in and out of our sight, and then vanished altogether, as if having passed over the lip of a cataract. The men rowing, did what they could, but we made little headway, having but four oars, and their every movement impeded by the heads or bodies of others. We were in fact so crowded that it was difficult for Hans and Joe to bail, which they did constantly, and I could scarcely move my arms sufficiently to handle the tiller yoke-ropes without knocking into some child, and these children frightened and crying most of the time. I could not leave the tiller to eat – there was not room to leave anyway so that Tookoolito had to feed me pieces of raw seal meat as I steered. After all that was done, the boat was still overloaded fearfully. It was with much difficulty through these changes that I preserved Captain Hall's writing-desk from destruction, as some of the men were bound to have Joe throw it overboard; but I positively forbade it, as it was all we had belonging to our late commander. Tookoolito, who reciprocated my feelings in this regard, argued in untypically open fashion with Kruger, who declared that she and I were being sentimental. One might expect a native to put survival before human sentiment at such a time, but Tookoolito in many ways is civilised, and she and Joe loved Captain Hall like a father. She rightly made the point that it is only our sentiments at a time like this, that keeps us from barbarism. Through hard work and some luck, we got about 20 miles through open seas and reached the pack, we were compelled to hold up on the first piece of good ice we could find. There we spread what few skins we had, set up our tent, and ate our ration of dry bread and pemmican. We were all exhausted.

April 4th. We are now encamped on a heavy piece of ice, and I hope out of immediate danger. But there is no ice to be trusted at this time of year. Our tent of course is not as good a protection from the wind as the snow-huts. Joe, with a little help, can build a hut in an hour, if the right kind of snow blocks can be procured, but on this floe there is little but bare, scraped ice. Still he intends to try, and with whatever snow remains he and the men knock together some meagre shelters and windbreaks. In the meantime, 19 souls crowd into our tent and the noise of the huffing canvas is terrible. If one attempts to rest the body, there is no rest for the mind. Blowing a gale from the north-east tonight, and a fearful sea running. We are all soaked to the skin and the rain lashes us from the northeast. Now and then for variety we have a snow squall.

For ten more days the starving castaways drifted on their new ice floe while their horrific living conditions worsened:

April 14th. Morning. I think this must be Easter Sunday in civilised lands. Last night I sat on my watch thinking over our desperation. The northern lights appeared in great splendour. The auroras seem to me always like a sudden flashing out of the Divinity; a sort of reminder that God has not left off the active operation of His will. So we must continue to trust. This, with my impression that it must be Easter Sunday, has thrown a ray of hope over our otherwise desolate outlook.

April 18th. Blowing strong from the north-east. At 9p.m. while resting in our tent, we were alarmed by hearing an outcry from Lundquist on the watch; and almost at the same moment a heavy sea swept across our piece, carrying away everything on it that was loose. This was just a foretaste of what was to follow; we began to ship sea after sea, one after another, with only a few minutes interval between each. Finally came a tremendous wave, carrying away our tent, skins and most all of our bed-clothing. Only a few things were saved, which we had kept in the boat. The women and children were already there, as they were every night, or the little ones would certainly have been swept away to watery graves. All we could do now was to try to save the boat. So all hands were called to man it in a new fashion, namely to hold on to it with might and main, to prevent its being washed away. All our additional strength was needed and we had to brace ourselves with all the strength we had. As soon as possible I got the boat, with the help of the men, over to that edge of the floe where the seas first struck; for I knew if she remained toward the farther edge, the gathered momentum of the waves as they rushed over the ice would more than master us, and the boat would go. It is well this precaution was taken, for, as it was, we were very nearly carried off, boat and all, many times during this dreadful night.

There we stood all night long, from 9p.m. to 7a.m. enduring what I should say few, if any, have gone through and lived. Every little while, one of these tremendous seas would come and lift the boat up bodily, and us with it, and carry it and us across the ice almost to the opposite edge of our piece; and several times the boat got partly over the edge, and was only hauled back by the strength of mortal desperation. Then we must push and pull and drag the boat right back across the floe to its former position, and stand ready, bracing for the next sea. Had the water been warm and clear of debris, it would have been hard enough. But it was freezing and full of loose ice, rolling about in loose blocks of all shapes and sizes, and with every sea would come an avalanche of these striking us on our legs and bodies, and bowling us off our feet like so many pins in a bowling-alley. Some of the blocks were only a foot or two square; others were as large as an ordinary bureau, or larger. And so we stood, hour after hour, the sea as strong as ever, but we are weakened from the fatigue.

April 22nd. Joe sees a bear, it was a period of intense, anxious excitement, the bear came slowly in, thinking undoubtedly that we were seals and expecting to make a good dinner upon us. Joe fired killing him instantly. We all rushed to the spot. Poor Polar. God has sent us food.

The blood of the bear was exceedingly acceptable; for though we had more water than enough on the outside, we had nothing to drink, and were very thirsty. His stomach was empty, and he was quite thin, but his flesh was all the better for that.

April 28th. 4.30p.m. A joyful sight – a steamer right ahead of our boat and bearing north of us! We hoisted our colours and pulled toward her. She is a sealer going south-west, and apparently working through the ice. For a few moments what joy filled our breasts – the sight of relief so near! But we have lost it! She did not see us, and we could not get to her; evening came down, and she was lost to sight. We boarded, instead of the hoped-for steamer, a small piece of ice, and once more hauled up our boat and made camp. The sea is quiet and we can rest peaceful; for although one steamer has passed us, we feel that we may soon see another, and that help can not be far off. The hope of relief keeps us even more wakeful than does the fear of danger.

April 29th. Morning fine and calm, all of us on the lookout for steamers, sighted one about eight miles off. Called the watch, launched the boat, and made for her. After an hour's pull, gained on her a good deal, but they did not see us. We fired guns hoping to attract their attention. We seemed to hear a response of three shots; at the same time the steamer headed towards us. Now we feel sure the time of deliverance has come.

We shouted involuntarily almost, but they were too far away to hear our voices. Presently the steamer changed her course, and headed south, then north again, then west; we did not know what to make of it. We watched, but she did not get materially nearer. So she kept on all day, as though she were trying to work through the ice, and could not force her way. Strange! I should think any sailing ship, much more a steamer, could get through. She being four or five miles off, we repeated our firing, but she came no nearer. All day we watched making every effort within our means to attract attention. Whether she saw us or not we do not know, but late in the afternoon she steamed away, going to the south-west; and reluctantly we abandoned the hope which had upheld us through the day.

April 30th. At 5p.m. Herron on the look-out spied a steamer cutting through the fog, and the first I heard was a loud cry. 'There's a steamer lads! Lads there's a steamer!' On hearing the outcry, I ordered the guns to be fired, and set up a loud simultaneous shout; fearing that, like the other ships she might not see or hear us, though she was much nearer, not more than a quarter of a mile off when we first sighted her. To my great joy and relief, the steamer's head was soon turned toward us. On her approach, as they slowed down, we gave them three cheers, in which all the men heartily joined in. It was instantly returned by a hundred men, who covered her top-gallant mast, forecastle and fore-rigging. The ship proved to be the sealer *Tigress* – a barkentine out of Conception Bay, Newfoundland.

Two or three of her seal-boats were instantly lowered, and the crews got on our bit of ice, shook our hands, and peeped curiously into the dirty tins we had used over the oil-fires. We had been making soup out of the blood and entrails of our last little seal. They soon saw enough to convince them that we were in sore need. They took the women and children in their boats, while we tumbled into our own, bringing Captain Hall's little desk, but leaving behind all else.

On climbing on-board, I was at once surrounded by sealers filled with curiosity to know our story, and all asking questions of me and the men. I told them who I was, and where we were from. But when they asked me, how long have you been on the ice, and I answered, since the 15th of last October, they were so astonished that they fairly looked blank with wonder.

The disbelieving seal-hunters were flabbergasted, but one had only to see the haunted look in their eyes, their emaciated faces, matted filthy hair and beards, the remnants of their clothing torn and threadbare, to understand the suffering these unfortunate frozen castaways had had to endure. In six months on ice floes this remnant of the Hall Expedition had travelled almost 1,800 miles on a cake of ice:

One of the *Tigress*'s crew looking at me with open-eyed surprise exclaimed, 'And was you on the ice night and day?'

The captain came along and invited me down to his cabin. There we sat talking of our wonderful or as he called it, miraculous escape. In the course of time breakfast came along, codfish, boiled potatoes, hard bread and coffee. I fell upon this plain food with a keenness which the reader may find it hard to grasp; in truth, no subsequent meal can surpass it to my taste, so long habituated to raw meat, with all its unclean accessories. No one, unless they have been deprived of civilised food and cooking for as long as I have, can begin to imagine how good a cup of coffee, with bread and butter, tastes! Never in my life did I enjoy a meal like that. Plain it was, I shall never forget that codfish and potatoes.

I have learned that the steamer we saw on the 29th ult was the *Eagle* belonging to St John's, commanded by Captain Jackman. Captain Bartlett says he could not have seen us, or he would have come for us, or, if he could not, he would have stood by, or in some way tried to save us; that Captain Jackman was noted for his humanity, and had more than once received medals for saving life in these waters. I am glad to know this.

On-board the *Tigress*, May 1st. How strange it seems to lie down at night in these clean quarters, and feel that I have no more care, no responsibility. To be once more clean, what a comfort! God bless the good and kind Captain Bartlett and his crew. We sail in a few more days for St John's.

On May 9 the group telegraphed the news of Hall's death to the outside world, and of their narrow escape from destruction on the ice and their uncertainty of the fate of the *Polaris*:

May 14th. The Consul has furnished all necessary funds for new outfits for all the survivors. Many ladies call at the hotel to see the Eskimo children, and asked Tookoolito and Merkut how did you take care of the children on the ice?
I shall always remember the kindness of the people of St John's.

There was huge public interest in the amazing story; many understandably disbelieved it could have happened, experts refused to believe their explanation of survival. That the expedition should have fallen apart so disastrously after Hall died and – apparently so incompetently – was incomprehensible.

The survivors were quizzed at great length down to the last detail. After all it was an amazing human-interest story. A few days later the controversy spilled onto the front page of the *New York Herald*, which raised the possibility that Hall had been poisoned. Under political pressure to account for the expensive mission, Navy Secretary Robeson promised President Grant that he would mount an Inquiry including interrogation of crew members. The Navy sent the steamship *Frolic* to Newfoundland to collect the castaways. On 5 June 1873, Tyson was called as the first witness before a four-man team of investigators aboard the USS *Talapoosa*, docked at the Washington Naval Yard. The investigating team was composed of Commodore William Reynolds, the senior officer of the Navy Department, Professor Spencer F. Baird, of the National Academy of Sciences, and Captain H. W. Howgate, of the Signal Service Corps, and presided over by the Hon. Secretary of the Navy, George M. Robeson.

Tyson gave forthright testimony on Budington's performance as captain, including the allegations of frequent bouts of intoxication. He was also scathing in his criticism of Dr Bessels. Tyson's evidence was corroborated by other witnesses.

After six days the questioning was complete. The Board of Inquiry judged they had insufficient evidence, as Budington and Bessels were still missing and unaccounted for. Ships were despatched to search the Greenland waters for

Polaris and the fourteen-member crew, among them the *Tigress* with Hans Hendrik and his family, who were returning home to Disko. George Tyson and Joe Ebeirbing were two of the crew. Finally, Littleton Island was declared to be the spot where the separation took place. The following is an edited version of George Tyson's description:

> Here the *Tigress* hovered around off shore, a boat was lowered for the shore, and then the distant sound of voices appeared to come from the shore and the wildest excitement prevailed, a few moments later the commander was heard to exclaim, 'I see their house – two tents; and human figures are on the main land near Littleton Island!'

But those in the boat soon discovered the mistake. The human figures were not the lost men of the *Polaris*, but native Eskimo (some of the men wore the clothing of civilised men). They told Tyson the *Polaris* was in a leaking condition after the storm, and Captain Budington had abandoned her on the day after she was separated from the floe; his party had built a house on the mainland, where they had wintered; they had fitted up with berths, or bunks, for sleeping fourteen in number (showing none of the party had died.); they had also furnished it with a stove, table, chairs, and other articles from the *Polaris*; during the winter the party had built and rigged two sail-boats, with wood and canvas from the ship, and it was about the time the ducks begin to hatch that Captain Budington and the whole party had sailed southward in these boats.

The chief witness among these Esquimeax also said Captain Budington had made him a present of the *Polaris* but that soon after the vessel broke loose in a gale of wind and had foundered.

Commander Greer in his report said the Esquimeax were in possession of the deserted quarters and also had two tents made out of canvas belonging to *Polaris*, situated at 78°23'N and in 73°46'W. The most diligent search failed to reveal any writing which indicated the time of their breaking up, or what route they meant to pursue. One important article was found, namely a logbook, out of which was torn all reference to the death of Captain Hall. The *Tigress* turned south, reaching Godhavn on 25 August. Here it was ascertained by whaling captains that had Budington kept to the east coast of Greenland he would have been rescued by now.

And so it proved. On 23 June Budington, Dr Bessels and the remainder of the crew had turned up safe and well. A Scottish whaler the *Ravenscraig* from Kirkcaldy in Scotland had found the survivors.

The Inquiry was reconvened, with Budington as the chief witness. Budington was surprised to learn the castaways had survived. He swore he did not see or hear the marooned group on the day they spotted and signalled to *Polaris*. Budington explained they had had almost as bad a time as the castaways on the ice floe. He claimed he had to abandon ship as it sank due to ice damage, forcing himself, Bessels, Chester and the remainder of their men to row to land on the west coast of Smith Sound where the Eskimo provided for their welfare over the winter.

When the weather improved they took to their boats, on which they travelled down the coast for hundreds of miles until they reached the whaling grounds and were rescued.

Budington contested Tyson's and the other witnesses accounts on nearly every detail. Budington insisted everything had gone well until Hall's death. He acknowledged that Hall suspected Dr Bessels of poisoning him and said Hall thought everyone was trying to poison him. Budington insisted Hall died from natural causes. In response to a question on Tyson, he called Tyson a useless sailor who complained bitterly about everything.

Dr Bessels was dismissive of all allegations of conflict or insubordination and claimed it was all a misunderstanding. He was not asked why Hall suspected him of poisoning him, furthermore Bessels claimed he never had any difficulty with Captain Hall, who in his opinion had died from natural causes. It was concluded by the authorities that Captain Hall died from natural causes, *viz.* apoplexy.

The finding of Navy Secretary Robeson on Budington stated that the facts showed that though he was perhaps wanting in enthusiasm for the grand objects of the expedition and at times grossly lax in discipline, and though he differed in judgement from the others as to the possibility, safety and propriety of taking the ship further north, he was an experienced and careful navigator, and, when not affected by liquor (of which there remained none aboard at the time of separation from the castaways), a safe and competent commander.

The US Government was eager for the embarrassing controversy of the failed polar mission to be finalised and forgotten about, and so ended one of the greatest epics in survival in the history of Polar exploration.

Captain Charles Francis Hall probably did die from apoplexy but there can be little doubt but that someone wanted to poison him. The great irony was that he was the only one to die on this truly amazing expedition. The strange circumstances of his death became one of the great Arctic mysteries. Apoplexy was the verdict of the history books for more than a hundred years. However, in August 1968, following delicate international negotiations, Hall's remains were exhumed by a team of investigators led by Chauncey Loomis, a young Dartmouth University professor. Loomis got permission to exhume Hall's body to determine once and for all the cause of his death. Loomis and three companions, Doctor Franklin Paddock, William Barret and Thomas Gignoux flew from Resolute in Canada in a Single Otter plane and landed on a flat plain at Hall's Rest. Chauncey Loomis describes at great length and in brilliant

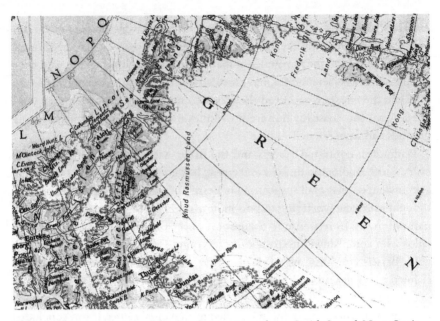

This map of north-west Greenland and its environs shows Smith Sound, Nares Strait, Kane Basin, Robeson Channel and Hall Basin.

detail the circumstances surrounding the gruesome autopsy. He noted that the two graves nearby were those of two men (Hand and Paul) who had died from scurvy while on the Nares Expedition and that close to the graves was a paleolithic Eskimo tent-ring. Hall's graveside autopsy was performed. Hall's body was eerily well preserved, the hair was there as was the beard, the skin was more or less intact and so were the fingernails. The results were startling.

Neutron activation tests run by Toronto's Centre of Forensic Sciences on his fingernails proved that during the last two weeks of his life Hall had received large amounts of arsenic (76.7ppm at the base of his fingernail). That the cause of his death was arsenic poisoning cannot be conclusively proved, although the dosage he had received was very large. Nor can it be proved that he was murdered. He owned a medical kit of his own and, distrusting his fellow crew members, he may have accidentally overdosed himself with an arsenical patent medicine. If Hall had been murdered there was no reason for it – by normal standards – but as those who experience the long Arctic night know, normal is in short supply. In spite of this new evidence pointing the finger at Bessels, Hall's death must remain a mystery forever.

In many ways the *Polaris* story was similar to the Franklin Expedition – a voyage of discovery into the unknown, the dead captain, the abandoned ship and the heroic escape on the ice floe – but happily for the *Polaris* survivors, no other fatalities. In a strange and ironic twist to the story, Dr Emil Bessels died from a stroke in 1888, at the young age of forty-two.

Tookoolito's young adopted daughter and only child Puney did not fully recover from her ordeal. She died from consumption on 18 March 1875, and is buried at Starr Burying Ground, Groton, Connecticut. On her grave marker are the words, 'Of such is the Kingdom of Heaven.'

Tookoolito, who was reluctant to return to Greenland and abandon Puney, remained in Groton. She bought a sewing machine on which she produced fur-skinned garments for her newfound American friends. Her iconic status enabled her to earn a modest living. Tookoolito, apart from the shortened name Hannah bestowed on her in America (in other records her name is spelt in several ways), remained faithful to the name used by Captain Hall in his book *Life With The Esquimaux*. Her husband Joe gained employment joining further expeditions to the Arctic and became quite a historic figure. Hans, Merkut and their children returned to Disko, Greenland.

George Tyson lectured on his experiences on the ice floe, charging an admission fee of twenty-five cents a head, and earning quite a decent living before returning to Arctic exploration. He died in 1906, aged seventy-seven and is buried in Glenwood Cemetery, Washington.

There was one more tragedy in connection with the *Polaris*. On 2 April the following year (1874) the *Tigress* was working through the ice when an explosion occurred which instantly killed ten of her crew – eleven others being so badly injured that they died the next day. Captain Bartlett was uninjured.

Chapter X

The Campaign of Osborn and Markham

On the death of Sir John Barrow, the baton of further Arctic exploration was taken up by Sherard Osborn, ably assisted by Clements Markham. The pair were originally two of Sir John's Barrow's 'boys'. The British Government had declared a moratorium on all further expenditure to find Franklin. The new Arctic goal was to reach the North Pole.

Sherard Osborn was born in Madras on 25 April 1822. The son of an army colonel, he joined the Navy and swiftly moved up the ranks. He captained the HMS *Pioneer* in the first search for the Franklin Expedition. Subsequently he was made a KCB and a Knight of the Legion of Honour, and became an influential figure in British maritime circles. Later in life he was promoted to Rear Admiral.

Clements Markham was born at Stillingfleet in Yorkshire on 20 July 1830. He joined the British Navy in 1844 as a cadet. In 1850–51 he served on the HMS *Assistance* in the search for Franklin. He later became Secretary of the Royal Geographical Society (RGS). He was knighted in 1896 and elected President of the RGS from 1893 to 1905.

Osborn and his friend Markham had been junior officers together and for ten years had been advocating a new strike at the Pole, pointing out that the Russians were now probing the area. They relentlessly badgered the Government and the RGS for support. Along with their influential friends, they lobbied far and wide in their campaign to force British politicians to renew Arctic exploration and to seek the North Pole. Risks were downplayed, rewards oversold and nationalistic fervour raised to fever pitch by the promoters and the press.

Among the maritime nations of Europe and the Americas, Britain's Royal Navy was the acknowledged master of ice travel and in Arctic exploration. In 1865 Osborn played the Union Jack card by appealing to Britain's patriotic instincts, pointing out the danger of another country raising its national flag on what should be British territory. Osborn accused Britain of dithering and prevaricating. While the British press and public lapped it up, the British Government and the Admiralty were still smarting from the Franklin fiasco. They turned a deaf ear to Osborn, Markham and their influential friends' pleas. The Admiralty intimated that they would not despatch any more men or ships to the Arctic, the implication being that if commercial interests wished to commit suicide they could do so, on their own ships, with their own men, and with their own money.

By now however some of the most vociferous critics of North Pole exploration were beginning to realise the possibilities and potential value to scientific knowledge of a successful expedition, particularly in such areas as astronomy, minerals, botany, marine and bird life, and of course the effects of the magnetic fields, which were proving a dangerous hazard to navigation.

The debate continued and despite being transferred far afield, each time he returned to Britain on shore leave Osborn continued to lobby and press his case. Support for the cause began to grow among the sceptics, the media, and the British public. The President of the RGS threw in his twopence worth when he wrote, 'To reach the Pole is the greatest geographical achievement which can be attempted, and I own I should grieve if it should be first accomplished by any other than an Englishman.'

In the early spring of 1871, much to their consternation, Osborn and his fellow campaigners learned that the American Charles Francis Hall on the USS *Polaris* was preparing to set sail for the North Pole, along with the US Navy ship carrying scientists and Inuit. From Hall's writings and experience of Arctic conditions they recognised that if anyone could reach the Pole, Charles Francis Hall was the man to do it. Osborn asked, was the great prize of being the first to reach the North Pole to be snatched from the grasp of its rightful owners? The search for the North Pole soon became an international obsession.

In the autumn of 1873, when the news of Hall's death, the disintegration of the *Polaris* Expedition, and the sensational story of the castaways hit the world headlines, Hans Hendrik, Merkut, little Charlie Polaris, the three children, along with Tookoolito, Joe and Puney, and Captain Tyson all became household names. The story of their epic voyage caused quite a sensation on both sides of the Atlantic, not least among Osborn and his friends when they noted that Charles Francis Hall had reached a farthest North of 82°38'N, less than 500 miles from the North Pole. The news had a most unsettling effect on the senior commanders of the British Navy. Furthermore, when the initial excitement had died down, George Tyson produced a blueprint on the ways and means of reaching the Pole.

Osborn renewed his pressure on the British Government with increased vigour.

Finally the sceptics were won over, realising the advantages and potential of Arctic exploration to British commercial interests. In August 1874 the British Government agreed to the possibility of a new Arctic expedition. The RGS, which had supported Osborn and Markham, was jubilant when the news was announced. On 17 November Prime Minister Benjamin Disraeli gave it his official approval. The objective was to reach the North Pole or the highest latitude achievable. The British Admiralty acted at once.

Arrangements were put in hand immediately. The expedition was scheduled to last for three years; provisioning and preparations would be a logistical nightmare. It was intended that the 1875 expedition would be better equipped and provisioned in all aspects than any other in the history of British exploration. It was a daunting project to organise the survival of two ships, each with a crew of sixty officers and men, on a three-year-long trip in difficult Arctic conditions. There would be no back-up in the event of shortages or emergencies. No communication with the outside world would be possible. Every single item down to the last and most minute detail had to be provided for. Recruitment of the most suitable personnel was top priority. Plans were drawn up to fill the necessary posts. Selection of officers and crews for the mission commenced.

The crews comprised the following:

Manpower, January 1875:
Commanders/Captains, 10
Lieutenants/Chief Principal Officers (including Boatswains), 14
Fleet Surgeons, 4
Scientists, Geologists, Astronomers and Botanists, 6
Chaplains, 2
Engineers, 4
Carpenters, 6
Stokers, 7
Cooks, 4
Sailmaster, 1
Paymaster, 1
Ice Quartermasters, 5
Signals Men, 2
Foretop/Forecastle Captains, 7
Colours Sergeant, 1
Bombardier, 1
Armourers, 3
Gunners, 6

Stewards, 4
Cooper, 1
Shipwrights, 2
Able Seamen, 27
Dog handler and Eskimo guide to be appointed, dogs to be purchased in Greenland *en route*.

Discovery Officers:
Captain Henry F. Stephenson
Senior Lt Lewis A. Beaumont
Lt Robert H. Archer
Lt Wyatt Rawson
Lt Reginald B. Fulford
Staff Surgeon Belgrave Ninnis, MD
Surgeon Richard W. Coppinger, MD
Charles E. Hodgson, Chaplain.
Chichester Hart, BA, Naturalist.
Sub-Lt C.I.M. Conybeare
Daniel Cartmel, Engineer
Matthew R. Miller, Engineer
Thomas Mitchell, Assistant Paymaster

Crewmen:
George R. Sarah, Ship's steward
George W. Emmerson, Chief boatswain's mate
E.C. Eddy, Chief captain's mate
Alexander Gray, Ice quartermaster
William Dougall, Ice quartermaster
Edward Taws, Ice quartermaster
George Bryant, Captain maintop
Frank Chatel, Captain forecastle
David Stewart, Captain foretop
Thomas Simmons, Captain forecastle
George Bunyan, Rope maker
William Ward, Armourer
James Shephard, Cooper
John E. Smith, Sail maker
Jonah Gear, Wardroom steward
George Stone, 2nd Captain foretop
James Cooper, 2nd Captain maintop

Henry W. Edwards, Able seaman
Daniel Girard, Able seaman
James Hand, Able seaman
Michael Regan, Able seaman
Thomas Chalkley, Able seaman
John Hodges, Able seaman
James Thornback, Able seaman
Alfred Hindle, Able seaman
Peter Craig, Able seaman
George Leggatt, Able seaman
Robert W. Hitchcock, Able seaman
John S. Saggers, Able seaman
Charles Paul, Able seaman
Benjamin Wyatt, Able seaman
Henry Windser, Carpenter's crew
James Phillips, Wardroom cook
Jeremiah Rourke, Leading stoker
Frank Jones, Stoker
William R. Sweet, Stoker
Hans Hendrik, Greenlander

Marines:
William C. Wellington, Sergeant
Wilson Dobing, Gunner
John Cropp, Gunner
Elijah Rayner, Gunner
William Waller, Private
Thomas Darke, Private
John Murray, Private
Henry Petty, Private

Alert Officers:
Captain George S. Nares
Commander Albert H. Markham
Fleet Surgeon E.L. Moss, MD
Fleet Surgeon Thomas Colan, MD
Revd W.H. Pullen, Chaplain
Senior Lt Pelham Aldrich
Sub-Lt George Le C. Egerton
Lt A.A.C. Parr

Lt G.A. Gifford
Lt W.H. May
George White, engineer
Captain H.W. Feilden, RA, naturalist

Crewmen:
George I. Burroughs, Ship's steward
Joseph Good, Chief boatswain's mate
John N. Radmore, Chief carpenter's mate
Vincent Dominics, Ship's cook
John Thores, Ice quartermaster
James Berrie, Ice quartermaster
David Deuchars, Ice quartermaster
Edwin Lawrence, Gunner's mate
James Doidge, Captain foretop
Daniel W. Harley, Captain foretop
Thomas Stuckberry, Captain maintop
Thomas Rawlins, Captain forecastle
Thomas Jolliffe, Captain maintop
Spero Capato, Captain's steward
George Kemish, Wardroom steward
John Hawkins, Cooper
John Simmons, 2nd Captain maintop
Adam Ayles, 2nd Captain foretop
Henry Mann, Shipwright
James Self, Able seaman
William Maskell, Able seaman
William P. Wooley, Able seaman
George Cranston, Able seaman
Reuben Francombe, Able seaman
John Pearson, Able seaman
William Ferbrache, Able seaman
Alfred R. Pearce, Able seaman
David Mitchell, Able seaman
Robert D. Symonds, Able seaman
Thomas H. Simpson, Able seaman
William Malley, Able seaman
George Winstone, Able seaman
William Lorimer, Able seaman
James Frederick Cane, Armourer

Robert Joiner, Leading stoker
John Shirley, Stoker
Thomas Stubbs, Stoker
William I. Gore, Stoker
William Hunt, Wardroom cook
Neil Carl Petersen, Eskimo interpreter
Frederick, Greenlander

Marines:
William Wood, Colour sergeant
William Ellard, Private
John Hollins, Private
Thomas Smith, Private
George Porter, Gunner
Elias Hill, Gunner
Thomas Oakley, Gunner

Two ships were allocated: HMS *Alert* captained by George S. Nares (who had been on previous expeditions searching for Franklin), with Lieutenant Albert Markham (nephew of Sir Clements Markham) as second in command, and HMS *Discovery* under Captain Henry Stephenson with Lewis Beaumont as first lieutenant. The two ships were quite small by modern standards, but in 1875 they were considered large.

The sixteenth ship of the Royal Navy to bear the name, the HMS *Alert* was built at Pembroke Dockyard in 1856. As Pembroke built hulls only, the uncompleted vessel was towed to Chatham Dockyard, which was then specialising in the application of steam machinery to wooden warships. One of six First Class Screw Sloops designed by Isaac Watts, Chief Constructor, the *Alert* was obsolete as a fighting ship almost as soon as she was completed. When built she had a wooden hull, copper sheathed, carried a full sailing ship rig, and was designed to steam in and out of harbour with horizontal engines of small power cramped low down in the ship. Her armament consisted of seventeen thirty-two-pounder smooth-bore guns, eight on each broadside with one fitted up on a slide as a bow chaser, and she carried a complement of 175 officers and men.

In 1874 the *Alert* was converted for Arctic exploration. The engines were removed and replaced and the armament superseded by a token battery of four Armstrong loaders. The hull was strengthened with felt-covered iron.

HMS *Discovery* had been built by Messrs Stephens & Sons, Dundee. Designed by the builders and engined by the Greenock Foundry Company, she was launched in 1873 and purchased in 1874. Her length was 166ft, breadth 30ft 2ins; load draught of water forward 14ft 6ins, aft 16ft 6ins; displacement tonnage 1,250; engine horse power, 365. The ship was built for seal hunting and initially named *Blood Hound*, but when purchased by the British Admiralty for the expedition, it was renamed HMS *Discovery*.

Captain George S. Nares was forty-five years old a the time of the *Discovery's* commission. Born in Aberdeen in 1830 he had been in the Navy since the age of fourteen. He was efficient and had Arctic experience. He was also acquainted with sledge travel and, having taken part in McClintock's monumental man-hauled sorties in search of Franklin, he was an experienced ice navigator. He was a tall, determined man; bearded, bold and serious. There could be no doubt as to his bravery, competence or courage. He would operate strictly by the book, but had the reputation of having a dour personality.

In 1874 Nares was in command of the Challenger Antarctic Research Voyage. He was chosen to lead the expedition because along with his other skills he was a strict disciplinarian. In many ways Nares was the ideal man for the task. He was considered by the Admiralty to be a safe pair of hands.

Second in command to Captain Nares was Commander Albert Hastings Markham. Markham was a vastly experienced officer. The son of a naval officer, he was born in France in 1841. He joined the Royal Navy at the age of fifteen and served in China, protecting British ships from pirates. He served in the Mediterranean, and was engaged in suppressing the illegal slave trade in South Sea Islanders. In 1873 he was appointed Commander.

The fitting out of the expedition was supervised by the vastly experienced Sir Leopold McClintock, assisted by Rear-Admiral Sherard Osborn and Rear-Admiral Richards. Each ship was provisioned for three years. The provisions we are told, were to be of the same high quality, or an improvement on those used in the Franklin Expedition. It transpired however that the Admiralty had learned nothing new in the intervening thirty years, particularly regarding scurvy and its prevention.

Alert and *Discovery* were to be accompanied as far as Greenland by the supply ship HMS *Valorous*, carrying mostly coal and other supplies to make up for what was expended by the two ships on the outward journey. Thereafter the *Alert* would push on through Smith Sound to Robeson Channel and beyond, while *Discovery* would anchor no farther than 82°N to act as a rescue ship in case the *Alert* became trapped in ice.

In 1875 the total cost of the expedition was £150,000. This outlay and commitment on Britain's part was a powerful reminder to other like-minded exploring nations that Britain was serious about being the first to reach the North Pole. It was considered by other nations a most impressive display of power and might.

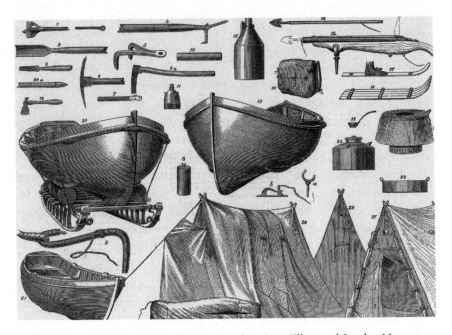

Implements and apparatus for the arctic exploration. (*Illustrated London News*, 29 May 1875.)

Nares's instructions were to give an idea of the matters which concerned contemporary scientists. He was asked to investigate subjects under the following headings: Ethnology, Mammalia, Ornithology, Ichthyology, Mollusca, Insecta and Arachnida, Crustacea, Annelida, Echinodermata, Polyzoa, Hydrozoa, Spongida, Rhizopoda reticularia, Botany and Geology. He was also to report on the Petermann Glacier, draw up a meteorological abstract, record tidal observations and keep a full game-book of everything the expedition captured or shot.

Among the officers, scientists and crew were four Irishmen. Henry Chichester Hart, born in Raheny, Co. Dublin, was appointed to the *Discovery*. Although principally known as a botanist, he was also an accomplished mountaineer and explorer. Dr Richard Coppinger from Dublin, was the fleet surgeon on *Discovery*. Born in November 1847 in Dublin, he was the son of a Dublin solicitor and qualified with an MD from Queen's University in 1870. Dr Thomas Colan (originally Coughlan) from Cork was the surgeon on the *Alert*. Born in November 1830, he changed his name from Coughlan to Colan in the 1860s. He had served as assistant surgeon aboard the *Royal George* during the Russian war in the Baltic, and had been active in major naval engagements through the years. Finally, there was Able Seaman James Hand from Bray, Co. Wicklow.

James Hand's naval record, updated during his service aboard HMS *Immortalite*

CAPTAIN G. S. NARES, H.M.S. ALERT, CHIEF COMMANDER OF THE EXPEDITION.

CAPTAIN H. F. STEPHENSON, COMMANDING H.M.S. DISCOVERY.

THE ARCTIC EXPEDITION OFFICERS.

The Portraits of Captain Nares and Captain Stephenson, and other officers of the Alert and Discovery, about to start on a voyage of exploring adventure towards the North Pole, are presented in this week's paper, and some of them in our next, as their friends in England must to-day bid them farewell, in the hope of a safe return after a successful performance of their noble task.

Captain George Strong Nares, who is chief commander of the expedition, and commands its leading ship, the Alert, entered the Royal Navy in 1845, having gained the annual naval cadetship given by the Lords of the Admiralty as a prize of merit to the boys of the Royal Naval School at New-cross. He served in the Canopus, in the Channel Squadron, until 1848, when he joined the Havannah, and served three years in her on the Australian station. Having returned with his vessel to England, he was appointed mate of the Resolute, employed in the Arctic expedition of 1852, under Sir Edward Belcher. With this ship he passed two winters in the ice. Upon the return of that expedition, he became Gunnery Lieutenant of the Glatton, the first of our iron-clad vessels. He afterwards held a similar post in the Conqueror.

under Admiral Sir Hastings Yelverton. When the present system of training naval cadets was instituted, Lieutenant Nares was placed in charge of those on board the Britannia, under the late Captain R. Harris. He held this appointment till promoted, in 1854, to the rank of Commander. With that rank he served in the Boscawen training-ship at Southampton.

his ship reached Hong-Kong, early in this year, he was ordered home to take command of the Arctic Expedition. The portrait of Captain Nares is engraved from a photograph by Messrs. J. Griffin and Co., of the Hard, Portsmouth, and of Cockspur-street, London.

Captain Henry Frederick Stephenson, who commands the Discovery, entered the Navy in February, 1855. He first served in the St. Jean d'Acre, at the blockade of Sebastopol. In September, 1856, he joined the Raleigh, sent to China as the flagship of Admiral Keppel, but was wrecked in that ship, off Macao, in April, 1857. He then served in the steamer Hong-Kong, bearing the Admiral's broad pennant, in the Canton river, and took part in the action of June 1, 1857, in the Fatshan creek. He was gazetted, in August, for his conduct in an action with the Chinese war-junks. In the Indian mutiny war he served as midshipman with the Pearl naval brigade, under Captain Sotheby, from September, 1857, to February, 1859. He took part in every engagement with the mutineers during that period. In the Gazette of April 23, 1858, he was praised for his gallant services, as aide-de-camp to Captain Sotheby, at the fort of Chandeepore. He was again gazetted, on May 21 of that year, for the affair at the fort of Bilwar, and for the general action with the

COMMANDER A. H. MARKHAM, H.M.S. ALERT.

and in the Salamander and the Newport, surveying-vessels. In the Newport, Commander Nares made a survey of the Gulf of Suez and of the entrance to the Suez Canal. He had made himself known to the public and to the profession as author of an excellent treatise on "Seamanship; including the fitting and rigging of ships, sailing, management of boats, &c." This volume, adorned with 400 illustrations, and with coloured sheets of signal-flags, was published at the price of one guinea. It has gone through five editions, with very high and general approval. In December, 1869, Commander Nares was promoted to be Captain, but retained command, in the Shearwater, of the Mediterranean survey. This he left in 1872, when appointed to command the Challenger in her voyage of scientific investigation round the world. Captain Nares took the Challenger to Australia and the Indian and South Pacific Oceans; but when

SUB-LIEUTENANT G. L. EGERTON, H.M.S. ALERT.

LIEUTENANT G. A. GIFFARD, H.M.S. ALERT,

The officers on Nares's Expedition. (*Illustrated London News*, 29 May 1876.)

in October 1872, tells us he was 5ft 10in tall, had blue eyes, brown hair and a fresh complexion. Subsequently we learned Jim filled out and became quite a big man. He smoked a pipe, took a drink, grew a beard and was known to his shipmates as J. J. Throughout his service his conduct was rated consistently good or very good. At eighteen, Hand signed on for a further ten years, serving on HM ships *Liverpool*, *Zealous*, *Excellent*, *Penelope* and *Duncan* before embarking on *Discovery* for his final fateful voyage to the North Pole.

Chapter XI

Portsmouth Harbour

In Portsmouth in the weeks prior to departure the excitement was mounting. Supplies and equipment arrived daily. Newspapers and journals informed the public of each development, such as the names and records of captains and officers, the backgrounds of the crews. During this time, on 9 May, James Hand had been granted three weeks shore leave from the HMS *Duncan*. It is a fair guess that he made what would be his last visit to see his parents. It is fair to assume that his parents would have been extremely worried about their son. Jim himself would have been well aware of the failed Hall Expedition, the names of the survivors, and what they had endured.

So why did Jim Hand volunteer for a Polar expedition? The ten-year tour of duty he had signed on for previously was ended so he could have walked away and followed John and his sisters to New York. There were probably a number of reasons, chief among them being the opportunity to be among the first to reach the North Pole. The prospect of adventure was probably high on the list also. Maybe there was a financial reason, such as a guaranteed naval allowance for his mother; others taking part in Arctic expeditions received double pay and double leave. Compared to normal naval pay, the bonuses were attractive, if not substantial. Being among the first to reach the North Pole would surely open doors in his future naval career. All things considered, and by the standards of his day, on completion of the three-year expedition he would have had a reasonably big pay day to look forward to.

Telegraphic communications were almost non-existent in 1875, but the written word abounded. If Jim Hand read the literature available to him on conditions in the Arctic he would have had a good idea of what lay ahead for him and for his shipmates. Before Jim signed on, he would have done his homework on the perils ahead. The reports, journals, records and diaries of previous expeditions were available to Navy personnel. Shipwreck, starvation, snow blindness, frostbite, desolation, despair and madness were all real possibilities. Would the elements be as appalling as the chroniclers described? He would surely have been concerned about a three-year sojourn in the Arctic and what effect the merciless cold would have on his mind and body. Jim Hand had good reason to be concerned but he must have placed his trust in his superiors, perhaps unwisely. With the exception of Captain Nares none of the officers on either ship had experienced Far North conditions.

That was the least of Jim's problems, however. The Admiralty had ignored the advice and the many reports that were available from experts on the correct diet for Arctic expeditions; the necessity for fresh meat or game, tinned vegetables and tinned fruit. They failed to realise how useless canvas footwear and outer woollen garments (where perspiration froze to the body) were in Arctic conditions. All this was known from people such as Captain Charles Francis Hall and Dr John Rae, who had more recent experience of Arctic conditions. Jim Hand would later discover that his clothing was of the wrong design and materials. The sledges he would be compelled to drag were far too heavy and would sink too deep into the snow. Snow shoes, considered so essential, were dismissed by the Navy as a joke. Jim would learn that the list of mistakes was a long one, and that some of them would have fatal consequences for himself and others.

The prospect of at least two winters anchored in ice, at temperatures of as low as 100° below was of great concern to Captain Nares and Captain Stephenson. But had they learned anything from Franklin's failure?

There is no clear evidence that the crews of *Erebus* and *Terror* had been taught survival skills of any kind. Franklin (due to his expeditions charting Northern Canada) and some of his officers were experienced in Arctic travel. He would have been aware of the necessity of Arctic survival skills, and yet his crew suffered fatalities from starvation in a more southerly area, where fish and animal food was available. None of his men had known how to use a harpoon for hunting seals or how to fish at holes or lanes of open water. The answer had to be that the British Admiralty did not consider the possibility that the men would have to survive on the ice.

Another important consideration was boredom. Boredom among crews had caused serious problems on other expeditions. The prospect of keeping over 100 inactive men in almost total darkness for twenty-four hours a day, for five months at a time was a daunting one. From the crew's point of view it must be remembered that they were naval service men subject to a rigid discipline and blind obedience, unlike some of the earlier privately sponsored expeditions, where there was a much more relaxed regime and more palatable food. The staple diet of the non-commissioned men was pemmican. Private expeditions had brought substantial quantities of alcohol (strictly for medicinal purposes they claimed). Understandably naval servicemen were strictly rationed.

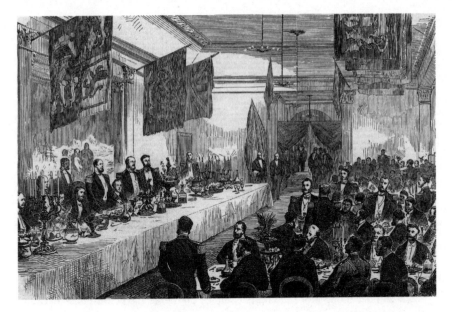

Banquet given by the Mayor of Portsmouth to the officers of the arctic expedition: Captain Nares returning thanks. (*Illustrated London News*, 29 May 1875.)

In the days prior to departure, Portsmouth's quays were hives of bustling activity; taverns and alehouses did a roaring trade, with visitors and locals alike enjoying the carnival atmosphere. Souvenir manufacturing was much in evidence prior to the departure of the expedition. A polar bear logo was adopted for the expedition and printed everywhere, even on the ships' dinner plates. At this time too, Captain Nares welcomed a gift of some pigeons, similar to those used in the Franco-Prussian War. The pigeons were intended to be used to convey messages from the sledge parties to the *Alert* and *Discovery*.

The following extracts from an editorial in *The London Times* of 29 May 1875, the day of departure, puts into perspective the views of what we may consider the prevailing approach to Arctic exploration and the North Pole in particular:

The departure of the Arctic Expedition makes this day in many senses an epoch in the history of the world. This is the first attempt made with a set purpose and elaborate plan, with the best possible preparations and a reasonable hope to reach the point which for ages has been the goal of universal aspiration.

There is, however, no point in which man has made so great a progress this century as in the science of expeditions, whether by sea or land, not to speak yet of the regions over our heads. Taught by painful experience, we have learnt to select the men and the kind of men, the materials whether for diet, clothing or fuel, and all the arrangements best adapted for the special purpose. We have learnt to calculate exactly weight, distances, and average difficulties as the most practised military commander would for an advance into an enemy's country. As far as possible, all contingencies, short of annihilation, have been provided for. So what we really begin this 29th day of May 1875 is in all probability a progressive series of operations for the discovery of this planet's most intractable and inaccessible quarter.

At present there lies within a few weeks of us and inhabited continents, a circle, 1400 miles across, of which we know not even whether it be land or water, or in what respects it is affected by some conditions wholly different from our own.

Is it anything more than a great refrigerator for the production of cold – that is, for the absorption of heat? Then what is the aurora? Is it of earth, or of heaven? Is it meteoric? Is it cosmic? Does it reveal a universal medium? Is it a magnetic phenomenon? At about the 70th degree of latitude the expedition will reach the other side of the Magnetic Pole, and will have to steer by rules the contrary of our own, and becoming more and more complex till the needle points finally to the centre of the earth.

Who would have guessed a few years ago that the interior of Africa was populous and delightful, that the ocean was full of life and undergoing change, or that the elements and fabric of the sun would yield to analysis. The expedition is a lottery, in which we know too well there are blanks, but in which there are sure to be some prizes, perhaps one or two great ones.

Maybe for several years, the men will be consigned to small, dark, stuffy cells, buried in ice and snow, to monotonous and unappetising food, taxing ordinary teeth and digestions, to utter exclusion from the world most of them love too well, and to equal share in a daily toil of which not the least part is the maintenance of one and other's spirits. The fortunately, or unfortunately, successful candidates have been selected by rules more stringent than any known to competitive examination.

For many months it is all winter evenings in the Arctic Circle, without the chance of a visit, or even the smallest incident – we must not say from day to day, for day there will be none – unless it be some accident, illness or death.

Time is certain to bring aggravations – less strength and less power of enduring cold, greater tendency to disease, and perhaps a diminished distribution of articles, more or less necessary, with a gloomier perspective. But all this will have to be done in a nutshell, in one and the same nutshell, possibly for years, with the intermission of sledging journeys of extreme toil and peril, across a frozen world. Each expedition is training for the next. If we advance henceforth as much as Captain Nares does on the Ross family, Parry, and Franklin and as they did on Cook and Phipps, it is hardly possible to say what the next century or half-century may witness.

The *Alert* and *Discovery* leaving Portsmouth for the arctic expedition. (*Illustrated London News*, 5 June 1876.)

Good and thoughtful people will remember them to-morrow, when they pray for all that travel by land or water. The Ark itself of sacred story was hardly a more mysterious and pregnant adventure.

Who knows what this may lead to? Even if it seeks not a new earth, or a better kingdom, it unquestionably seeks some addition to our knowledge and opportunities, and to extend Man's primeval and converted dominion over all the powers of Nature.

Chapter XII

Sailing for Disko, Greenland

In the year 1875 the art of photography was in its infancy and so its importance may have been underestimated by the Naval Command. Consequently, there was no professional photographer appointed to the expedition, although two officers, George White, an engineer on the *Alert*, and Thomas Mitchell, the assistant paymaster on the *Discovery* were assigned to photograph aspects of the expedition. The pair had been tutored by Captain de Abrey of the Army School of Photography in Chatham, a pioneer of the 'dry plate process' which was launched to the public only a few years before.

The following is an extract from the log of George Bryant, Boatswain, HMS *Discovery*:

> April 15th HM *Discovery* was put in commission at Portsmouth. We store and provision from the 15th of April till the 28th of May and on the 29th we sail from the jetty under the cheers of thousands of people both in boats and on land, when we got clear we made sail 5.30p.m. Sent letters in by Mr Conabers Fathers at 8.45p.m. and then got the screw. May 30th Sunday 12a.m. Admiral Cepple and staff came onboard to look at the two ships. 1a.m. Left after three hearty cheers in the evening. We got the screw down and furl sails. 10p.m. Made sail on the starboard tack.

The day the ships set sail, 29 May, was a pleasant sunny day. There were an estimated 200,000 people gathered at Portsmouth Harbour. Nares's ships prepared to leave at noon, but departure was delayed by the loading of coals and other stores. The Prince of Wales visited the ships and lunched with the captains and officers. The departure was postponed until 4p.m. The Military and Naval brass bands played rousing marches. The inns and hostelries were packed. There was much boisterous laughter, back and thigh slapping in the ale houses and a great sense of pride as the ships left the harbour to resounding cheers and applause. Captain Nares commented:

None on-board our two ships can ever forget the farewell given to the discovery vessels on that occasion. Closely packed multitudes occupied each pier and jetty on both sides of the harbour. South sea beach was thronged to the waters edge, the troops in garrison paraded on the common, men of war in port manned their rigging and as we passed, greeted us with deafening cheers, whilst the air rang with shouts of encouragement on shore, and from on-board the steamers, yachts and small craft which crowded the water.

The excitement had even reached Buckingham Palace; in his hand Nares held a telegram from Queen Victoria the contents of which read, 'I earnestly wish you and your gallant companions every success, and trust that you may safely accomplish the important duty you have so bravely undertaken.' It was a magnificent send off and probably heady stuff for Jim Hand, no doubt dwelling on success and the prospect of an even more momentous homecoming reception.

At 4p.m. the ships raised anchors and cast off. Nares and Stephenson were compelled to sail and lift all impediments into their places as they sailed down the channel. On passing through Spithead, HMS *Valorous*, the expedition's coal supply ship joined the company. The fires were banked and all sail made before a northerly wind. By 8p.m. the ships were south of the Needles, with only one friendly yacht left, belonging to the Revd Mr Conybeare, the father of one of the officers of the *Discovery*, which naturally gave the ships a lingering farewell. By midnight the ships were abreast of the Portland Lights, running down the Channel under sail, at the rate of six knots an hour. The following day they passed the Eddystone Lighthouse. Captain Nares takes up the story:

In the evening the *Valorous* parted company for Queenstown [Cobh, Co. Cork] to complete loading additional coal and sail onwards to Bantry Bay where she rejoined us. The ships called into Bantry Bay on 1st-2nd June. From there the crews despatched final farewell letters and telegrams to loved ones.

The ships had a rough passage and encountered gales and a cyclone while crossing the Atlantic. One of the boats of *Discovery* was destroyed and another badly damaged, the heavily laded ships were rolling 20 and 30 degrees each way.

Before the storm the *Discovery* was staggering along behind us but now was nowhere in sight, and as her boats were even more exposed than those of the *Alert* we were naturally somewhat anxious as to how she got through the cyclone. Many thoughts were also directed towards the live sheep on-board the *Valorous* and doubts were expressed as to whether their lives could have been saved. The *Valorous*, although she set every possible bit of canvas and disconnected her paddles from the engines to permit them to revolve, could not keep up under sail alone with the Arctic ships. I accordingly gave her permission to part company

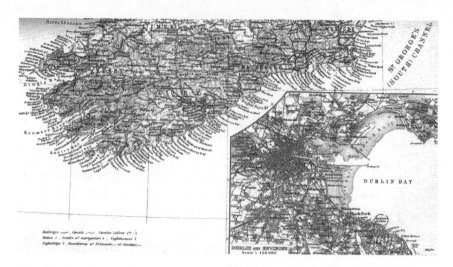

This old map gives the older names of Queenstown and Kingstown to Cobh and Dún Laoghaire respectively. (*Encyclopaedia Britannica* Cambridge 1911, 11th Edition.)

and to rendezvous at Godhavn (also known as Lievely) in North Greenland, early in July.

On 29 June I found we had run deeper into the ice stream than I had intended and was forced to haul out from five to ten miles farther away from the land. A few seals and a single walrus were observed asleep on the ice.

Nares goes on to write about his astonishment at the unusual massiveness of the ice and ceases to wonder at the misfortune which overtook the *Hansa* belonging to the German expedition six years previously in that location:

On our arrival on 6th July at the Danish settlement of Lievely, on Disko Island, we were received with a salute from three brass cannons in front of the inspector's house. We also found the *Valorous* at anchor, all was well and the sheep had survived. *Discovery* also arrived safe and well. I was much pleased to meet Herr Inspektor Krarup Smith the Governor of North Greenland who was most anxious to meet our every need. Disko is a regular rendezvous of the English whaling fleet. The island is nearly 50 miles square. The population of the port was 96, composed of Danes and Eskimo, a mixed race whose occupation was catching seals. The ships anchored in the commodious harbour for ten days, replenished coal stocks from *Valorous* and the crews availed of a last opportunity to send home despatches. The houses in Disko are built in wood, some of the poorer inhabitants lived in hovels built of turf. Sixteen children attend the local school which is of

Lutheran denomination, a pastor comes from Upernavik which is farther north, whenever any of the more important religious ceremonies are to be performed such as marriages or christenings. The weather was seasonal for an Arctic summer, daylight for a full 24 hours, the crews enjoyed it all immensely, trekking excursions in the mountains, visiting their first glacier and had a great deal of sport and recreation with the locals, fishing and shooting.

If Jim Hand was an astute observer of the Eskimo guides he would have learned a great deal from them. He would have noticed their extremely high level of unwavering concentration, which is absolutely vital in the unforgiving environment. Every slip, slide, or trip could be the one to break an ankle or a leg. In the case of an Eskimo hunting alone, incurring an injury could render him a frozen corpse, never to be found.

Jim would have learned that a dog team and sled is the highest acquisition of an Eskimo man, and that the Eskimo husky is the only dog in the world that can live solely on a diet of snow and frozen seal meat. Jim would also come to know that the fatigue and privation that the Eskimo dog can endure borders on the incredible and their intelligence is matched by their capacity as thieves. Dogs are not allowed inside houses because they would overheat.

During Jim's enjoyable ten days ashore he would have seen the most obvious form of Eskimo culture – carving – a historical tradition with Eskimo. Eskimo children learn the skills from their parents at an early age. This art form has been handed down through the centuries and enables them to produce fantastic carvings in bone and tusk. On a more practical level, they are expert at producing bone blades and ivory arrows.

In conversations with the Danish settlers Jim may have learned of the 'Piteraq'. Greenland is frequently hit by powerful storms. In the coastal areas the wind from the inland ice blows at a staggering 200mph, harder than a tropical hurricane, with a temperature that will freeze the eyeballs in your head – this is the Piteraq.

Another realisation for Jim Hand on his visit to Greenland was that if he needed anything other than fur skins, fish or bone, he should have brought it along himself.

Captain Stephenson bought a kayak from a native. It was a little gem. To the vastly experienced sailors it was an amazing piece of engineering, long, slender and silent, therefore easy to paddle, cost-effective and energy free. It was an ecologist's dream, made from bone, sealskin and small pieces of driftwood. Stephenson didn't realise it at the time, but it proved to be an enormous boost to the morale of the crews. Hilarious scenes followed. The Europeans considered it a strange construction in comparison to a canoe. Taking it in turns slipping, sliding, and tripping on the slippery ice while wearing heavy clothing, they had great difficulty entering and extricating themselves from it as it bobbled in the water, much to the amusement of their fellow crew members.

The kayak, in the icy Arctic waters could be a silent killer among Eskimo men. Down through the ages the kayak has been the cause of countless accidental deaths by drowning. If for any simple reason one fell into Arctic water, even in the height of summer, one had about two minutes before the cold took its grip and numbed the brain. There is no margin for error, no second chance.

The officers and crews exchanged civilities with the Governor and socialised with the locals. As for the Eskimo – what did they make of the arrival of large numbers of foreign white men? They did not feel threatened. Unlike the Native American, the Eskimo possessed nothing the white man desired (though it may have been a much different story if they had). The white man only needed assistance to reach a place called the North Pole, or the Great Nail as the Eskimo ingeniously named it. Evidently it was of some bulk or of great value to the white man. Iron was worth its weight in gold to the Eskimo in the Far North, when its advantage over bone-hooks and knives had been demonstrated, and they were wise enough to realise there might be something in it for themselves in the long term. In the meantime, they thought it strange that the white men should bring vast quantities of food a thousand miles when there was so much fresh food available for a white man with a gun. Captain Nares continued:

On Sunday 11th July the opportunity was taken of holding a sacrament service in the chapel on the shore. Most of the officers and a number of the crews of the three ships attended.

In the course of a conversation with Krarup Smith he invited me to visit a spot where Professor Nordenskiold discovered the so-called meteoric iron-stones, some of which were removed in 1871 by the Swedish Expedition under Von Otter. Smith was of the opinion that the iron masses detected were precisely similar to some of those taken away by the Swedes. I organised a party to inspect the iron but much to our disappointment the roughness of the sea prevented an inspection.

The ships raised anchors, destination Upernavik. On 16 July they sailed first for Ritenbenk, thirty miles north. Here, the *Alert* took on additional supplies, and Captain Nares bought thirty dogs. The dogs further encumbered the narrow, congested gangways between the piled-up provisions. Captain Stephenson purchased twenty-five dogs.

One afternoon Captain Nares arranged for Neil Petersen and Hans Hendrik to give a demonstration to the men on how to handle a dog team. This session

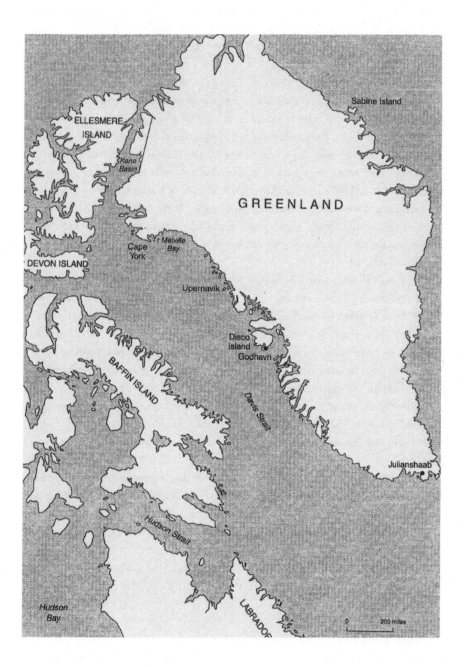

was even funnier than the kayak episode. Sled-dog handling requires a great deal of skill and infinite patience. The sailors had neither, and the dogs sensed it. It was a mystery how the seamen didn't break any bones. The experiment was a cause of great merriment, but it did not auger well for the future. Captain Nares alluded to the dogs thus:

Being in strange quarters they are in concert, the distracting noise frequently diversified by a sharp howl as a sailor in forcing his way through their midst uses the toe of his boot. The packs collected from different settlements are strangers to each other. The king-dog of each team is necessarily tied up, his subordinates of both sexes clustering around, and crouching at his feet. In their anxious endeavours to protect their followers, the females of whom are rather given to straying, and if possible to maintain their rights, these king-dogs are straining their very utmost at the ropes, snarling and lifting their upper lips, evidently longing for the time to arrive when they may fight it out, and decide who is to be ruler over all.

By sheer fighting each has worked his way up to a position he now holds, the most determined and enduring animals gaining the day. A long series of combats will be undertaken before the supreme head is acknowledged, and hereafter many an attempt at revolution will be fought out by rising aspirants for power, as old chiefs become worn out from age or from other causes. It would appear as if fighting were an enjoyment or natural condition of their existence. In maintaining discipline among the weaker sex, punishment is left entirely in the hands, or rather the mouth of the favourite queen, who, except when jealousy may occasionally warp her judgement, uses her prerogative pretty fairly, whilst it frequently happens that the king-dog himself submits without resentment.

To the consternation of the crew the stench of dog excrement was overpowering, the dogs frequently took fits, and were constantly whining, barking and yelping. These unfortunate seasick animals were confined twenty-four hours a day on a small congested heaving ship, protected only by a tarpaulin covering tied to the ship's rail, in minus temperatures.

Both ships sent parties on a shooting expedition for wild birds, they returned with a considerable number, a welcome addition to their fresh food stocks. Nares continued:

When at Godhavn, Disko, we remarked how densely each fresh-water pool was inhabited by the larvae of mosquitoes just on the point of changing their condition to the winged state. A few days later at Ritenbenk the mosquitoes were intolerable, and when getting under way, the weather being calm, these persistent annoyers fairly took possession of the upper deck.

On July 17th we left Ritenbenk, waved off by the crew of *Valorous*, a signal was hoisted on all three mastheads 'Farewell, Speedy Return'. They disappeared into the Arctic fog. This was the last we saw of the *Valorous*. Two days later the ships arrived at a settlement named Proven, the inhabitants number about 106 souls; where the Dane Neil Petersen joined the expedition. Petersen had previously accompanied Dr Kane and Dr Hayes.

Nares considered Petersen invaluable as a guide and interpreter in his attempt to reach the North Pole. Captain Nares also welcomed the Eskimo hunter Hans Hendrik on-board. Nares knew Hans Hendrik would be indispensable to the expedition. A hero of Captain Hall's *Polaris* Expedition, he was vastly experienced and resourceful. One other experienced Eskimo named Frederick also joined up. Nares continued:

Hans was an accomplished kayaker who also had assisted Kane and Hayes on their expedition up the Smith Channel. Hans, when a lad of 19, joined Dr Kane's expedition in 1853. After rendering invaluable services to his companions during their two winters' stay at Rensselaer Harbour, Smith Sound, he married Merkut, the daughter of Sanghu, one of the Arctic Highlanders. He had remained with his wife when Dr Kane abandoned the *Advance*. They travelled south to safety at Upernavik in one of the boats. [Isaac Hayes had also taken Hans, his wife and child on-board the United States on his 1860 expedition.]

Hans bade farewell to his wife Merkut and the children. We left Proven on the evening of 21st July, the scenery is superb; magnificent cliffs of gneiss rise sheer from the water's edge to a height of 1,000 to 1,200 feet; the rich colouring of the rocks presented an almost inconceivable richness of hues, and formed a striking contrast to the glaciers and mer de glace.

We entered Upernavik Harbour and met the Governor Fliescher and Sophie his wife; the latter the considerate friend of all English voyagers since the first of the Franklin search expeditions. I had the pleasure of presenting her with a thoughtful present of crockery from Sir Leopold McClintock.

I am afraid that few of the transient visitors to these North Greenland Settlements think of the dreary winters which the Danish inhabitants must necessarily pass. Disko and Ritenbenk are in the same latitude as Igloolik, where Sir Edward Parry wintered between 1821 and 1823 and as King Williams Land, where Franklin's two ships were lost. Upernavik is a little south of Lancaster Sound, where so many expeditions have passed their winters. With a well-found naval expedition newly arrived from southern climes the monotony of a long dark winter, which appears something dreadful and dismal in the anticipation, is considerably relieved by the charm of novelty. The Danish inhabitants, who are obliged to endure a yearly recurring period of equal darkness with only one or two associates, can but contrast the monotony of one winter with the past; life under these circumstances must be hard indeed, and the Danish officials and missionaries who voluntarily undergo it are entitled to our liveliest commiseration.

Nares commended the Danish Government:

Since 1721, the year of Egede's settlement at Godhaab in South Greenland, the Danes have consistently endeavoured to improve and ameliorate the condition of the Eskimo inhabitants of Greenland. Their efforts have been crowned with marked success, and the paternal rule of the Danish Government has been conducted with such complete regard for the interests of the Greenlanders, that we find the native population scattered along the coasts of that inhospitable land enjoying the blessings of religion, law, order and a considerable degree of civilisation. This enlightened policy has been carried out by a succession of worthy officials and missionaries, whose self-denying labours reflect the utmost credit on themselves and the country to which they belong. While the *Discovery* was secured to the land-ice inside the grounded icebergs, a female narwhal with a well-developed tusk, was killed, also a great number of little auks. Seventeen natives, 15 men and two women, with three dog sledges visited the ship. They appeared poorly clad in hooded seal-skin jumpers and bear-skin trousers cut off at the knees; wearing nothing underneath, they showed a broad margin of body between the two garments.

On being given the narwhal they ate it in great quantities, tearing the raw flesh asunder with their teeth. Their hair was long and matted, but their splendid row of even white teeth showed to advantage out of the setting formed by the flat mahogany coloured visage. They were given a supply of lucifer matches, biscuits, knives, etc., which appeared to please them greatly. We also encountered some Arctic Highlanders who arrived in dog sledges over the ice-floes, those met were barbarous in their habits when eating. They wear an upper garment made of seal-skin with trousers of bear-skin, they build dog sledges but have not advanced so far as to make kayaks. They had met with very few Europeans previously, as far as the crews could make out.

Our two ships left Upernavik on July 22nd and proceeded north through Baffin Bay arriving at Cape York on July 25th, rejoining the *Discovery* and laying down depots of supplies on land in the event of an emergency. Expecting to find a southerly current in the offing, where there were few icebergs, I steamed along the Greenland shores within a couple of miles of land and inside a long line of immense bergs lying around parallel to the coast, trusting to the grounded ice to point out any hidden dangers. At this season little snow remained on the Beverly Cliffs though behind them the inland ice-cap was visible, and down the ravines between the dark walls of rock many glaciers made their way to the sea. A few Iceland gulls were seen perched on the bergs, and this was the most northern point where we recognised that species. Guillemots were abundant, a large loomery being visible near cape Parker Snow. These would have been more convenient if placed on Northumberland Island or on the mainland, but I was much afraid of the Eskimo finding and plundering the depot.

July 28th. We were steering close under Cape Alexander and as far northwards as Cape Ohlsen and Lifeboat Cove, and as far as we could see inland grantoid and gneissaid rocks prevail. The total absence of drift-ice between Cape York and Smith Sound and the fact that a strong northerly wind was bringing no ice down, led me to conclude that the main pack to the northward had not yet broken up and that we had arrived at Hartstene Bay at the most opportune time, when the ice at the head of Baffin Bay had drifted south and before the northern ice, which breaks up later in the season, had drifted south through Smith Sound. A few days subsequently the sea between Littleton Island and Cape Sabine, which now permitted free progress was so ice-encumbered as to prevent any vessel crossing the channel. The *Alert* proceeded on her way towards the Cary Islands, there to establish a depot of provisions and deposit a boat for use should we unfortunately be fated to retreat from South Sound, leaving our vessels behind us, as two out of three expeditions which preceded us were forced to do. The crew of the *Alert* landed a depot of 3,600 rations in an almost inaccessible location, fearful of Eskimo hunters plundering the supplies. Before leaving Disko we left a notice for Captain Allen Young, or anyone likely to follow our footsteps. We placed a boat in a crevice of the rocks, more information and letters were placed in a cairn on the summit of the island, which attains an altitude of about 600 feet.

As a northerly wind prevented our advance except at a large expenditure of coal, I took the opportunity to visit Life Boat Cove, where a part of the crew of the USS *Polaris* wintered in 1871–73. I was in hopes of finding the pendulum and other instruments which were necessarily abandoned on the retreat of the party in small boats to the South. There is so little depth of water in Life Boat Cove, that the *Polaris* must have grounded close to the entrance of the bay. We had no difficulty in finding the locality where Captain Hall had built his onshore depot. Many relics from the *Polaris* were lying about, such as clothes, pieces of books, ice-chisels, fish hooks, and bottles. A large amount of seal and walrus-rubber was cached in the neighbourhood.

A dog-sled made entirely of bone, with runners ingeniously constructed of pieces of tusk of the walrus, was found hidden in a cleft of the rock; it was of course not interfered with. Arrows were found in the Eskimo huts and in the neighbourhood. The remains of numerous ancient settlements are scattered along the shore between Jensen Point and the village of Etah; the sites are marked by enormous quantities of bones lying around, which speaks forcibly of the animal wealth of this neighbourhood. It would be difficult to assign any definite age to these remains, but evidently Port Foulke must have been a favourite and productive station of the natives for a long course of the years. Reindeer and walrus bones were the most prominent in these kitchen-middens. Remains of seals were very abundant with bone of foxes and hares, also thousands of the sterna of little auks.

Unfortunately no fossil organisms were found. The ships were obstructed by ice. The ships passed by the Crimson Cliffs and after several days arrived at Port Foulke, the winter quarters of Dr Elishia Kent Kane. The crew spent a day at Brother John Glacier [so called after a brother of Dr Elisha Kane according to Captain Nares]. A journal belonging to Kane was found there but no remains of his party. There was no wind, the ships steamed for several days expending valuable coal stocks at times hemmed in by ice. On the morning of July 29th the ships crossed Smith Sound under sail steering direct for Cape Isabella. The snow clad coast of Ellesmere Land was very clearly defined. Cape Sabine, which is formed of red syenite, differs much in colour from the headlands north and south of it and is very conspicuous. I had at first determined to send the *Discovery* direct to Cape Sabine, there to establish a station, while the *Alert* erected a cairn at Cape Isabella; but considering it important that all the officers and men in both ships should be acquainted with the exact position of each cairn and depot of provisions, I kept the two vessels in company. However exact the description of the position of a depot may be, it is extremely difficult for a traveller during the spring to find a cairn or mark which has been established during the period of the year when the land was wholly or partially free from snow.

The choice of a spot on which to build a cairn that can be readily found by a stranger is not so easy a matter as may be supposed. In the present case it was rendered more difficult in consequence of the Eskimo, who are said to wander round the shores of Ellesmere Land. To obtain this safety for the provisions destined for our travellers it was necessary to hide them away in clefts of the rock at some distance from the cairn which contained directions for finding the depot. At 5a.m. on July 30th we observed the *Discovery* close to the land, with five or six miles of heavy pack ice cutting us off both from her and the shore. Although the land was hidden by fog the atmosphere at sea was clear. Perceiving a likely-looking channel we steamed towards it, but before reaching the entrance it closed up and prevented our advance. Observing the *Discovery* was not moving, we bore into the pack and succeeded with a little trouble in gaining the land and securing the ships in a convenient harbour formed by a group of rocky islands.

Captain Nares continued the journey to Payer Harbour (called after Lt Julius Payer from an earlier expedition). In his book, Nares describes the differences between the various ice floes and bergs, their likely origin, age, colour, thickness, those that were honeycombed, those that were rotten, their shapes and their line of flotation since they first separated from their parent glaciers.

Captain Stephenson, meanwhile, was engaged in landing a depot of provisions consisting of 240 rations for the use of any sledge party in need in an emergency. A cairn was built on the summit of Brevoort Island, on which a record paper was subsequently placed. It would be fair to say the crews must have been impressed at the precautions taken by Captain Nares. Clearly there would not be a repeat of the Sir John Franklin fiasco.

Progress was proving extremely difficult amidst the ice pack. Captain Nares glimpsed a very tempting channel about two miles long leading to Cape Hawks, with only six or eight miles of ice apparently open between it and a large water space stretching out from the south shore of Grinnell Land. He was forced to make a vital decision. Nares continued:

The pack, lately opened and driven to the eastward by the westerly wind was sure, on the subsidence of the pressure, to work its way back again and in all probability would close up the water channels. The northern sun, shining brightly and casting a dazzling glimmer on the ice and water alike, rendered it difficult to distinguish the most open channels; but with such a prospect of reaching the mainland few could resist the temptation; so at the risk at being beset, I pushed on towards the north through the pack. But by the time we had reached the end of the two-mile channel the ice had closed everywhere, our retreat was cut off and we were caught in a trap. No choice was left to me but to secure each ship in a notch or bight in the heaviest floe that I could reach, and wait for a change either favourable or otherwise. No one of the floes was sufficiently large to permit the two ships being docked near each other; neither did I deem it advisable, surrounded as we were by numerous icebergs, so to imprison the ships. After seeing them secured in a fairly large pool of water, I had just entered my cabin when the officer of the watch following me stated that the ice was closing in on every side. On reaching the deck I found that the *Alert* was surrounded by the ice and drifting towards an iceberg only a quarter of a mile distant. Signalling to Captain Stephenson take care of the iceberg he was able to haul the *Discovery* a hundred yards ahead; but his ship was then similarly caught in the pack, and immovable either by manual labour or by steam power. Both ships immediately prepared for a severe nip; the rudders and screws were raised, the boats tuned inboard, the yards braced fore and aft, and all possible precautions taken. At first the *Discovery* was apparently in the more dangerous position; but shortly the ice by wheeling around brought the

HMS *Discovery* (left) and HMS *Alert* at Cape Prescott.

Alert directly in the path of the iceberg, against the side of which the intermediate surface ice was piling itself up as it forced its way past it. Had the pack consisted of ordinary ice from four to six feet in thickness, which would have crumbled up against the side of the berg, the danger would have been even more imminent, but the great thickness of the floe to which the ships were secured proved their safety; for on its advanced edge reaching the iceberg, it stood the strain without splitting and for the moment checked the main drift of the pack.

Very shortly afterwards the accumulating pressure in the rear, exerting its force alternately on either side of the floe as it hung unequally balanced across the face of the berg, broke off large pieces, some of them one hundred feet in diameter. These being heavy enough in themselves to withstand a considerable pressure, became collected in front of the iceberg, and formed as it were a point of heavy ice sufficiently strong to divide and split up the floe and to act as a buffer to fend off the ship; this it did in our case most successfully. As the ship began to heel over with the increasing pressure, and officers and men working alike had given the last haul to the screw purchases, and when there was nothing left for anyone to do but to look on as calmly as possible waiting for what might happen, the corner of the floe split off and the ship, amidst a collection of debris ice, slid past the side of the berg without damage; the *Discovery*, hidden from view on the other side of the iceberg, reading the signal all safe the ships were then secured by ice anchors to the leeside of the iceberg, where the faster drift of the surface left a small pool. The next 30 hours were spent in constant struggles with the pack, the ships being moved from the shelter of one ice-berg to another as circumstances rendered necessary; and, owing to the unsteady wind and the variable tidal currents, we were never quiet for more than one hour at a time. Had I allowed the ships to drift with the ice we should have been carried to the southward deeper into the pack; there was therefore no alternative but to get up full steam and be prepared to take instant advantage of every change that might occur in our favour. The ships were seldom separated for long, and now, as on many other occasions, they assisted each other. The *Discovery* was handled in the most masterly and daring manner combined with great judgement, qualities essential in Arctic navigation. She as well as the *Alert* ran not a few hairsbreadth escapes and in particular when in following us through a closing channel between an iceberg and heavy floe-piece, before getting quite past the danger she was caught and nipped against the berg fortunately without suffering severely.

Having less beam than the *Alert*, a finer bow and an overhanging stem, the *Discovery* proved to be best adapted for forcing her way through the pack.

We found that floes up to four feet in thickness and in a soft state, melting not freezing, might be charged with impunity; thicker or harder ice had to be left alone. It speaks well for our chronometers, and the manner in which they were secured, that their rates were little affected by the frequent concussions on this and many after occasions. It must be obvious that the commander of an Arctic expedition can obtain but little rest during the navigable season. In ice-navigation one false decision may imperil the chance of further advance, he therefore can depute his responsibility to no one, but must be constantly on watch himself. Fortunately for his health an Arctic season only lasts from three to six weeks. Today Commander Markham harpooned a walrus which was towed back to the ship and hoisted on an ice-floe. Its dimensions were, length twelve feet six inches, girth eleven feet six inches, tusks eighteen and a half inches in length.

The flesh and blubber when cut up filled five casks of 250 pounds weight each. The meat when fried was much appreciated by all of us, and the liver was pronounced to be excellent. The dogs made a hearty meal off all the scraps. The ice remaining stationary, all hands turned out in the evening on the smooth ice-floe for a game of football, the dogs poor things, also being landed for a run. Some of them being harnessed gave the novices an opportunity of practising the art of sledge-driving. With each dog pulling in a different direction the starting was a ludicrous sight, and was seldom effected without the aid of a friend enticing the dogs on with a piece of meat. After struggling on for about half a mile they invariably obtained their own way, dragging their would-be guiders through many water-pools in spite of the frequent application of the long hide whip which, in inexperienced hands, was more frequently felt by the riders than the dogs.

The ships were making heavy weather of their journey through the ice and fog. In the event of the ships becoming separated, Nares ordered Captain Stephenson to rendezvous in Dobbin Bay. About this time the dogs aboard the *Discovery* showed the first signs of disease, owing probably to close confinement, wet decks, and want of natural exercise. Fits were frequent, and a few deaths occurred after symptoms of madness. Dr Colan and Dr Ninnis took great trouble to discover the nature of the disease and to arrest it. It was evident that this alarming and very often fatal malady could not be true rabies or hydrophobia, for in several instances the affected dogs recovered.

Nares continued:

Although the weather was calm during 17th August the pack had a general tendency to drift towards the south-west at the rate of about five miles a day. In consequence of the floe to which we were attached being held stationary the moving pack outside ground its way past, tearing off the exposed corners in a very alarming manner. As the exposed parts of the border of our floe were broken up one after another the line of nip was steadily but surely nearing us; but as the same kind of terrific combat was going on a quarter of a mile to the southward, on the other side of the ships, it was unwise to move sooner than we were compelled to. As the position of the nip advanced so the two ships gradually retreated before it, losing much to the regret of all, a portion of our hard-won advance towards the north. By the evening of the 18th we had been forced back into a small pool of water close to the two grounded ice bergs, against which our floe was resting with the outside pack nipping against the whole length of its outer edge in anything but a reassuring manner. The water pool in which the two ships floated was steadily contracted in size until at last it became so small that had a nip occurred both must have been destroyed at the same moment. Although the greatest danger was imminent, entrapped as we were, our anxiety was lessened by the knowledge that as human beings we were powerless and must leave the result to providence. This was the first time the ice-quartermasters – experienced men in the ice-navigation of Baffin Bay – realised the vast thickness and power of the Polar ice as compared with that with which they had hitherto been acquainted. The closing together of two polar floes upwards of 50 feet in thickness may be appropriately compared to the closing of the two sides of a dry dock on the doomed vessel. Over the next 48 hours of relentless probing, nudging and ramming to find a weakness, man-hauling the ships, finally with the assistance of our gunners and a hefty supply of gunpowder, we eventually broke free amid the resounding cheers of the officers and crews to a great expanse of open water from where we could see Cape Constitution, a view similar to that seen by Mr Morton of Kane's Expedition in the same locality. Morton's description of Cape Constitution with the relative positions of Franklin and Crozier Islands rendered it easy to recognise the spot where his remarkable journey from Rensselaer Harbour terminated in 1854.

In the evening when the two ships were abreast of Cape Constitution, the wind lulling, we took in the fore and aft sails, passing to the westward of Franklin Island.

At 4a.m. on August 24th, the officer of the watch reported that the southerly wind in the channel was dying away, and hoping that a lead might open at Cape Lieber, I with Thomas Rawlings landed and ascended Cape Morton. After a very severe climb to the summit, a height of 2,000 feet, we were amply repaid for our labour and loss of breakfast by the grandeur of the view. It was a beautiful morning with scarcely a cloud in the sky, I was able to work without gloves though the temperature was down to minus 20. The warmth engendered by our rapid ascent passed off, and our damp underclothing proved anything but agreeable. The panorama was certainly superb. Sixty miles distant in the SW, were the Victoria and Albert Mountains. Nearly due north a slight break in the continuity of the land showed where Robeson Channel opened into the Polar Sea. On the eastern side of the strait at a distance of 40 miles, Cape Lupton, a notable landmark, terminated Polaris Promontory; then came Polaris Bay. At my feet lay Cape Tyson and Cape Cleverly, on the northern shore of Petermann Fiord, rising to an elevation of 1,500 feet. The southerly wind had left fairly open ice in the Kennedy Channel between our position and Cape Lieber, with a large space of open water in Lady Franklin Sound. Robeson Channel, Polaris Bay and the entrance to Petermann Fiord were closely packed.

Offley Island, at the Northwest of Petermann Fiord, being within reasonable proximity of the localities where the *Polaris* Expedition procured their supplies of musk-oxen, had been looked upon by me as likely to afford good winter quarters for the *Discovery*, although the disadvantage of its being on the eastern side of the channel was very great; but now the condition of the ice preventing any approach to Offley Island left me no option but to take both ships to the western shore.

We ran quickly across the channel under sail where the edge of the pack led us round towards the north shore of Lady Franklin Sound. On a nearer approach we discovered a large and well protected bay, inside of an island the outer point of which formed Cape Bylot.

Nares described the ships' arrival:

There the ships were secured close to the shore at 2a.m. of the morning of August

25th. Lady Franklin Sound, with its grand precipitous cliffs, which we hoped would prove to be a channel leading to a western sea, appeared to our regret, to be considerably narrower than it was depicted on the chart. I named the anchorage Discovery Bay. I at once saw the value of the natural harbour we had attained as a wintering place for the *Discovery*, but in consequence of the quantity of newly fallen snow lying on the ground, the neighbourhood presented so desolate an appearance that we could not but feel compassion for her crew to spend a year, if not longer, in such a place.

Preparations were made at once for our parting company. Lt Wyatt Rawson and a sledge crew including Neil Petersen [Jim Hand was one of those chosen], joined the *Alert* to strengthen her crew and as far as possible to share the honours of a struggle towards the Pole. If the vessels did not separate too far, some were to return to their own ship with details of *Alert*'s winter anchorage. It was impossible for two ship's companies to have worked together for a common end more harmoniously than those of the *Alert* and *Discovery*, and one and all regretted that duty rendered our separation necessary. A few species of wading birds still lingered, but as a rule they were in flocks and evidently on their way south. Snow buntings were flocking and they chirped in a sad disconsolate manner about the frozen streams, residents in temperate climes, who enjoy throughout the year the presence of many birds with their joyous notes can scarcely realise the feelings of the sojourner in the Arctic wilds when the first notes of the snow-bunting,

The *Discovery*, August 1875, anchored at Lady Franklin Sound at the beginning of the winter freeze.

harbinger of summer and returning warmth, awaken in him vivid recollections of the far-off south. With such a one, the snow-bunting must ever remain an especial favourite, and the preparations of this sweet songster for a departure to more genial regions are a reminder of approaching darkness and the monotony of a long Arctic winter.

The ships had reached the Polar Cap of the World and the crews were about to begin their sojourn – a return to living in the Ice Age. They had the entire Arctic to themselves, bereft of humanity, a desolate, hostile vastness of ice. On 31 August Jim Hand celebrated his twenty-eighth birthday on the *Alert*.

Nares continued his narrative:

Arctic navigation is so greatly dependent on the wind that there was still sufficient of the season left to give us a reasonable certainty of reaching the northern land which on the report of the *Polaris* Expedition had been placed in latitude 84°N. [*Polaris* had drifted back to 82°11'N.] On the morning of August 26th having left my orders with Captain Stephenson concerning our future movements, the two ships separated; those in the *Alert*, if the public charts and statements of our predecessors proved correct, having the cheering feelings of, in all human probability, successfully completing the chief duty assigned us; those on-board the *Discovery* although rejoicing at the prospects of their comrades, having also the depressing sensation of being left behind to play what they could not but consider at the time a secondary part in the general programme.

Captain Nares sailed for Cape Sheridan:

Our crossing from Bessels Bay to the western shore had given an opportunity for a joke about musk-ox grounds having been left behind; but it was destined to be short-lived, for on entering the harbour, Dr Moss, always on the look out for game, espied a herd of musk-oxen near the shore. They were first mistaken by some for black boulders, but soon our doubts were removed by the animals moving. Amidst great excitement, half a dozen hunters were landed and succeeded in shooting the entire herd, numbering nine. Our intense gratification at this result was enhanced by the news our sportsmen brought back that the countryside was fairly vegetated, and that numerous tracks of hares, foxes and ptarmigan had been seen. In the evening I ascended a hill on the north side of Discovery Harbour, a height of 1,200 feet by aneroid. It was the worst ground for walking over that I ever met with; the level plots were cut up by the frost into large clods, like a deeply ploughed field with cross ridges; the whole was covered with a smooth carpet of snow, which while hiding the irregularities from sight

The *Discovery* on shore in Discovery Bay. (*Illustrated London News*, 11 November 1876.)

HMS *Alert*, frozen in at her winter quarters. (*Illustrated London News*, 4 November 1876.)

Embedded in ice: HMS *Alert* pictured in 1876, when James Hand was on board.

was not solid enough to bear one's weight. The footing was so extremely uncertain that several times I fell headlong.

At this period of our voyage we supposed Robeson Channel to be a narrow strait connecting Hall Basin with a similar sea to the northward, and the difficulties experienced by the *Polaris* when navigating this channel demonstrated that we could not hope to advance through it except when a westerly wind blew the ice off the western shore. On the termination of the westerly wind, or a shift to any other quarter, the ice would naturally close in again, with the prevailing southerly running current. This afterwards proved to be the general movement of the pack, except in the narrowest part of the strait between Cape Beechey and Polaris Promontory. There, with a slight northerly pressure during calms, the large floes jammed against each other and blocked the passage. The ice to the south of the block being carried onwards, water pools were formed under the same sea which gave birth to the heavy ice met with off the coast of America by Collinson and McClure, and which sealed up the *Investigator* for ever in the Bay of Mercy, after her memorable and perilous passage along the north west coast of Banks Land. It was the same description of ice that Parry encountered when attempting to pass to the westward of Melville Island in 1820, and which conquered him and his experienced companions; that passing down McClintock Channel, beset and never afterwards released the *Erebus* and *Terror* under Franklin and Crozier; and which streaming along the eastern shore of Greenland destroyed the *Hansa* of the last German Arctic expedition. As our only hope of north against the general set of the current through such ice (to say nothing of the extreme hazard of remaining in the pack) consisted in regaining the shore, both boilers were lighted and full steam kept ready in order to take immediate advantage of any opportunity that might arise. At 10.30p.m. the pack which previously had been drifting in a compact body to the southward, eased a little near the edge of the large and deep-floating floes, in consequence probably of a difference in speed between the surface and undercurrent, but before we were able to clear away a space of water at the stern sufficiently large to enable the rudder to be shipped, the ice closed and obliged us to dismantle again. A second time at 11.30p.m. just at the top of high-water, the pack showed signs of opening, but after moving the ship half her length ahead, we were again obliged to unship the rudder. Fully expecting a change with the flood-tide on the morning of the 31st, with much labour a working space was cleared under the stern, but owing to the rudder being badly balanced we nearly lost our opportunity. At 9.30a.m. during a momentary slackening of the ice, with steam up to its greatest pressure, we commenced to move. By going ahead and astern alternately, the ship formed an ever increasing water space and at last pushed her way to where the ice was more open, and shortly afterwards entered a narrow water-channel which led to Lincoln Bay. Few occurrences are more trying to the temper of the commander of an Arctic ship than an accident which prevents him taking immediate advantage of a momentary change in the ice, on which the success or failure of an expedition may depend. Had the shipping of the rudder delayed us another five minutes, the ship would in all probability have remained in the pack during a heavy gale which shortly after set in from the south, and continued for two days.

When in the pack, I regretted that the ship was not near a floe to which we might have escaped in case of being nipped; for although a large one was within a quarter of a mile of us, such was the rugged state of the broken-up intermediate ice, that had the ship been destroyed, it would have been quite impossible to have transported any provisions or stores to it, even had we succeeded in reaching it ourselves. After our late escape we all could appreciate Captain Budington's recommendation, when the *Polaris* was placed in precisely similar circumstances, to get out of the Polar pack as quickly as possible. It is either affectation or want of knowledge that can lead anyone seriously to recommend an attempt being made to navigate through such ice. I can answer for all on-board the *Alert* having been most thankful again to reach the land. During the late struggle, as well as on many previous occasions, it was noticeable how futile the efforts of the crew were to clear away the ice which impeded the movement of the ship on the bow or quarter, compared to the enormous power exerted by the ship herself when able to ram her way between the pieces even at ordinary speed. Thus, steamers are enabled to penetrate through a broken-up pack which the old voyagers, with their sailing vessels, necessarily deemed impassable. At the same time there is a limit to the risks which are advisable to be run; no ship has been built which could withstand a real nip between two pieces of heavy ice.

Shortly after the ship was secured in her former position to the firm ice in Lincoln Bay, the wind gradually freshened from the SW, blowing slightly off the land; accompanied with a snowstorm and a threatening appearance of the weather. So far as we could distinguish through the snow and mist, the main pack was driven by the gale to the northward up the channel; but knowing that it would take some hours to produce a navigable passage past Cape Union, I waited until the morning of September 1st, when with steam at hand ready if requisite, we passed up the straits, running before a strong gale, nine knots an hour, between the western shore and the pack, which was driving quickly to the northward, at about three miles distance from the land. By noon, having arrived in latitude 82°24'N, a more northerly position than any vessel had ever previously attained, the ensign was hoisted at the peak amid general rejoicings. With such a strong wind blowing off the shore we enjoyed the pleasing certainty of not being again stopped by ice so long as the land continued to the northward. We therefore had very sanguine hopes that we should at least attain to latitude 84°20'N, the reported position of President's Land, without another check. At 1p.m., we came suddenly and unexpectedly to a block. On hauling to the westward, at what afterwards proved to be the northern entrance to Robeson Channel and the shore of the Polar Sea, the wind headed us from the Northwestward, and then died away. The breadth of the water-channel also considerably lessened, until off Cape Sheridan the main pack was observed to be touching the grounded ice, making farther progress impossible. Running close up to the end of the water-channel, the ship was secured to a large floe which rested against the cape. The weather at this time remained very misty. During a partial clearance we observed every appearance of land due north, and reasonably supposed that we had reached Army Fiord of the *Polaris* chart, and that some local cause had prevented the ice being driven off shore by the gale; our stay was therefore thought to be only temporary.

At 2 pm., finding that the ebb-tide was setting towards the Northwest, along the land, and that in spite of it the pack was slowly nearing the shore, I moved the ship to a more protected position inside of some pieces of ice lying aground close to the beach. Since entering Smith Sound I had remarked the almost total absence of a continuous line of shore, hummocks similar to what is usually met with in the western channels of Lancaster Sound. Such a ridge, by protecting the water space from disturbance that lies between them and the shore, admits of the formation of perfectly smooth ice. The advantage in sledge travelling of finding smooth ice extending between the shore and a line of outside hummocks is incalculable. I therefore foresaw that when our sledging parties had to journey along these unprotected shores, the daily distances travelled would necessarily fall short of those accomplished during the Franklin Search expeditions. In Robeson Channel, except in a few places where the cliffs rise precipitously from the sea and afford no ledge or step on which the ice can lodge, the shore line is fronted at a few paces distant by a nearly continuous ragged-topped wall formed by accumulated ice pressed up by the pack on top of the original ice-foot, and rising from 15 to upwards of 35 feet high. Opposite the large ravines the water carried down by the summer floods melts a way for itself through the barrier and occasionally breaks the continuity of the wall; but immediately the pack closes against the shore with pressure, a newly formed pile of ice is quickly raised and closes up the gap. The debris brought down the valleys, being unable to escape out to sea, is deposited inside of the ice-barrier, forming a raised beach, which, where the land is steadily rising and the incline of the shore favourable, attains a considerable thickness.

To the north of Robeson Channel, where the land trends to the Northwestward the coast line loses its steep character, near Cape Sheridan the heavy Polar ice becomes stranded at a distance of one hundred to two hundred yards from the shore, forming a border of unconnected masses of ice from 20 to upwards of 60 feet in height lying aground in from eight to 12 fathoms water. We had one frightening escape when the ship narrowly avoided being struck by an iceberg which I considered to be 30,000 tons in weight. It was then I decided to travel no further than Cape Sheridan.

The *Alert* had sailed, probing through the ice, and pressed on up the western coast of the Robeson Channel, passing 30ft ice floes aided by a southerly gale which cleared the ice in front of the ship. Nares reached 82°24'. Fifteen days later on 1 September he achieved 82°27' where, just before the freeze began, he anchored in a bay safe enough for wintering at Cape Sheridan. Within hours the vast blocks of ice through which he had steered, some weighing 30,000 tons or more, coalesced into a solid pack that enclosed the bay completely.

The *Alert* was not an ice-breaker; its engines could carry it through loose floes, but any prolonged stretch of ice – even a few feet thick – brought it to a halt. In front of it there now rose a barrier 50ft high through which they had no hope of breaking until the next thaw. Still, it was a good anchorage in which to spend the winter, shallow enough to keep bergs at a distance while at the same time protected by the barrier seaward. Nares made several unsuccessful attempts to sail as far north as possible before the onset of the Arctic winter. He described the anchorage thus:

> On the 1st September we anchored at Cape Sheridan roughly 70 miles or seven days sailing from the *Discovery* at Lady Franklin Sound. I named the anchorage Floeberg Beach. Off an open coast, with no more protection than that afforded by such pieces of ice, the *Alert* was fated to pass the winter. Most providentially during the 11 months she was thus exposed the *Alert* never once experienced a gale blowing towards the shore.

Chapter XIII

The Anchorage at Cape Sheridan

Preparations were put in place for the various operations and functions required to ensure the safety and well-being of the ship and crew until the spring of 1876, when the attack on the Pole was scheduled. Although separated by seventy miles, the climatic conditions were similar for the two ships, and both were in great danger of being crushed to pieces by the ice.

Captain Nares sent teams inland to seek a source of fresh water, a lake or a river, and find suitable locations to safeguard their supplies. Preparations were made for laying down of supply depots for teams assigned to explore the areas surrounding the anchorage.

At 2p.m. on 16 September 1875 the pack ice reached Cape Sheridan and effectively closed in the *Alert*.

Among the priorities was the construction of the sledges. They were mainly constructed of Canadian elm, with crossbars of ash. The upper and lower pieces were called the bearer and the runner. The uprights had tenon joints, shoeing an eighth of an inch thick, iron three inches wide and slightly convex on its under surface. The length of a sledge depended on how many men were to work it; a 13ft sledge required ten men, a 9ft required six (in addition to the officer who would scout ahead). Each sledge weighed 125lb and carried a waterproof tray or boat for ferrying the sledge across water. This weighed 115lb.

The crew prepared and fitted out their winter clothing. The light sails were unbent, the running rigging unroved, and the heavy sails were left bent to the yards. Captain Nares organised sledge exploration parties to experience Arctic travel. During the worst of the weather the surviving ravenous dogs suffered from cramp and fits brought on by the atrocious conditions, the rapidly falling temperature and their diet of small blocks of frozen pemmican.

On shore the really hard work commenced. A special snow-house was built with particular care some distance from the ship to store the gunpowder, guns, ammunition, lifeboats, and coal. Located so far north, beyond human habitation, Captain Nares was confident the food supplies were safe from marauding Eskimo. Transportation of the stores was both a difficult and dangerous operation. The impending and inevitable loss of daylight hours added an air of great urgency to the task. The dogs proved themselves useful on short journeys, ferrying the supplies from ship to storage. Much of the ship's rigging was dismantled and carried ashore. If loaded with ice, the weight could break or tip over the ship. Fire holes were cut in the ice (and kept clear all winter) to ensure the availability of water in the event of fire. To add to insulation a wall of snow was built around the hull. They were a group of tired and relieved men when the operation was completed. However Nares was happy in the knowledge that if the worst was to happen to his ship, difficult, dangerous and uncomfortable as their predicament might be, they had at least preserved the means of survival until the arrival of Captain Sir Allen Young and his supply ship the *Pandora* in the summer of 1876.

The removal of the stores from the congested main and lower decks provided the crews with increased living space and enabled them to make their living quarters a little more comfortable for what would be at least up to six months of a cold, dark and relentlessly dull Arctic winter before the spring (with the distinct possibility of an additional eighteen months' tour of duty on top of that). For the following four months until the sun reappeared the crew would have to endure freezing conditions on-board the ship and eat every single meal or snack in the gloom of oil lamp or candle light, a most depressing prospect. There was one advantage; the ship was higher in the water which reduced the risk of being crushed by the ice.

None of the crew had ever seen such darkness at noon time, and certainly never experienced an outside temperature of −99°F and −82°F. There was also the uncertainty of not knowing if the *Discovery* with all their friends on-board was safe and well. The crew, in their quieter moments, must have often discussed their predicament. Civilisation was thousands of miles away. It was hundreds of miles to the nearest Eskimo settlement in Greenland. To the north, closer now to them than the distance between Edinburgh and London, lay the North Pole. They marvelled at the eerie beauty of the snow, and were awed by the cold and by the extent of the sunless winter. Jim Hand witnessed events that he had never before experienced, a beard that stuck to a tongue when licked, the butter that could only be carved with an axe and the debilitating effects of the lack of sunlight. One dog's tail froze to the ground, another's tongue stuck to the inside of a meat can.

In freezing fog, icicles formed on the men's headgear, eyebrows, nostrils, and beards. When a group of men moved in unison the ice formed in clumps on their outer garments. When they bumped into each other in the dark they rattled like chandeliers. And at times it was terrifying, the ominous creaking sounds of young ice against the ship's bows, the constant fear of the *Alert* being crushed, the awesome size of the surrounding ice floes – some a mile wide and weighing more than a million tons rearing, splintering and meshing as they piled on top of each other. Then came the wondrous spectacle when the midnight sun came out, kindling various coloured fires on every part of the surface and making the ice around them one great mosaic of gem work, a filigree of rubies, diamonds, silver and molten gold.

During the winter the crews amused themselves with the carefully pre-prepared programmes of Captain Nares. British captains had always emphasised the importance of keeping the men occupied during the sunless months. Kane's, Hayes's and Hall's Journals had all described the monotony of an Arctic winter – monotony which had possibly contributed to their undoing – and Captain Nares was not going to let his men drift the same way. A programme of entertainments was arranged for each ship. They had board games such as roulette, chess, draughts, etc., musical instruments, drums, tin whistles, fireworks, puppets, books, costumes for plays, masquerades and card playing.

Dances were organised, at which some of the crew men dressed in drag. Lt Aldrich played the piano and sea shanties were belted out, much to everyone's enjoyment. Boxing matches were staged and evening classes were arranged. Lt Aldrich also organised the publication of a newspaper with regular editions. Anchored on a small ship, out of communication with the outside world for months, one might ask the question, what news did Pelham Aldrich write about?

Every week there was Thursday Pops, semi-educational entertainments which comprised of songs, readings and tableaux. Captain Nares re-instituted The Royal Arctic Theatre, which had last seen service on the Franklin rescue expeditions more than twenty years previously. From time to time during the winter, plays were produced by the officers and men. These were interspersed with variety nights when all joined in, performing their party pieces, songs and recitations.

A walk a mile in length was constructed by shovelling away the snow and this was used as an exercise ground. It was christened 'The Lady's Mile' and was lined with guide ropes and tin cans as a safety precaution against wandering away in the darkness.

Captain Nares had orders to set up supply depots of provisions as far north as possible, thus reducing the loads to be carried by the returning sledge parties in the following spring. On 26 September travelling parties were ready to start, led

HMS *Alert c.* 1875-1876.

by Commander Markham and Lieutenants Parr and May. Sledges were drawn by twenty-five men and provisioned for twenty days. At 9p.m., after prayers on the ice floe, they set off in the best of spirits. Each sledge weighted to 200lb per man.

On 29 September at Floeberg Beach and at Discovery Bay, a long spell of misty weather set in with frequent falls of snow which lasted until 10 October. Captain Nares continued to relate his experiences:

Arctic scenery is naturally expected to be somewhat desolate in appearance, but few are prepared for the utter dreariness which a long continuance of misty weather and a snow-charged atmosphere produces. No shadows or sky-line visible, no measure or height or distance can be formed. The land and ice-covered sea, masked alike with snow, are indistinguishable. Being anxious to communicate with Captain Stephenson if possible before winter set in, I despatched Lt Rawson, Neil Petersen as guide, Egerton and several men on 2nd October. Egerton, who had accompanied Rawson for two miles, reported on his return that the new ice was still so thin the sledge was obliged to take

Preparing to start on a sledge journey. (*Illustrated London News*, 29 May 1875.)

to the land. I therefore could scarcely expect Rawson would make a success-ful journey. In the evening Lt Aldrich who had been exploring the area since 22nd September reported the dogs sinking frequently in the soft snow up to their muzzles. They proved to be almost useless, but for the help of the men the sledge would have had to be abandoned. The dogs suffered much from fits, one had been shot and two others had wandered from the party when temporarily mad.

On 27th September. Aldrich succeeded in reaching 82°48'N, a somewhat higher latitude than had ever before been attained, our gallant predecessors Sir Edward Parry, Sir James Ross, Admiral Edward Byrd, and the coxswain James Parker in their celebrated boat-journey towards the North Pole from Spitzbergen in 1827 having advanced a little beyond latitude 82°45'N.

On 7th October heavy snowfall and drifting to such an extent as to hide everything from view that was more than a ship's length distant. On-board the snow had collected in drifts as high as our hips. On 12th October Rawson returned and as I fully expected had been unable to reach the *Discovery*. Rawson and his men on some days could only cover a single mile in a day so soft and deep was the snow. On the 14th October Commander Markham and his three sledge crews struggled home. I did not expect Markham on-board until the following day; but so great was the discomfort of passing another sleepless night in the stiff and shrunken tents, the hard frozen blanket-bags and clothing, that he made a forced march to get on-board. Although all were able to walk several men were severely frost-bitten. The journey had been most severe; but Markham had succeeded in establishing his depot of provisions at Cape Joseph Henry.

Out of the party of 21 men and three officers no less than seven men and one officer returned to the ship badly frostbitten, three of these so severely as to render amputation of fingers and toes necessary, the patients being confined to their beds for the greater part of the winter. By this time a heavy mortality had occurred among our dogs. We have lost 15 out of 30. All the men had returned safely.

After consulting with Dr Colan regarding the scale of diet which our stock of provisions would permit us to issue during the winter, the allowance of preserved meat was increased. As the travellers in the spring could not carry bottled fruits while absent from the ship, the winter ration of that item was increased, an arrangement much appreciated by everyone.

Captain Nares, with all hands back on-board, began his recreational winter programme:

There were three or four crew members unable to read or write. I arranged lessons, instruction to be given by Dr Colan. On Sunday Church is over by 10.30a.m., all hands are then started for a walk. School was commenced this evening. On October 17th the crew saw the last of the sun, it would not reappear until March. Sledge travelling in autumn is accompanied by great hardship and discomfort, the temperature falls and each day adds a modicum of dampness to the tent, blanket-bags, and clothing, until at last they contain so much moisture and become so frozen and contracted in size as to be almost unserviceable. The sodden blanket-robes frozen as hard as boards can scarcely be unrolled, and the stockings and foot wrappers put on damp in the morning, are by night frozen so hard into the canvas boots as to refuse to separate unless cut apart or melted inside the blanket-bag by the heat of the body. As the season advanced and the temperature decreased the usual troubles of Arctic ships were experienced, cold draughts, dampness, condensation and a chronic lack of ventilation, this is a deeply troubling combination, and makes living conditions most trying. The temperature of the lower deck ranged between 35°F and 55°F, that of the outer air being 21° and −32°F, a mean difference of about 55°.

November 1st. Much to the crew's delight a glass of beer was now issued in the evenings twice a week, on the other five evenings a second allowance of rum will be issued during the winter.

November 5th. Shut in as we are there is great difficulty in finding suitable prizes for winners in our games of chance; one does not wish to stop cards, roulette, and other games among the crew; in fact I encourage these pastimes; but whereas the officers can establish a scorebook at one penny a point, the men I fear, cannot so readily institute a recognised stake. How great a need there is for some article of currency is shown by games being played in the wardroom jokingly for matches, candles have been thought of; but they are of too much importance for their loss to be risked.

Captain Nares did not refer to it, but the candles were rationed out at an inch a day per man.

A course of lectures, with popular readings and songs in character, to last about two hours on each Thursday evening, was commenced. I opened the course by a lecture on astronomy. At the end it was scarcely necessary to remind such a steady thoughtful body of men, that astronomical subjects lead us to consider how God employs the numberless objects around us to contribute to our wants, and how after creating the sun, moon, earth, and stars − God saw that it was good.

The frostbitten patients are all doing well, but continuous darkness or rather lamp-light is evidently not the best restorative for invalids.

November 18th. The snow on the land is at last sufficiently hard to allow us to extend our walks on shore to wherever we please; but the cold and darkness combine to keep us from straggling far. Dr Colan's Lady's Mile walk, half a mile in length with rows of empty preserved meat tins placed 30 feet apart, forms an excellent exercising ground.

Mercury frozen for the first time, temperature down to minus 45°F. An attempt was made to train the carrier pigeons which were brought on the expedition. They are of little or no use during fogs, strong winds or heavy rains. Pigeons are therefore practically useless for explorers advancing over a new country.

A moving prologue was written and recited by our chaplain, the Revd H.W. Pullen and was spoken at the re-opening of the Royal Arctic Theatre. The acting was excellent and everything went off well. Aldrich's frequent and pleasant performances on the piano were most enjoyable. He plays dance music much to the delight of the numerous dancers.

The total consumption of coal is almost a ton a week; with this consumption, the average temperature of the lower deck is $49°$. On November 22nd the sun attained its most southern position. Yesterday, at noon it was as dark as any previous English expedition had experienced, we have yet 87 days of intense darkness to pass through.

A crew member wrote:

Today the moon reappeared above the southern horizon. She is truly the presiding goddess of the long Arctic night. During some period of her stay, a full moon occurs and she displays her greatest beauty. Thanks to her we can never realise what existence would be like if totally deprived of light.

The men were captivated by the climatic changes. During blizzards visibility was down to a few hundred yards, yet above them, the moon and stars were clear and bright. In early December there was a decided change in the complexion of a number of crew members in consequence of the want of sunlight; in a few instances noticeably so. The dogs lived on the ice floe, even though the changes in the temperature were rapid and quite remarkable, sometimes varying $60°$ in a few hours. At Christmas especially, James Hand would have thought of home and loved ones.

The Christmas morning service took place on deck. A muffled Chaplain preached to his bearded congregation amidst the yellow glow of an oil lantern, while ice hung in feathers from the canopy above the deck. Jim Hand had entered a world of freezing isolation. On his Atlantic voyages in the past he would have experienced loneliness, but this was different. It was his first Christmas in the Arctic and he was experiencing for himself all he had read and heard about, wondrous scenes seen for the first time from a latitude not previously reached. Captain Nares continued:

December 25th. Apart from the absence of the sun it was a splendid Christmas Day, with a perfectly clear starlit sky, the faintest twilight glimmer at noon, and just sufficient movement of the air to render our walk on the ice the more bracing, with a temperature of minus $34°$. Christmas Day was a time of great celebration. The morning begun with a small group, the sergeant, mate, and three others wandered round the ship singing carols to suit to the occasion, in the forenoon there were prayers. Shortly before our departure from England, a box arrived from Queenstown [Cobh], containing presents for everyone in the expedition, from Mrs Coote and her friends and other members of Sir Edward Parry's family. Unfortunately, one parcel had been stowed in a damp place, I was obliged to distribute its contents a few weeks ago; the rest of the presents were given out to-day, and expressing as they did the kindly forethought and interest of the donors. I need scarcely say how greatly they were appreciated. The lower deck was appropriately decorated, the dinner tables being laden with as good and ample a meal as they could wish. The Captain and officers visited the mess in the lower deck, tasted the pudding, inspected the decorations and so on. Then the boxes of presents given by friends in England were brought out and presented by the Captain to each crew member. Ringing cheers were given for the donors of the presents and for absent friends, loved ones at home, wives, mothers and sweethearts. Not forgotten were Captain Stephenson and the crew of *Discovery* who they hoped were safe and well but had no way of knowing if they were alive or dead.

The crew had a sumptuous meal for once. On that day they ate dinner at noon and the officers dined together at 5p.m. Each ship had brought along fish, beef, and mutton. They also brought some live sheep from England which were killed from time to time. Six sheep were still alive when they anchored at Discovery Harbour but on being landed they were worried by the dogs and had to be slaughtered. The food had been preserved by hanging it from the masts where it became frozen solid in the outdoor natural freezer and was perfectly fit to eat.

The remainder of December was uneventful except for the most uncomfortable combination of condensation and lack of ventilation (each and every crack in the ship's woodwork was sealed). The incessant dripping condensation was the biggest problem, soaking the crew's hammocks and bedding and then freezing on everything it had landed upon.

The crew was facing into a very long and boring January and February. Apart from their normal duties maintaining the ship, periodically starting up the engines and checking vital equipment, they had to endure twenty-four hours of nightfall. Dense fog and blizzards confined them to the ship. The men played cards, and games and amused themselves as best they could in the unforgiving conditions. They read with great difficulty by candlelight and generally coped to the best of their ability in their icebox home named the *Alert*. Captain Nares went on:

The recovery of the frostbitten is slow. Although we are only 453 miles from the Pole it is still no misnomer to call this the shortest day, for at noon there was an indistinct greenish tint brightening the southern sky. The twilight was sufficiently strong to put out the stars forming the Milky Way within 30° of the north and south horizon. To escape completely beyond the limit of twilight we must yet journey northward 120 miles before the sun sinks 18° below the horizon, the measure by which the garrison twilight-gun is fired throughout the world. The decided change in the complexion of each of us in consequence of the want of sunlight continues. It is difficult to keep the heels of the cloth boots from slipping; consequently the heels of the socks and boot-hose wear out very quickly. The officers walking briskly can wear blanket-wrappers and moccasins without feeling cold in the feet, but the crew while at work, and having to stand about a great deal, are necessarily unable to wear the thin-soled moccasins, and are obliged to keep to the warm but clumsy cork-soled cloth boots. As usual in Arctic ships all of us expected that during the winter there would be ample time for reading and writing; now, the general complaint is how little can be done in that way.

The men breakfast at 7.30a.m., then clear up the lower deck. After an hour's work on the ice we muster at divisions and read daily prayers at a quarter past 10a.m. The officers breakfast at 8.30, after which there is too little time to settle down to any particular occupation before the general muster on deck at 10a.m. After prayers, all hands leave the ship, the men for work, and the officers for exercise. The crew dines at 1p.m., then out on the ice again until 4p.m., when their official work is over for the day. The officers generally remain on the ice until about 1p.m.; between which time and dinner at 2.30p.m. the time slips away in a surprising manner. After dinner and a smoke the ship is very quiet, so probably many take a siesta; but there is plenty of noise at teatime at seven. Then comes school on the lower deck until 9p.m., after which one sits down for the first time in the day perfectly ready for study, and with a certainty of not being disturbed. We need not wonder then, if when the regular lamps are put out in the wardroom at 11p.m. most of the cabins remain lit by private candles for some time longer. An early dinner is necessary on account of the want of fuel obliging us to put out the cooking fires at 4p.m. Tea is made on one of the warming stoves. The old year is dying away calmly. There is perhaps more excuse for us than for many in looking forward anxiously to the next one, for if any can be pardoned for wishing the present time to pass quickly it is those undergoing their term of voluntary banishment in these regions. Not that the time is hanging heavily, for I can confidently say that no former collection of officers or men met their monotonous and lonely Arctic life more cheerfully and contentedly than those under my command are meeting theirs.

December 31ˢᵗ. Making due allowance for the difference in time, at 7.55p.m., it being midnight in England, we drank a Happy New Year to all absent friends, with earnest wishes for as happy and successful a coming year as the old one has proved.

In early January both ships were lashed by a succession of snowstorms, gales and squalls. One day there was a bizarre change in the weather pattern; although anchored further north than *Discovery* there was a −36° difference recorded on the *Alert* compared to the *Discovery*.

January 16ᵗʰ. The ship is now heeling over from two to three degrees to port, as the tide rises and falls, she is pressed over by the tidal motion exerted on the ice-hinge lying between us and the floe berg on the starboard side and by the weight of the snow bearing down the ice on the port or inshore side. The smokers complain greatly about their tobacco pipes freezing. Unless the stem is very short it soon becomes clogged with frozen tobacco juice which defies all attempts to remove it by wires.

January 24ᵗʰ. Mercury frozen all day, temperature down to minus 58°. A comforter covering the lower face freezes to the beard. One officer was frostbitten in this way for some time, without his companion telling him. He is now suffering the consequences. Afterwards we found *Discovery* experienced temperatures of between minus 56° and minus 63°.

February 1ˢᵗ. Our nearest unfriendly floe berg has rolled over towards the ship, proving that the inshore ice is still contracting with the colder weather, in consequence of the movement of our neighbour, the snow embankment has fallen away from the starboard side of the ship and will require a considerable amount of labour to repair it.

February 3ʳᵈ. The Thursday Pops are as much appreciated as ever. The 'ladies' have now become perfectly at home in their dresses. Dr Colan this evening gave us an interesting lecture on the composition of the food supplied to us. He was very happy in making such a dry subject amusing as well as instructive. The last of the patients who were frostbitten and those who had fingers and toes amputated in the autumn got on deck today, after spending nearly four months on the lower deck and the greater part of the time in bed.

February 8ᵗʰ. During a break in the weather which I must say is improving, I walked towards Cape Rawson with the chaplain Mr Pullen. We obtained a very fine view of the pack for a distance of six miles from the land. It will be as difficult to drag a sledge over such ice as to transport a carriage directly across England. When looking down on this icy sea, my companion remarked how impossible it was to realise that water would ever exist there again. The temperature is still minus 50°. The daylight is improving, enabling us to extend our walks. Returning to the ship it feels like approaching one's home, and however tired, once on that well beaten track we forget that we are weary. Everyone, without exception is complaining of shortness of breath. I certainly do not remember experiencing the same at Melville Island. We suppose it is due to the excessively cold temperature. In more than one instance severe running has been followed by blood-spitting from otherwise healthy men.

One has to wonder, could these symptoms have been the first signs of scurvy?

Chapter XIV

Spring, 1876

Each team of men was equipped with a tent, 8ft high, 15ft long and erected with four poles, seven sleeping bags, a groundsheet, a single buffalo-skin robe, a spirit cooker, a kettle and stand, to which was added food and fuel. The provisions and fuel for seven men for forty days weighed 876lb, which when combined with the constant 440lb, gave a total starting out weight of 1,316lb or nearly 220lb hauling weight per man. Captain Nares continued his narrative:

February 12th. Preparations are being made for the spring travelling campaign.

Today all the tents were spread out on the ice to ascertain whether further alteration was necessary. In the autumn we found that none of them reached the full measurement; they have now been altered, allowing sixteen and a half inches to each man, or rather thirty-three inches between two men sleeping head to foot as they are obliged to do when sledging. Less space may be conducive to warmth, but probably also to cramp.

Today at noon we could distinguish the outline of a man at half a mile distant and faint blue and green tints were observable in the ice-hummocks; since 1st November up to this date the ice has been perfectly white and colourless. All the frostbitten crew have at last been taken off the sick list. The temperature remains steady at minus 48° with calm weather. A few of us walked to the southward beyond the Gap of Dunloe (so named by one of the officers).

Markham's dog Nelly, the only dog that is permitted to live on the lower deck appears only to feel the severe cold in her paws, which become clogged with ice-balls between the toes; she does not complain much unless her walk is extended beyond a distance of four or five miles, when the ice, having time to accumulate, cuts into the flesh. The similar troubles of our poor Eskimo dogs are now close at hand; they will commence exercising during the coming week. During the winter several weakly dogs have died from fits or been shot, leaving one strong team of nine dogs, as many as we can possibly feed on the ship's ration. Yesterday they commenced exercising preparatory to a trip to *Discovery* in March.

February 27th. The crew have lately been employed in transporting the coal which was stacked on shore in the autumn, ready to be put on-board in the summer. Although the sun is still absent, so bright is the light at mid-day that on first descending to the lamp-lit deck it is some time before the retina has accommodated itself to the change and enables us to see our way.

Gifford and Egerton, with Simmons had a long and cold journey to-day with the dogs. They reached Cape Union, and ascertained that the despatches which Rawson left there last October have not been disturbed by any party travelling north from the *Discovery*. This proves that they, like us, were unable to journey along the shores of Robeson Channel. Rawson and Egerton saw the upper limb of the sun returning to awake nature from its long repose. Temperature remains at minus 60°.

We have experienced a considerable advantage in consequence of the ship floating in water throughout the winter. By carefully covering the engine-room hatchway, and preventing the cold air descending to the ship's holds, the temperature has been very seldom below 28°, the same as that of the water beneath the ship. In this we are far more fortunate than Lieutenant Weyprecht and his companions on-board the *Tegetthoff*. Completely cradled in ice as that ship was during two winters – between 1872 and 1874 – the temperature of the holds became so lowered that most of the provisions froze.

March 1st. In arranging my plans for the sledge travelling during the spring, I naturally took into consideration the result of our previous geographical discoveries. We had ascertained that the land to the westward of Cape Joseph Henry trended in a Northwesterly direction for a distance of not less than 80 miles from our position The coast of Greenland was in sight trending to the north-east for about 80 miles; beyond that distance its direction was doubtful. Immediately to the northward was a very heavy pack, decidedly impenetrable for a ship, and of a description which former Arctic travellers had considered impassable for sledges.

In my orders it was impressed on me that the primary object was to attain the highest northern latitude, and if possible, to reach the North Pole.

The more I considered the character of the ice in our neighbourhood, the more convinced I became that the only way to carry out my instructions was by advancing along a coastline; and that unless we discovered land trending to the north, neither the ship nor our sledges would be able to advance far in that direction. Our great object therefore was to discover land leading towards the north. I accordingly decided to explore the shores that were in sight, in order to ascertain if either coast turned in the desired direction, and at the same time to send a secondary party over the ice to the northward; to discover whether or not the pack was in motion in the offing, and if stationary, whether, in the event of our not finding land towards the north, it would be feasible to journey over it the following year with the combined strength of the crews of the two ships.

When organising the party to proceed directly to the north across the pack, little or nothing was known with certainty regarding the nature or movements of the ice, but the experience of the *Polaris* expedition led us to expect that if the pack was not already in motion it would certainly break up early in the season. Accordingly in order to ensure the return of the party in the event of the ice breaking up in its rear and endangering the retreat, it had to be supplied with boats suitable for navigation. But such a boat weighs within a few pounds as much as the total amount usually dragged by a sledge crew, and at once completely disarranges the plans usually adopted in the Arctic travelling along a coast-line. When a boat is added to the necessary equipment of the sledge the constant weights become raised to about 200lbs for each man, and therefore only allow provisions for two or three days to be added. To advance 15 or 20 days the maximum weight of 240lbs a man must be transported. It is thus evident that if the crew of each sledge is to be provided with a boat, the usual mode cannot be adopted of pushing forward one sledge to an extreme distance by provisioning it through a system of relays, and supporting parties, which return to the ship one at a time. After calculating the weights most carefully, I finally decided to follow the plan of Sir Edward Parry, namely for the travellers to advance the requisite weights each day by stages; first dragging forward the boat, then to return and transport a second sledge laden with provisions. This method is described as banking. From my former experience I well knew, as is stated in the 15th paragraph of my orders that in the absence of continuous land, sledge travelling has never yet been found practicable over any considerable extent of unenclosed frozen sea.

Nevertheless I trusted that we might advance such a distance from the land as would enable us to ascertain the nature of the pack ice in the offing, and learn whether it could ever be travelled over a reasonable distance, on a future occasion with or without boats. There was also the chance of a northern land being sighted. Knowing well how extremely irksome such a journey would prove to all concerned in it, I determined to despatch two sledge crews to mutually support each other. As the Northwestern exploration promised to be the most important I offered the command of it to Commander Markham; but he, considering that the land would probably not be found to stretch in the desired direction, elected to take command of the party whose duty it was to ascertain the nature of the pack ice to the northward. I then arranged for Lts Aldrich, and Gifford, with 14 men, to explore the coast of Grant Land, whilst Commander Markham with Lt

Parr and 15 men, supported by two additional sledges until they left the land, were to advance directly towards the north over the ice. Captain Stephenson and the officers and crew of the *Discovery* were to explore the northern coast of Greenland, endeavour to ascertain whether Petermann Fiord was a channel leading to an eastern sea, and to examine Lady Franklin Sound, which was reported to be a channel.

The *Discovery* being upwards of two hundred miles north of the arranged rendezvous at Cape Isabella, I considered sending a party there but decided it would be so much strength thrown away; for in the event of a ship from England visiting Cape Isabella during the summer of 1876, and finding that we had not communicated with the post at the southern entrance of Smith Sound, it would be at once understood that our two ships had advanced far to the northward and were well placed for exploration. Sir Allen Young on visiting Cape Isabella in August at once drew this inference. In order to communicate my intentions to Captain Stephenson, Sub-Lieutenant Egerton was prepared to proceed with the dog sledge to Discovery Bay, as soon as the sun returned. As Lt Rawson would be employed in the exploration of the coast of North Greenland, it was desirable that he should confer with Captain Stephenson, under whose directions the Greenland party would be organised; accordingly Rawson was to accompany Mr Egerton and Petersen.

Captain Nares later recorded:

As the expedition subsequently experienced a severe attack of scurvy, which has been attributed in some quarters to errors in the sledge dietaries, I may here conveniently refer to the subject, and give my reasons for adopting the scale of diet used by the travellers from the *Alert* and *Discovery*. In doing this I fear I shall leave the actual cause of the outbreak of scurvy in as undefined a state as others who have endeavoured to explain it. [At this point Captain Nares presented a detailed explanation of his actions. As the matter is dealt with at the subsequent Naval Inquiry the explanation appears later.]

The sun which had set in October, returned on March 1st 1876, after 142 days – the longest period that we know any mortal has spent without the sun according to Markham. I now continue the extracts from my journal relating to the proceedings on-board the *Alert*.

March 1st. The temperature is down to minus 64°F. It is far too cold for human beings and judging from the movements of the dogs for animals also; they refuse to go into an enclosure, they are glad enough of any shelter obtainable between them and the wind. The weather prevented any work being undertaken outside the ship except what was absolutely necessary, and the walking parties were contented with shorter exercise than usual; every possible kind of face protector being tried. The preserved meat for the use of the dogs while travelling has been taken out of the tins and broken up into pieces of about two pounds in weight; exposed to the cold this has become frozen as hard as marble, and in that state has been stored ready for use in a canvas bag. As it is impossible to thaw the food when travelling the poor creatures will have to swallow these lumps of food at a temperature 60 and 70 degrees below freezing point; it is therefore not only surprising that fits occur but rather that any dogs are left alive.

In consequence of the saving of lime-juice which will occur during the absence of the travellers in April, the ration has been doubled. The evening issue is not compulsory, but I am sure that very few will neglect to take it.

Owing to the gradual accumulation of newly formed ice on the starboard side of the ship, caused by the freezing of the water which over-runs the surface when depressed by the tide, she is now forced over to port, heeling four and a half degrees; a very decided incline. It is quite impossible to remedy matters before the thaw commences. We must be thankful that the rise and fall of the tide is not greater; otherwise we should be as badly placed as the *Polaris* was under similar circumstances at Thank God Harbour.

March 2nd. The sledge preparations occupying the whole of each evening, to-day was the last of the Thursday evening gatherings for lectures and other entertainments. These have been kept up throughout the winter with unflagging interest. The cold however had been intense. For most of February the mercury froze in the thermometers. In early March the temperature dropped to 101° below freezing, the boxing matches had to be cancelled because the combatants were unable to see each other through their breath.

March 4th. 11.30. To-day had been fixed for the departure of the dog-sledge for Discovery Bay, but the cold weather prevented the start. The mean temperature for the last two days has been minus 69.6°F; yesterday two reliable thermometers registered below minus 73°F, the mean being minus 73.75°F, or more than 105 degrees below the freezing point of fresh water. The appearance of the southern slopes of the Greenland hills which were to-day tinted a warm crimson afforded a rich treat to all of us, and the feeling of intense cold was greatly modified by feasting our eyes on the glorious shades of colour.

March 5th. When falling in for muster on the ice, although the men were permitted to keep moving until the last moment, several were frostbitten about the face. It is amusing to notice how angry anyone becomes when informed that his nose is frostbitten; being uncertain whether he is the victim of a joke or it is really the case. The frozen breath collects so quickly, and the ice is so excellent a conductor of cold that those who cover their noses and mouths with a comforter are certain to suffer. Masks for the face are not recommended, it is better to wear nothing when walking near the ship. There is a widespread popular notion concerning the treatment of frostbite by applying snow, but our snow is far too cold for such a purpose. When frostbitten the object is to restore circulation gradually, With superficial frostbite the best remedy is the gentle application of the hand to the affected part; the slightest friction would certainly remove the skin.

March 9th. Yesterday on the temperature rising to minus 45°F, the dog sledge was made ready to start, but to-day it has fallen again to minus 58°F so I have countermanded the order for its departure. A puppy born three days ago has mysteriously disappeared; it has doubtless been eaten, as usual, but in this case the mother herself is suspected of being the culprit. The men are employed daily in cutting a ditch in the ice on the starboard side of the ship, in the hope of reducing the pressure, and keeping her from heeling over any farther to port. The ice has again sunk suddenly away from the ship at the stern, or rather she has suddenly jumped up one foot, tearing her stern clear of the ice.

March 12th. A misty morning, a rising temperature risen to minus 30°, gave notice that the extremely cold weather was at an end. Accordingly Mr Egerton and Lt Rawson, accompanied by Neil Petersen and nine dogs, started for the *Discovery*, the sledge being weighed to 51lbs per dog.

It was in these appallingly low temperatures that on 12 March Captain Nares despatched the three men to travel south to contact the *Discovery* to check if all was well. The party encountered an atrocious snowstorm. They returned after four days having covered only sixteen miles in a blizzard. Nares continued:

March 16th. This evening I was astonished at the return of Mr Egerton's party, and much distressed to learn that it was occasioned by the severe illness of Petersen. He was taken ill on the second march with cramp, and afterwards, being unable to retain any food whatever, nothing could keep him warm, and he became badly frostbitten. By depriving themselves of their own warm clothing and at great personal risk the two officers, his only companions, succeeded in restoring circulation. The following day, Petersen being no better, they wisely determined to return with him to the ship. But the gale of the 14th rendering it impossible to travel and the tent being very cold − temperature minus 24°F − they burrowed out a hole in a snow bank, and with the aid of a spirit lamp raised the temperature inside to minus 7°. With noble disregard of themselves they succeeded in retaining some slight heat in the man's body by alternately lying one at a time alongside of him while the other was recovering his warmth by exercise.

On the morning of the 15th the patient being slightly better, and the weather permitting, they started to return to the ship with the sledge lightened to the utmost. During the journey of 16 miles over very rough ground, although frequently very seriously frostbitten themselves they succeeded in keeping life in the invalid until they arrived on-board. He was badly frostbitten in the face and feet.

The three men were severely frostbitten, especially Neil Petersen whose feet particularly had been badly affected. The medical team aboard the *Alert* were

The road between *Alert* and *Discovery*. (*Illustrated London News*, 11 November 1876.)

shocked at the condition of his feet.

The mechanics of frostbite are depressingly simple. In extreme cold, the blood vessels constrict to conserve heat. The lack of circulation allows ice crystals to form inside and around the watery cells of the human body. The ice expands, rupturing the cells. When blood starts circulating again, whether from warmth or exercise, it clots on the damaged cells and blocks the flow. Slight frostbite, signalled by a tell-tale whiteness accompanied by blisters, is reversible. Severe frostbite, when the white turns black, indicates gangrene. Modern antibiotics can deal with gangrene, allowing the infected parts to atrophy without infecting the rest of the body. In Neil Petersen's time however, antibiotics were unknown.

Peterson suffered, watching impatiently as his feet blistered and wept. The traditional remedy was a cold massage of snow – a trick which lets the blood come back gradually, without impeding circulation. This was the method adopted by Rawson and Egerton on Petersen and one of the reasons why they also suffered frostbite. If it does not work the toes blacken, crack and have to be amputated. If the condition worsens the heels literally fall apart, chunks of flesh dropping off to expose bone and tendon. The last resort is to amputate the foot or feet.

Fleet-Surgeons Colan and Moss worked tirelessly night and day to save Petersen's feet but to no avail. The two doctors decided to amputate, otherwise Neil would die in a matter of days. The amputation was carried out under the most difficult conditions imaginable. To everyone's immense relief the operation was a success, though Petersen's condition remained grave. Nares continued:

During severe weather Arctic travelling of any sort, at a distance from all other human help, is only just bearable for strong men when all goes well. The slightest mishap is sure to entail serious consequences, and a severe sickness, which providentially has seldom occurred amongst the hundreds of travelling parties, is almost certain to terminate fatally.

Mr Egerton whose own conduct was beyond all praise, thus speaks in his official report of Lt Rawson's behaviour on this occasion: 'It is with great diffidence that I presume to say anything regarding the very valuable assistance that I received from Lt Rawson, but I feel I should fail in my duty if I omitted to bring to your notice the great aid I derived from his advice and help; without his unremitting exertions and cheerful spirit my own efforts would have been unavailing to return with my patient alive to the ship.'

Later Nares went on to write:

When walking with Aldrich we crossed the tracks made by the dogs when exercising yesterday, and noticed the numerous frozen pellets of blood lying on the floe which always form between the toes of these animals when working during severely cold weather. On-board the *Resolute* in 1853, we endeavoured to fit our dogs with blanket pads on their feet, but these were found to increase the mischief by first becoming damp and then freezing, when the hardened blanket cut into the sinews at the back of the leg.

We commenced to-day taking down the upper deck covering, in order to let in as much light as possible. The cold will prevent the hatchways or skylights being uncovered for some time. To-day I published the programme of the spring sledging parties. It is eminently satisfactory to find how every officer and man, after a long and severe experience during the autumn of what Arctic sledging really is, has been anxiously pushing his claims for employment with the advanced parties, those bound north over the ice, a journey thoroughly well known to entail the most trying and tedious work, being the most favoured. The popular supposition that sledge travelling with dogs in the Arctic region is a comfortable, expeditious and exciting method of locomotion is very far from the truth. With a light sledge, a skilled handler, perfectly smooth ice and a team of good dogs, rapid journeys may be made over great distances where supplies of food for only a few days have to be carried on a sledge. Dog sledging as practised by naval expeditions in districts where food cannot be obtained on the road, is necessarily of a different nature.

The object frequently being to prolong the journey to the utmost extent, or, in other words, to enable the sledgers to be absent from their ship the greatest number of days, the sledge at starting is loaded to the full amount of provisions and gear that the dogs can draw with the aid of men. The driver walks or runs at the side of the sledge, guiding the animals with his whip while another of the party runs ahead, choosing the best path through the piled-up hummocks or rough ice, the rest of the crew pushing the sledge from behind, but very frequently they have to use their drag-belts. Owing to the repeated delays among rough ice where the dogs stubbornly refuse to do any work whatever, and the men facing the sledge have to drag it three or four feet at a time by standing pulls, the rate of advance is seldom over two or three miles a day. In fact, the crew of a dog sledge have even more laborious work to undergo than those who drag a man-sledge. The dogs should never be permitted to advance faster than the travellers can walk themselves with comfort and without losing breath. During Egerton's return journey with the lightly-laden sledge there was great difficulty in preventing the dogs running away when they knew that they were homeward

Sledging party, Cape Rawson, 1876.

bound. In passing the deep snow slope at Cape Rawson, the invalid Petersen being fortunately off the sledge at the time, they could not be restrained, and the sledge rolled over the side of the bank a depth of 30 feet. After the sledge was righted, and while Egerton was employed clearing the entangled harness, the dogs suddenly broke away, dragging him more than 100 yards and bruising him severely before they were stopped by his body becoming jammed in between two pieces of ice.

Egerton reported:

During the journey all the dogs except Bruin worked very well, and no fits occurred. I picketed them each night and they remained quiet, only one dog Flo breaking adrift. I found no difficulty in giving them their food – two pounds of preserved meat each, daily. They appeared to enjoy it thoroughly.

Captain Nares took up the story on 19 March:

To-day the skylights above the lower deck and my cabin were free from snow, and daylight introduced an inestimable blessing but with it the cold also finds its way in. The difference in temperature between the inside and outside of the glass was sufficient to crack one pane before the quickly accumulated frozen vapour on the inside formed in sufficient thickness to protect the glass. Previous to this taking place owing to the quick conduction of cold through the unprotected glass, snow-flakes formed and an actual fall of snow took place in my cabin. We have had great trouble finding the snow-house containing the gunpowder which was landed for greater security in the autumn. During the winter the house has become covered by snowdrifts, and in the darkness the pole marking its position has been lost.

March 20th. I despatched Mr Egerton with Lt Rawson accompanied by John Simmons and Michael Regan, one of the original crew of the *Discovery* to make another attempt to contact *Discovery* at winter anchorage, with a sledge drawn by seven dogs; the dogs dragging 78 pounds each. The sledge crews have commenced exercising for their long journeys. In order to utilise their labours I intend to form a large depot of provisions near the Crossing Floe ready for Beaumont's use. The weather was so calm, and the sun so powerful that, when standing still and facing it, although the temperature was actually minus 30°, it felt appreciably warm, yet ice formed on our eye-lashes thick enough to impair our sight considerably. After a six-hour exposure the cold had penetrated so far into our apparel that a woollen waistcoat, worn inside a thick box cloth coat and a **duck** outer covering had ice on it thick enough to brush off. This may enable people to realise the condition of a traveller's clothes after 11 hours hard work and how quickly his garments, which he can never dry, or indeed ever change night or day, become saturated with moisture.

March 24th. Today Markham's crews, with their boats lashed on sledges, went out onto the pack for exercise. After much labour with the pickaxes they were enabled to advance one mile and a half in the same number of hours, but that was with boats alone. If they journey at the rate of three miles a day they will do well, their worst enemy will be the misty weather. We hope that as they advance north the floes will become larger, and hedged with narrower lines of hummocks than those in our neighbourhood.

March 25th. Temperature minus 37°, the sun is only ten degrees high at noon, and yet the glare was intense when walking towards it over the snow. It afforded much relief to our eyes to occasionally face about and gaze at one's own shadow, the only dark object to be seen. The accumulations of ice about our eye-lashes and on fur caps act as a number of prisms, refracting the light into the eyes. The white painted boats being objectionable for snow-blind travellers to gaze on, Dr Moss has been painting those belonging to Markham's party with diversified colours, but the paint does not appear inclined to dry. The backs of the travellers white-duck jumpers have also been marked with appropriate designs in order

HMS *Discovery*, summer 1875, Lady Franklin Sound.

when pulling at the sledge-ropes each man may have some colour to rest his eyes on. Every individual is free to choose his own crest, the variety and originality displayed is somewhat quaint.

For several days past there has been an animated scene on the cleared part of the lower deck. One or other of the officers, and the leader amongst the crew of his sledge, styled captain of the sledge, have been alternately in possession of the weights and scales, preparing the provisions for the spring journeys. As Arctic sledge travellers are entirely dependent for subsistence on what they drag, the preparation of the provisions is a serious undertaking. Once started from the ship on a journey lasting from 80 to upwards of 100 days, there is no means of rectifying a mistake or neglect for nothing can be obtained from the ice but water, and to get that, fuel has to be carried for melting it. Carrying too much entails more weight being added to the already heavily-laden sledge. I need not mention the consequences of taking too little. In a matter of such vital importance the commander of each party must rely only on himself. Every article has to be weighed with the greatest nicety, and the lightest material procurable used for wrapping up the parcels; for this purpose a raid has been made on all the private linen. After three days work in weighing out groceries, which were tied up in some yellow calico, Dr Moss discovered that the dye used to colour it contained arsenic, and this wrapping had to be discarded.

March 29th. A gale last night, force 8. Today the *Fox* instrument was taken on shore in order to obtain base observations; but the parts froze so solidly together that the instrument could not be used. No traces of Eskimo have yet been discovered in our neighbourhood, and as it would be quite impossible for them to sustain life here during the winter we can scarcely expect to find any. Probably at Polaris Bay, and other favoured places in Smith Sound pools of water remain open, and seals may be procured; but here, since November, and for at least another month – making half a year altogether – they certainly could not be obtained.

Chapter XV

Aboard *Discovery*, Lady Franklin Sound, Winter 1875/6

On the first day they landed, a hunting party succeeded in shooting a herd of eleven musk oxen. This may appear to be a large amount of fresh food, but shared among a few score of famished and hard-working men it was devoured within a very short time. It was likely to be the last musk oxen they would eat until the following spring. As a precaution Captain Stephenson ordered most of the ship's coal to be transported ashore. A fresh water iceberg was found within a mile of *Discovery*. Once again the dogs earned their keep transporting the heavy loads of ice to the ship to be melted by the crew when required.

The anchorage and natural harbour were surrounded by hills almost 2,000ft in height. Captain Stephenson was hugely impressed by the vista – a beautiful sight when the hills were visible. Then the temperature dropped dramatically.

Captain Stephenson despatched a sledge party along the shoreline north to attempt to contact the *Alert*. He was confident Captain Nares would also attempt to make contact, but freezing temperatures, snow-storms and blizzards forced the unsuccessful party to return to ship. A few days later the frost set in and the sea was completely frozen around the ship.

As soon as the ice could bear it, the crew commenced building a multi-purpose wooden structure on shore, to use as a smithy and carpenter's workshop for building sledges, to house a magnetic observatory and a small workshop/theatre. The building had a roof made of coal bags, cemented with ice and was 60ft long by 27ft broad. According to Captain Stephenson it had a green room and a stage, and he christened it the Alexandra. The Alexandra Theatre opened on 1 December, the Princess of Wales's birthday, with the farce *My Turn Next*.

For exercise and recreation the crew also constructed an ice rink. Ice skates were manufactured by the blacksmith. The men cleared away the snow in a circle of 7ft in diameter, made a hole in the ice, through which they drew water in buckets and poured it on the rough ice which quickly froze, and then extended the rink to a suitable length.

HMS *Discovery*, Ellesmere Island, 1876.

Conditions on and around each ship were by and large similar, each crew waiting impatiently for spring. Christmas on-board *Discovery* was as lonely for the crews as it was for those on the *Alert*, all missing their loved ones. Despite the atrocious, unrelenting cold, the boredom and the restricted living conditions, the days and weeks passed without incident.

It was expected that the sun would be visible on the horizon on the last day of February. The crew assembled on the surrounding hills at noon in eager anticipation of its arrival, but they were disappointed as this sight was prevented by mist and fog. It was not until several days later they at last espied that most welcoming of God's great gifts.

Captain Stephenson, two officers and three men, with a dog-sled, set out across the Robeson Channel to Hall's Rest, the winter quarters of Hall's *Polaris*, to report on the stores left there by that ship, which had been placed at Nares's disposal by the United States Government. They returned in five days reporting that they had found biscuit, pemmican, preserved meat, molasses and various other useful items. While there, the men lived in Captain Hall's wooden observatory/depot which they had found there. It had taken the five men over half a day to clear the snow off the tiny wooden structure.

Captain Hall's grave looked quite fresh and in a good state of preservation. The head-board made from the door of a cabin, with Captain Tyson's inscription upon it, was still in place to mark the grave. A small flat piece of upright

Skating rink at the winter quarters of HMS *Discovery*. (*Illustrated London News*, 4 November 1876.)

stone was at the foot, and the willow mentioned by Tyson as having been planted there was still alive. Hans Hendrik the dog handler, and one of the heroes of the *Polaris* expedition could explain his experience of the tragic events that had taken place only five years previously.

Near the end of March a sledge party of Lt Rawson, Egerton, Simmons and Regan arrived from the *Alert*. After a journey of six days, the joyful news of the well-being of all their friends on the *Alert* was somewhat dispelled by the distressing news of the amputation of Petersen's feet.

Captain Stephenson welcomed the new orders passed on to him by Lt Rawson outlining totally unexpected instructions from Captain Nares: crew members from *Discovery* would be required to participate in the attack on the Pole after all. Based on new the orders, Captain Stephenson detailed the sledge crews. Lt Beaumont's men were to cross the Robeson Channel to explore North Greenland and seek a route to the North Pole from that direction. Meanwhile back on the *Alert*, Captain Nares continued his diary:

March 31st. To-day, with a temperature of minus 30° in the shade, we observed that the sun, for the first time this year, had a visible effect on the surface of the snow, rendering it glazed and slippery. The moccasins, soled with thin upper-leather cut from our long fisherman's boots are serviceable, so long as we walk only on snow, but the sharp slaty shingle on the bare patches of land cuts them badly.

The sledges are now drawn up alongside of the ship, already packed for a start on Monday the 3rd of April, should the weather be favourable.

During the last few days officers and men have clipped all the hair off their faces ready for travelling, and it is now difficult to recognise individuals by a casual glance.

If the beard and moustaches are worn the moisture from the breath settles on them and quickly forms into a fringe of icicles, which after two hours exposure have grown large enough to effectively prevent anything being drank out of a tumbler until it has been thawed off. The comforter worn round the neck also freezes to the beard, and after returning on-board has to be thawed off before a fire. When such a circumstance happens in a tent, with the temperature many degrees below zero, nothing can be done except to cut the beard away close to the skin. As the eye-lashes if removed may not grow again, Arctic travellers have to put up with the annoyance of ice forming on them; if not removed gradually this unites at the corners of the eye and eventually seals up the eyelids. The usual remedy is to thaw it away every now and then by the application of the bare ungloved hand. In very extreme weather when the hands of the travellers cannot be thus exposed instances have occurred of men being temporarily blinded in this manner, and unable to see their way.

Chapter XVI

Contact with *Discovery*: The Sledge Teams Set off from *Alert*

Later in March Captain Nares arranged for another attempt to be made to make contact with the *Discovery*. The following extracts are from Egerton's journal describing the journey from the *Alert* to the *Discovery* via Cape Rawson, Black Cape, Cape Union, Black Cliffs, Cape Beechy, St Patrick's Bay, and finally Discovery Bay:

March 20th. Left the *Alert* at 9.45a.m., we got over the difficulties at Cape Rawson and The Black Cape without unpacking the sledge, travelling was very good. By 6p.m. we were all in our bags, we are able to cook in the tent. This raises the temperature slightly and is much more comfortable for the cook, the only objection to it being that it makes the air in the tent rather thick; between this and four smokers the atmosphere becomes much like a London fog; of course we tied up the ventilation holes, as we had no intention of letting any warmth inside escape into the cold air without. Temperature in the tent minus 7°, in the air minus 42°.

March 21st. Under way by 9a.m. What we considered difficulties before when returning to the ship with Petersen, were now comparatively easy, having two good working hands with us. The travelling now became worse; we were keeping to the land, and the whole of the drift between the slope of the cliff and the hummocks was at a considerable angle sometimes very steep, up and down hill, always the latter we did not object to, though the sledge capsized frequently, but the former gave us much trouble, unless there had been four of us our progress would have been very slow, for the dogs are of little or no use in this kind of travelling; one man walks ahead to lead them, while the other three, having cut a footing with a pickaxe, sit down and with 'one, two, three, haul' drag together, until the sledge is up, when the dogs, finding the strain eased, start off at a full swing down the hill the other side; the sledge slides down a short way sideways and then capsizes, sometimes turning over three or four times; this style of thing went on incessantly until we became rather more knowing, and found it better for one to walk down the hill very slowly in front of the dogs with the whip in his hand; by doing so we sometimes avoided the usual capsize, being able to ease the sledge down gradually.

After half a mile of such work we came to the conclusion that, although the pack beneath us was nothing but what is commonly called rubble it could not be much worse than what we were then having, and determined to try it. To get the sledge down from our position, which was about 20ft above the pack, we un-toggled the dogs, secured the drag-ropes and tent guys to the back of the sledge, and then all having obtained as firm a footing as possible, we lowered the sledge over; unfortunately our backing ropes were not long enough, but there was nothing for it but to let go, trusting to Providence for the rest; the sledge being uncommonly strong stood the blow it received at the bottom splendidly. After getting the sledge over a short distance of the boulder ice we came to a lane of perfectly smooth ice running along just underneath the cliffy wall of ice formed by the grounded hummocks and floebergs, the outer sides of which were cut as straight, and polished as smooth as a piece of marble, with parallel lines scored out by the pack grinding against them when in motion. The travelling over the smooth ice was excellent, but we seldom came to more than a hundred yards or so of it without hummocks intervening, which generally had to be cleared away with pickaxes. As we got farther on we found water on the top of this lane of ice, which appeared to be continuous; and the pack being too hummocky to attempt, we were compelled to take to the land again just opposite the third ravine from the cairn on Cape Union. Half a mile farther on the slopes became too much for us, so we lowered the sledge on to the floe once more, preferring the 'one, two three haul' and getting something to the same with no result. When we came to any good travelling, Lt Rawson and I walked on ahead, the dogs keeping close to our heels, while the men took it in turns to sit on the sledge and to steer. At 6.15 we reached the depot at Lincoln Bay, and camped beneath it, men and dogs pretty tired. Temperature of the air, minus 37°; tent minus 3°.

March 22nd. Across Lincoln Bay the travelling was very fair, here we had slight misfortune; the toe of the sledge runner caught under a ridge and sprung. As we approached Cape Frederick VII getting under the land, the travelling became more hummocky and the snow was just too hard to bear. We all suffered considerably from cramps in the legs last night more so than usual.

The party continued their punishing journey without respite, each day as difficult as the previous one.

March 25th. Crossed St Patrick's Harbour on a large blue-topped floe. After rounding numerous small points, which shut out the ship from view, we at length

The *Alert* nipped by the ice against the shore off Cape Beechey. (*Illustrated London News*, 11 November 1876.)

sighted the *Discovery* and gave three cheers as loud as we could. We were all in very high spirits at the thoughts of seeing our friends on-board, and the prospect of a comfortable night instead of the usual cold and cramps. We were about half a mile from the ship when we cheered and we could see one or two figures alongside the ship stop and look in our direction; we gave another cheer, and presently we saw all hands running out to meet us, there was bear-hugging, back slapping and the shaking of many hands. We answered questions by the hundreds. When we could get a word in we were very glad to hear that they were all well and had survived the winter.

Lt Rawson gave the crew of *Discovery* the news of Aldrich's and Markham's exploratory journeys. But Captain Stephenson and crew were shocked to learn of the tragic plight of shipmate Neil Peterson.

There was much excitement at Discovery Bay, and great rejoicing on the part of both officers and men on learning that they were to join in the exploration of the northern coasts. Lt Aldrich's sledge party had departed to the north-west, Commander Markham's had gone directly to the North Pole, and now the sledge crews of the *Discovery* would travel by way of the Northeast of Greenland, the three parties thus forming a pincer movement.

The *Discovery* sledge crew assignments were as follows: Lts Beaumont and

Rawson, with three sledges and twenty-one men; Dr Coppinger and Hans Hendrik were to accompany Beaumont on part of the journey, they were then to return to base; Dr Coppinger, Fulford, Chatel and Hendrik would then explore and chart Petermann Fiord; Lt Archer and Mr Conybeare, with two sledges and eighteen men were to explore and chart Lady Franklin Sound.

As a precaution, on Conybeare's return to the *Discovery* after the provisioning of Lt Archer's sledge with supplies, he and his men were ordered to transport a boat across Hall Basin, which would enable Lt Beaumont and his men to return later in the season to Discovery Bay should the ice in Robeson Channel have broken up.

On 30 March Egerton, Rawson and their two companions left the *Discovery* to return north to the *Alert*, at the same time intending to smooth the way for Lt Beaumont's heavier sledges. The conditions were as trying on the return journey as they had been on the journey south, with the sledge continually capsizing. A blizzard confined them to their tent where they huddled for a day and a night. They called it twenty-four hours of misery. Such confinement is considered to be one of the most trying hardships of an Arctic journey as with temperatures as low as minus 44°, they suffered severe frostbite to hands and feet and severe cramp to shoulders and legs, and also swollen ankles. Lt Rawson and Egerton deserved great credit for their heroic endeavours on this particular assignment.

On 4 April at 8p.m. they arrived back on-board the *Alert*, disappointed at finding the main sledge parties had departed on their missions the previous day, but very thankful for returning to the ship safe and well.

Lt Rawson reported to Captain Nares that Beaumont's Greenland division would be unable to drag their heavy sledges through the barrier of ice hummocks at Black Cape. The ice was heaped up to a two-storey height above the level of the floe, forming a barrier a quarter of a mile in width, without one flat spot large enough to rest on in an even position. Captain Nares organised a work party to prepare a smooth path for Beaumont's sledges. Captain Nares noted:

The news received from Captain Stephenson is most cheering, with the exception of one man who has suffered from scurvy in January, all our friends are well and have passed a happy and comfortable winter. Over 30 musk-oxen have been shot during last autumn, and frequent rations of fresh meat have been issued to the crew throughout the winter.

The morning of 3 April was the day that had been fixed for the departure of the sledge travellers. Captain Nares described the occasion:

General disappointment was felt at the non-arrival of Rawson and Egerton with news of the *Discovery*. We had hoped that the dog-sled would have returned by that date, and that our parties might have left the ship with the gratifying knowledge that our friends on-board the *Discovery* had passed a comfortable winter. The weather, however, being settled and favourable, with the temperature ranging between minus 25 and minus 30 degrees below zero, the temperature usually experienced by Arctic travellers early in April, I gave the order for departure. The party consisted of 53 officers and men, all apparently in robust health; those remaining on-board the *Alert* numbered six officers and six men. All hands assembled for prayers on the ice alongside of the laden sledges, which were drawn in line.

It was a rousing departure, the silk banners lightly fluttering in the breeze. bearing heraldic emblems and imposing names such as Marco Polo, Victoria, Bulldog, Challenger and Bloodhound. Every man of our company was present, the ship being tenanted only by poor Petersen, who was bearing his sufferings and trials most patiently. Mr Pullen ended the usual daily prayers. The entire crew joined in a hymn before the sledgers picked up their ropes and moved off to three loud cheers.

A most impressive scene recorded Nares; each heart inspired with enthusiasm, and with a feeling of confidence that the labours, privations and hardships that the travellers were about to undergo would be manfully battled with. They donned harness and started at 11a.m, each man in the northern division dragging 230lbs and those of the western division 242lbs. The itinerary was as follows: Lt Aldrich, assisted by a sledge crew under the command of Lt Gifford, was to explore the shores of Grant Land on Ellesmere Island towards the north and west, along the coastline he had discovered the previous autumn; Commander Markham, seconded by Lt Parr, with two boats, and equipped for an absence of seventy days, was to force his way to the northward over the ice, starting off from the land near Cape Joseph Henry, with three sledge crews under the command of Dr Moss and Mr George White accompanying them as far as their provisions would allow. Nares continued:

April 8th. George Bryant [who had been assigned to travel part of the journey with Commander Markham] returned to-day having accompanied Markham as far as Cape Richardson. Markham reports that a few of the men were suffering from the severe and unaccustomed work, and the want of sleep occasioned by the extremely cold weather; a great deal of double manning [two journeys instead of one] had been necessary with the heavy sledges. One of the crew returned frostbitten.

April 10th. Lt Rawson and Mr Egerton started this evening to return to *Alert*, with two light sledges, four men, and seven dogs, to search for an available road across the frozen Robeson Channel, in readiness for the heavier exploring sledges under Lt Beaumont, expected shortly from *Discovery*. Beaumont's party will travel by night to escape the glare of the mid-day sun which is now considerable and to avoid snow-blindness; also for the great advantage of sleeping during the warmest part of the 24 hours. They started after an afternoon sleep and a good supper, which to them was in reality breakfast. Although many of those remaining onboard were drinking a glass of spirits and water before going to bed, the voyagers, both officers and men, preferred tea or coffee knowing from experience that spirits are bad to travel on. Parties starting as they did, with dearly bought experience, carry neither more or less weight than is actually necessary. The men know the value of taking care of themselves, and of the sledge on which their lives depend. The most minute attention is given, therefore, to every article of dress, equipment and provisions. The sun during the day is becoming very decided, and owing to the extreme cold it is difficult to protect our eyes. When wearing neutral-tinted spectacles the evaporation from the eye condenses so quickly on the glasses that they have to be taken off and wiped every few minutes. A gauze veil is even more useless.

The following is an account Lt Beaumont's sledge journey from the *Discovery* to the *Alert* with extracts from his official reports:

Although this journey does not form part of our exploring campaign, it requires some brief notice in consequence of its being our first experience in sledging. The party set out in good health and in excellent spirits; but the extreme cold, minus 40° to minus 30° Fahrenheit making it difficult to sleep at night, together with the unaccustomed food and hard work, soon told upon some of the less trained men, and for the two following days our progress was slow, considering the nature of the roads. George Leggat, ship's cook, was the worst, and for half-a-day had to walk by the side of the sledge; but as there was nothing more serious than over-exertion, they soon began to recover their strength. Leggat's indisposition was chiefly due to his dislike of pemmican, and he, and many others, would not eat it until hunger compelled him to do so. The road, with a few exceptions, was a very rough one, there seemed to be no choice but to follow the line of the high and very steep cliffs along the ice. Once we tried the land-foot, but after passing some inclines so steep that we had to cut a groove for the hill-side runner, we were forced to lower both sledges and crews down an ice-wall 25 feet high, which caused such a delay that for the future we preferred working through the hummocks. Floes were rare and of no great size, consequently our progress was only moderate.

We passed Lincoln Bay on the 11th of April, and arrived at Black Cape on the 14th, where we were detained one day by a gale of wind, reaching the *Alert* on Sunday the 16th, which by this time was almost deserted, 53 of its 61 man crew under Commander Markham and Lt Aldrich having departed on their separate missions.

The harrowing ten-day sledge journey from the *Discovery* to Cape Sheridan must have made the sledge party aware of the weeks or maybe months of hardship and deprivation that they were about to endure. The four days of rest enabled the sledgers to recover some strength and gave them time to consider the future and its unknown implications.
Beaumont continued:

> This trial trip was of great use to us, for the sledges not being heavy enabled the men to get into the work without undue effort, and gave them time to get accustomed to the food and novelty of the life, so that we reached the *Alert* in excellent condition, and ready to begin work in earnest.

Captain Nares reported:

> On April 19th, that noon, when the atmosphere was unusually clear, Lt Beaumont and I thought that we could distinguish cliffs forming the Greenland coast about Cape Stanton, where previously I supposed that the travellers would find a low shore and fair travelling; but as the land is upwards of 30 miles distant, we hope we are deceived. In consequence of the drift of the pack towards the east before the prevailing winds which appear to blow continuously from the westward, the coast between Cape Brevoort and Cape Stanton, lying at right angles to the course of the ice, is sure to be an extremely wild one with regard to ice-pressure. Should there be cliffs and the sledges be forced to take to the pack, the travelling will necessarily be extremely heavy.
>
> Lt Beaumont has been extremely busy all day weighing out provisions for his journey, and also some for a more lengthened trip in the spring of 1877. Three of his crew are too tall for their blanket bags, which therefore have to be lengthened.

The following are extracts from Captain Nares's orders to Lt Beaumont:

> Equipped and provisioned for an absence of 56 days, you will cross the Robeson Channel and explore the coast of Greenland towards the north and eastward. Your party, although not as strong [numerous] as I would wish, admits of two sledges being advanced for the time mentioned, under the command of yourself and Lt Wyatt Rawson, an officer in whom I have the fullest trust, and of two others

placing a depot of provisions for your use when returning.

During your advance you are to endeavour to keep one of your sledges on the northern shores. Your best guide for doing so will be to follow the line of heavy stranded floe bergs, which border the coast, in whatever direction they may lead you.

Should you experience smoother or lighter ice than that in your neighbourhood, you may reasonably conclude that some protecting land exists to the northward. In such a case you should divide your party; one sledge endeavouring to reach the northern land, and the other continuing the exploration of the Greenland coast. But as you are not provided with a boat, anyone detached should return to the mainland before the 1st of June.

Should you discover any deep inlet, which in your opinion might prove to be a channel affording an easier journey to the eastward than the coast-line of the Polar Sea, it is desirable that it should be explored this year.

Your party, on returning to the *Discovery* must necessarily cross the Robeson Channel after the ice has broken up. This part of the work before you will require more than usual skill and judgement; but I know of no officer in whose hands I would more willingly leave its accomplishments, having the utmost confidence that, with your great ability and aforethought, your interesting journey will be successfully accomplished.

Dr Coppinger in addition to his medical duties, will take executive command of the two sledges thus employed; George W. Emmerson, taking charge of the sledge *Alert* under his orders.

Captain Nares recorded:

On the 20th April, Lt Beaumont accompanied by Lt Rawson, Dr Coppinger and a dozen men, dragging four sledges weighted to 218lbs per man, started for Greenland, the officers themselves, as usual always dragging whenever not employed in selecting a road through the rough ice.

With the exception of Rawson and two of the men who had only rested for two days, the whole party under Beaumont enjoyed the great advantage of a thorough rest of four days, after a preliminary ten days' journey, and started in apparently most excellent health. Had the Committee of Inquiry appointed to enquire into the outbreak of scurvy amongst the crew of the expedition considered this fact, they would doubtless not have introduced the following paragraph in the report:

'How far, with due regard to the length of the travelling season, these evils could have been mitigated by a recourse to short journeys, utilised for laying out depots of provisions, and other preparatory purposes, prior to those of a more extended character undertaken to effect the main objects of the Expedition, we are not prepared to say, but it is obvious that the adoption of such a system would have afforded an amount and description of that previous training so essential to the success of sledging, far more efficacious than the exercise obtained during the winter, but limited by its severity.'

Nares continued:

The invalids who are unfit to join the sledges have a great press of work to perform in the necessary duties on-board the ship. They have far too little exercise. The officers are obliged to help in many ways, and anyone who will turn a hand to manual labour can readily find useful employment.

Where dampness was prevalent during the winter, mildew is now collecting, and would do so to a very prejudicial extent if left undisturbed. This mildew grows rapidly on the hammocks, beams, clothing, books, papers, et cetera.

Over rough ice a large team of 12 dogs is too many for one sledge. If their traces are all of equal length the dogs become collected too close together, and those who keep on the outside of the crush are forced to drag with their trace at a considerable angle, while several of the weak dogs being unable to push their way into the crowd cannot tighten their rope at all. A large party of dogs should certainly have traces of different lengths; but then in rough ground those in advance would turn the corners too sharply, and get out of sight of the driver. Amongst hummocks, the frequent sharp turns require the dogs to be as close to the sledge as possible.

Lt Archer started from Polaris Bay on his return journey and arrived on-board the *Discovery* on the following day. Hans Hendrik, accustomed to hunting seals in the open water pools, was much astonished to find firm ice for the whole distance across the strait with no water anywhere. Captain Nares took up the story on 22 April:

Lt Rawson returned unexpectedly from Lt Beaumont's party for a new five-man sledge, one having hopelessly broken down while crossing the barrier hummocks, although a roadway had been made through them. The heavy eight-man sledges stood the great strain in what would be a surprising manner even to the carpenters who made them. They are certainly a great triumph of ingenious workmanship, but the small sledges are far too light for our work, indeed they were never intended for it, even Sir Leopold McClintock never expected that we should have to travel over such heavy ice. They are broken by sliding too quickly down an inclined hummock, and striking the front horns against the next ridges, the weight of the cargo acting like a battering ram. The drag ropes reversed would of course enable the sledge to be eased down; but in misty weather the snow-road is so deceptive that the crew do not become aware of the declivity until they have floundered to the bottom of it themselves, it is as much as they can do to escape out of the way of the descending sledge; fortunately at the bottom of most of the inclines there is usually soft snow in which it buries itself and so generally escapes. The eight-man sledges being longer and stronger are better fitted for the rough work than the smaller ones. The sledge which has been to the *Discovery* and also to Greenland and back this season, after all the perils and numerous capsizes it has gone through without being much damaged, is naturally a favourite one with both Egerton and Lt Rawson. Many jokes are made that the latter broke his own before starting on his long journey on purpose to obtain Egerton's well-tried one. If so he was successful, for while Egerton was out of the way Rawson obtained possession of the coveted article with which he quickly disappeared to rejoin his own party.

April 23rd. Captain Stephenson and Thomas Mitchell, Hans Hendrik with William Dougall, ice quarter-master, and Henry Petty, a marine, arrived with 12 dogs from the *Discovery*. They experienced strong icy northerly winds during the journey, and like the other travellers, a very rough road, but with the exception of the leader who is severely attacked with snow-blindness, are in good health.

Chapter XVII

Commander Markham's Diary

The following are extracts from Commander Markham's diary on the attempt to reach the North Pole:

April 3rd. Left the ship at 11a.m. The western division, under the command of Lt Aldrich in company, the travelling by no means good; snow deep, and the sledges dragging very heavily. This being our first march, the men showing signs of fatigue, a halt was called at 5.30p.m., the tents pitched on the eastern side of the neck of land connecting Mushroom Point with the main.

April 5th. Although the temperature inside our tent was minus 25° we all slept a little more comfortably, or rather a little less uncomfortably, though deprived of all feeling in our feet. Double banked all the sledges over the land, we found hard work with our heavy sledges; the travelling around and beyond Harley Spit excessively heavy and laborious. Men getting tired and appear a little stiff, and complain of having suffered a good deal last night from pain in their limbs, and to-day suffering from great thirst. Another cold sleepless night, to use Admiral Richard's simile, our sleeping bags resembled sheet-iron, while the curry paste, as our cook observed, was exactly like a piece of brass, and was equally hard. Distance marched ten miles; made good six miles, temperature minus 35°.

April 7th. The sledge Bloodhound having fulfilled the duties entrusted to her, was despatched to the ship at 8a.m. Gave her three cheers on parting.

A few slight frostbites were sustained yesterday. The travelling to-day is a fore-taste of what we are to expect; heavy floes fringed with hummocks, through and over which the sledges have to be dragged. Land very much distorted by mirage. Temperature remains extraordinarily low; minus 41°. Distance marched 14 miles; made good four and a half.

April 8th. Care has to be taken in selecting the road so as to avoid the hummocks as much as possible; occasionally we are brought to a standstill by a belt of more than ordinarily large ones through which we have to cut a road with pickaxes and shovels. Sledges double banked as before. The large sledge, on which is the 20ft ice-boat, drags very heavily. This is caused by the overhanging weight at the two extremities. Glare from the sun has been very oppressive. A few of the party, including Parr and myself, suffering from snow-blindness.

April 10th. Parr's snow-blindness is no better. Although the temperature is minus 30° the sun has sufficient influence to dry our blanket wrappers and other gear; the yards of the boats being very convenient for the purpose of tying up our robes, etcetera. The snow is still very deep on the floes and between the hummocks, materially retarding our progress. From its Northwestern edge the depot at Cape Joseph was plainly visible; a great relief to our minds, as thoughts of its being buried in deep snow-drift would frequently occur to us. Distance marched thirteen miles; made good four.

Leaving tents pitched, we started with an empty sledge for the depot, distant about two miles. We experienced heavy work cutting a road through the line of shore hummocks that girt the coast, and did not succeed in reaching the depot until eleven o'clock. Sending the party back to camp, Aldrich, Gifford, Moss and I ascended View Hill (650ft) whence we obtained a good look-out. The prospect was anything but cheering. To the north-ward was an irregular sea of ice, composed of small floes and large hummocks. Our anticipations of slow travelling and heavy work seem about to be realised as the snow thawed under our feet, making the travelling more unpleasant. We shall start to-morrow morning with provisions complete for 63 days. Thus loaded, the sledges will drag uncommonly heavy, over the rough hummocks we are certain to encounter; our only mode of advancing will be by a system of double-banking which simply means one mile made good for every five actually marched. If we accomplish two miles a day it will be a fair days work. Parr is still affected by snow-blindness and my sight not quite the thing. Snow still falling. I was greatly indebted to Moss for his efficient aid in assisting me to choose a road for the sledges. Aldrich has very wisely determined to return to the land and try his luck through the Snow Valley, instead of rounding Cape Joseph Henry. At one o'clock, displayed all colours, and parted company with Aldrich's division and our two supporting sledges amid much cheering. They were soon lost sight of amongst the hummocks.

Parr in advance with half a dozen men cutting a road with pickaxes and shovels, the remainder of the men dragging up the sledges singly. Got on to a heavy floe and then in amongst a mass of heavy hummocks, through which appeared no road or outlet; but the steady and persevering exertions of Parr and his roadmakers performed wonders, and the sledges were soon travelling over a road that had before looked impenetrable and impassable. The floes are small but very heavy. It is difficult to estimate their thickness, but it must be considerable. They appear to have had a terrible conflict, one with another, the result being what we are now encountering, namely a great expanse of hummocks varying in height from 20ft to small knobbly pieces over which we stagger and fall. Between these hummocks the snow-drifts are very deep, and we are continually floundering up to our waists, but the men struggle bravely on. Possibly when we leave the vicinity of Cape Joseph Henry, and get well clear of the land, we may experience better travelling; larger floes and less snow. One thing is pretty certain, we cannot have much worse, and this is a consolation. Encamped amongst the hummocks, after a very hard and weary day's work. The men appear a good deal done up. The road making was incessant the whole afternoon. Distance marched ten miles; made good two and a quarter.

After breakfast, commenced with a half a dozen road-makers cutting a road through the hummocks, leaving the remainder of the party to strike the tents, pack, and bring up the sledges one by one as far as the road was practicable. Parr's eyes are improving and he has worked like a slave with pickaxe and shovel. After lunch, emerged from the hummocks on to a small floe, and then through another mass of hummocks, having only made half a mile during the afternoon. The surface snow on the floes sparkles and glitters with the most beautiful iridescent colours, the ground on which we walk appearing as if strewn with bright and lustrous gems; diamonds, rubies, emeralds, and sapphires being the most prominent.

Camped for the night, the men being rather fatigued. We are all suffering from cracked skin, the combined action of sun and frost, our lips, cheeks, and noses being especially very sore. Travelling through hummocks is most unsatisfactory work; it is a succession of standing pulls – 'one, two, three, haul!' – and very little result. Distance marched nine miles made good one and a half. Temperature minus 28°. John Shirley has to be put on the sledge. George Porter is rendered *hors de combat*, and is suffering a good deal more of pain. He is just able to hobble after us. Our force is much weakened by the loss of these two men. The snow being deep, we found the travelling on the floes very heavy indeed; the large boat comes along very slowly, and it is seldom we can advance many paces without resorting to standing pulls. Some of the floes are thicker than others, and it is of no infrequent occurrence that we have to lower the sledges a distance of six or seven feet from the top of one to the surface of another or vice versa. After lunch, George Porter, being unable to walk any farther has to be carried on the sledge. This is sad work; it makes our progress very slow and tedious. Distance marched; nine miles made good one and a quarter. Having made a slight alteration in our weights by lessening those on the heavy sledge, we resumed the march, Shirley has slightly improved, and is able to walk slowly in our rear. So hard were our sleeping-bags frozen last night, that the operation of getting into them was positively painful. We seemed to have quite got away from the smooth level floes surrounded by the dense hummocks, and have reached those of gigantic thickness with a most

The highway to the North. (*Illustrated London News*, 11 November 1876.)

uneven surface and covered in deep snow. The travelling has been rough and heavy. The Victoria capsized, but was quickly righted without damage to either sledge or boat. The foremost batten of the Marco Polo was also carried away. Temperature minus 33°. We have to be cautious about frostbite. Distance marched ten miles; made good one mile.

April 19th. Experienced great difficulty in getting from one floe to another some of them being with the snow on the surface, as much as eight or nine feet above the others. After labouring and toiling for three and a half hours, standing pulls nearly the whole time, during which period we had barely advanced 300 hundred yards, I came to the determination of abandoning the 20ft ice-boat. I did not arrive at this decision until after very mature deliberation, and from my own conviction that amongst such ice as we were then encountering, should a disruption occur, the boats would be of little avail to us, except to be used as a ferry from one floe to another. For this purpose the smaller boat will suffice. Distance marched eight miles; made good one mile.

April 20th. Weather so thick with fog that we experienced great difficulty in making any headway, crossing small floes and through hummocks that appear interminable. Snow very deep; prospect anything but cheering as nothing but hummocks can be seen. Compelled to deviate to the eastward of our course in order to avoid a mass of heavy hummocks, through which it would take

A sledge party camping for the night. (*Illustrated London News*, 11 November 1876.)

days to cut through. After lunch we were forced to put Shirley on the sledge again in order to prevent him getting frostbitten, as he was unable to move fast enough to keep himself warm. The wind is so keen and cutting that the cold feels more intense to-day than on any day since we left the ship. It almost cuts one in two. In consequence we halted an hour earlier than we otherwise would have done. Numerous frostbites among the party. Some of the greatest enemies that we have to contend with in crossing the large floes are the numerous cracks and fissures that radiate in all directions and are concealed from view by a treacherous covering of snow. Into these we frequently fall, sinking up to our waists. Porter still has to be carried on a sledge his condition is a constant worry. The men are an uncanny lot to look at; very dirty, faces and especially noses scarified and disfigured, lips sore and tips of fingers senseless from frostbite. We crossed the 83rd Parallel to-day. Distance marched eight miles; made good one and-a-half.

And so Commander Albert Markham and his sorely pressed crew continued their relentless march, day after day with no let up from interminable hummocks, frostbite, icy winds, freezing fog, and blizzards that confined the crew to their tent, with invalids to be carried, battering roads with picks and shovels oftentimes in deep snow up to their waists, thoroughly fatigued in temperatures of –30°.

Back on the *Alert*, Captain Nares noted:

Lt Beaumont's auxiliary parties returned from Repulse Bay to the *Alert* for a second load of provisions. While crossing Robeson Channel Beaumont had severe work, both the small sledges were damaged and one crew member was injured by being jammed between the laden sledge and an ice hummock; otherwise the journey was progressing. Neil Petersen is still in a critical condition, everything that can be done for him is being done bearing in mind the ship's location, anchored in the Arctic embedded in ice and relief still months away.

Mr Egerton, taking charge of the *Discovery's* auxiliary sledge, started for Greenland, the crew dragging 161lbs a man. He carries orders to Dr Coppinger to proceed to Polaris Bay, visiting on his way all the cairns erected by Captain Hall and the other members of the *Polaris* expedition. Mr Egerton also carries canvas boats for Beaumont's use later to facilitate his return to the *Discovery*.

May 7th. Dr Colan is becoming increasingly anxious about poor Petersen, who bears his trials cheerfully and patiently but is very weak.

May 14th. Poor Petersen died this evening, passing away quietly and without pain. Dr Colan has been incessant in his attendance, not only in a medical capacity but as a nurse; so perfectly self-sacrificing is he that I am seriously alarmed for his own health.

May 19th. Neil C. Petersen was buried to-day at Cape Sheridan on the brow of a hill a quarter of a mile from the ship where the snow never collects; the grave will therefore always remain conspicuous. No documents are buried near it, it need never be disturbed.

Commander Markham's report continued:

May 1st. A fine bright morning has ushered in the month of May, Latitude 83°10'30"N. The invalids are not improving, John Hawkins totally unfit for duty, Shirley very weak and faint. Porter's symptoms appear to be scorbutic. We are inclined to believe that they are all attacked with scurvy, although we have not been led to suppose that there is any probability of our being so afflicted and are ignorant of the symptoms. Our strength is rapidly decreasing. Reuben Francome feeling so bad that he is obliged to be put on the sledge. More of the men are complaining of pains in their legs which we fear are only the premonitory symptoms. A dreary scene surrounded us; a cold desolate, and inhospitable-looking scene. Everything of the same uniform colour; nothing to relieve the eye; nothing but one sombreness uneven and irregular sea of snow and ice. Distance marched four miles; made good three-quarters of a mile. Alfred Pearce is now unable to walk and it is evident Shirley is in the same condition. Under these distressing circumstances there was nothing to be done but to advance with one sledge, unload it, return with it empty, and then bring on the remainder of the gear and the invalids. The snow being very deep, the continual walking backwards and forwards is very fatiguing on the men; they find it easier to drag a sledge through the deep snow than to walk without the support of the drag belt. Distance made a quarter of a mile. The interiors of our tents in the evening have more the appearance of hospitals than the habitations of strong working men. In addition to the cripples [sic] our men belonging to the Marco Polo are suffering from snow blindness, although in a mild form.

May 9th. We have at length arrived at the conclusion, although with great reluctance, that our sick men are really suffering from scurvy, and that in no mild form. Should our surmise be correct, we can scarcely expect to see any of the afflicted ones improve until they can be supplied with fresh meat and vegetables. We are unwilling for the men to suspect that they are suffering from this terrible disease, but at the same time are issuing to those attacked a small quantity out of the very little lime juice we brought away with us. It is given to them in lieu of their grog, as being a better blood-purifier. We have only two bottles on each sledge of this excellent anti-scorbutic.

May 10th. After very serious consideration I arrived at the conclusion, though sorely against my inclination, that this must be our most northerly camp. With five of our little force totally prostrate, and four others exhibiting decided symptoms of the same complaint, it would be folly to persist in pushing on. In addition to which the greater half of our provisions have been expended. It was a bitter ending to all our aspirations.

Tomorrow will be our fortieth day out; only thirty-one days' full allowance of provisions remain, so that prudence and discretion unite against our own desire of advancing, and counsel a return. Markham planted the Union Jack where he stood. It was the farthest north any human being had stood – indeed in Markham's estimation it was a higher latitude than will ever be attained and with this the country must be satisfied.

On this being duly announced three cheers were given, with one more for Captain Nares; then the whole party, in the exuberance of their spirits at having reached their turning point, sang 'The Union Jack of Old England', 'The Grand Palaeocrystic Sledging Chorus', winding up, like loyal subjects, with 'God save the Queen'. These little demonstrations had the effect of cheering the men. The instruments were then packed, the colours furled, and our steps retraced to the camp. On arrival the flags were hoisted on our tents and sledges and kept flying for the remainder of the day. A magnum of whisky that had been sent by the Dean of Dundee, for the express purpose of being consumed in the highest northern latitude, was produced, and a glass of grog served out to all. It is needless to add his

The *Alert* hoisting colours in honour of having attained the highest latitude of any ship on record. (*Illustrated London News*, 11 November 1876.)

kindness was thoroughly appreciated, nor was he forgotten in the toast of absent friends. We all enjoyed our supper, for we had the hare shot by Dr Ed Moss at Depot Point, equally divided between our two tents, cooked in our allowance of pemmican, making the latter uncommonly good and savoury. After supper a cigar was presented to each man by Lt May. And the day was brought to a close with songs, even the invalids joining in.

A complete rest to the invalids of a couple of days may be productive of much good. With this we must be content, having failed so lamentably in attaining a much higher northerly latitude.

May 12ᵗʰ. Breakfasted at 8.30, immediately after which, leaving the cooks behind at the camp to attend upon the invalids, the remainder of the party carrying the sextant and artificial horizon, and also the sledge's banners and colours, and started northwards. We had some very severe walking, struggling through snow up to our waists, over or through which the labour of dragging a sledge would be interminable, and occasionally almost disappearing through cracks and fissures, until twenty minutes to noon, when a halt was called. The artificial horizon was then set up, and the flags and banners displayed. At noon we obtained a good altitude, and proclaimed our latitude to be 83°20'26"N, exactly three hundred and ninety nine and a half miles from the North Pole.

May 13th. Our outward-bound tracks nearly obliterated. The invalids appear no better for their long rest. Started with two sledges, leaving the tents pitched and the sick inside, and commenced our march southward.

Having advanced the two sledges for some distance they were unpacked and dragged back to camp empty. The tents were then struck, and putting two invalids on each of the small sledges, and one on the boat on the large sledge, again advanced by short stages, dragging the lighter ones single-banked six hands to each, the whole party returning to drag the heavy one. As this will be our future mode of travelling, no further reference will be made regarding the details of our order of marching. Distance made one mile and a half miles. It is impossible to see many yards ahead; this makes following the old road a task of great difficulty.

It is a curious fact that for the last week or ten days our appetites have been decreasing in a marvellous manner. For the first three weeks after leaving the ship the majority of us were perfectly ravenous, and could easily at supper-time have devoured an extra pannikan full of pemmican. Now we are seldom able to consume what is served out to us although little more than half the allowance is cooked. It is with great difficulty the patients can be induced to eat anything, their mouths being too tender to eat the biscuits, although well soaked. Distanced made good one mile.

May 18th. Our appetites are still on the decline and to a rather an alarming degree. At breakfast to-day, in one tent, scarcely a pannikan full of pemmican was consumed by the whole party. On the other hand we seem to be assailed by an unquenchable thirst, that can only be alleviated at meal-times, as we are unable to spare fuel to make extra water. After serious thought, we have resolved, should any more men be compelled to fall out from the drag ropes, upon abandoning the boat. We look upon it as a dernier resort, but an imperative necessity. If any more men are attacked our only chance of reaching the shore, before our provisions are expended will be by lightening the sledges as much as possible, and the first thing to be discarded must be the boat. We must take our chance of the ice remaining stationary, and hope that no disruption will take place before we gain the shore. Old Joe, as the men irreverently term Cape Joseph Henry, is looming larger and darker, and Mount Pullen was seen to-day for the first time for some days. Our small modicum of lime juice is nearly all expended, although it has been most carefully husbanded, and only issued to the sick every other day. Ominous signs predicting a movement of the ice were visible. Snow falling heavily. All the party are more or less suffering from stiffness and aching bones. Distance made good one mile and a half.

May 24th. A bright sunny day. The land is plainly visible. Being the Queen's birthday, the colours were displayed at lunchtime, the main brace was spliced, and Her Majesty's health drunk by her most northern, though not the less loyal subjects. Travelling over an extensive floe, but with very deep snow, with numerous hard snow ridges and hillocks that made the operation of dragging the sledges up very laborious, whilst the coming down was just as bad, as the cripples had scarcely time to jump to one side before the sledge was on top of them. William Ferbrache appears very bad, but pluckily sticks to the drag ropes; not, poor fellow, that he is of much use there, as he can hardly keep pace with us, much less pull, it serves however as a support to him. Thomas Rawlings and Thomas Simpson are not much better. Out of the 34 legs in the whole party we can only muster 11 good ones and even some of these are shaky. Distance made one mile and a half.

May 26th. Blowing a strong SW gale accompanied by a heavy fall of snow an a dense snow-drift, had breakfast, holding ourselves in readiness for a start should the weather permit. In this however we were grievously disappointed and were again doomed to a day of idleness. To pack the sledges and place the invalids on them without their being almost buried in the blinding snowdrift was quite out of the question, and even if there was a chance of advancing it was impossible to see a sledge's length ahead. This delay causes us great anxiety, as every day, every hour, is of importance to us, as we know not when we may, one and all, be attacked and rendered useless for further work.

May 27th. Made a start. The large fall of snow that has fallen renders the travelling very heavy, in addition to which the high temperature causing a partial thaw, has made the snow assume a sludgy consistency which clings tenaciously to our legs and sledge runners. The men are no better for their rest of yesterday, indeed may be said to be worse; the only two men at present scathe-less, with the exception of the officers [which was very telling] being John Radmore and William Maskell. This diminution of our forces was an event which we were quite prepared for, therefore preparations were made for abandoning the boat and all superfluous weights. Our object now must be to reach shore as speedily as possible. Left the boat as conspicuous as possible, and depositing a record in a tin cylinder stating the approximate position of the floe and our reasons for deserting the boat. Our appetites still on the wane, some go without a meal altogether, and these latter are not allowed to smoke or to have their grog. Shortly before the tents were pitched, much excitement was caused by the appearance of a little snow-bunting, which fluttered around us for a short time, uttering its, to us, rather sweet chirp, and then flew away to the northward. This was an event of no small interest to our party, as it was the first bird seen by the majority for a period of nine months, even the sick men on the sledges requested they might have their heads uncovered and lifted, so as to obtain a glimpse of the little warbler (a touching incident in its simplicity). Distance made good one mile.

At lunch the colours were again displayed and the main brace spliced, to commemorate the first anniversary of our departure from England. Crossed a fringe of hummocks, which had evidently been in motion since we passed them on our outward journey; but what was more alarming, whilst dragging the sledges over a small patch of young ice the heavy sledge broke through, and we had no little trouble in saving it from complete immersion, which might have resulted seriously to one of the unfortunate invalids who was securely on the top. As it was the whole of the rear part of the sledge was immersed in water. We were all wet through, and very wretched and uncomfortable, the falling snow and drift thawing on our clothes as quickly as it fell. Our old track is completely obliterated and it is only occasionally by seeing evidence of our former journey, such as tin pots, et cetera, that we know we are still adhering to it. Travelling altogether very heavy. Snow in places up to our waists. Distance made good half a mile.

June 2nd. A sad list of sick this morning. Rawlings and Simpson completely done up, and utterly incapable of further work. It is marvellous how they kept on so long. Edwin Lawrence is also attacked in his arms as well as legs. We are now reduced to only six men, and they anything but healthy or strong, and two officers. Five men are carried on sledges, and four can just manage to crawl after. The weather has at last proved triumphant and has robbed us of our road. The track was lost despite our utmost efforts to adhere to it, we now have to renew the arduous task of road making and with a drastically depleted crew. Unless the weather clears sufficiently to enable us to pick up our track, our intention is to make straight for the land in the direction of Snow Valley.

The condition of George Porter is a cause of grave concern.

June 4th. Leaving the road-makers to follow in our track Parr and myself pushed on for the shore. We here observed the recent traces of a dog-sledge and human footsteps. On reaching the depot we learned to our disappointment that Captain Nares, Lt May and Captain Feilden had only left for the ship the previous day. This was unfortunate. Twenty-four hours earlier and we should have met them. They had obtained three hares, which they kindly cached in a crevice between two hummocks for our use. The tents pitched for the night on a small piece of ice about 300 yards from the shore. Our supper consisted of the three hares and will doubtless do good. Next morning we were on *terra firma*, after an absence of over two months. Strong gales moderated during the night, but not before it had nearly blown our tent down, one of the bow lines gave away, and a tent pole started, and we were momentarily expecting to have our house down about our ears; fortunately for us it resisted all efforts. We really need urgent assistance, or lives will be lost. After a long consultation with Parr it has been resolved that we shall proceed to-morrow morning, if fine, and walk to the ship. Our only chance of saving life is by receiving succour as soon as possible, although the distance from us to the ship is nearly thirty miles, over floes covered with deep snow, and girt by heavy hummocks. Parr has nobly volunteered to attempt it, and has confidence in being

Lieutenant Parr setting off to bring help to the northern sledge party. (*Illustrated London News*, 11 November 1876.)

able to accomplish it. He is the only one of the party strong enough to undertake such a march, we all have the utmost confidence in his judgement and ability to perform it. Parr started off as lightly accoutred as possible. We all wished him God-speed and will be anxious to hear of his safe arrival.

Captain Nares described Parr's arrival:

On the evening of June 8th Parr made his appearance aboard the *Alert*. As he crossed the quarter-deck, silently nodding to the one or two who chanced to meet him, his grave and weary expression was unmistakable, and in a very few moments the certainty that some sore calamity had occurred had spread throughout the ship. So travel-stained was he on entering my cabin that I mistook him for his more swarthy friend Beaumont, then on the Greenland coast, and therefore anxiously questioned him concerning the disaster which had occasioned his totally unexpected return. I then received the distressing intelligence that nearly the whole of Commander Markham's men were attacked by scurvy and in want of immediate assistance. Markham and the few men who were able to work had succeeded in conveying the invalids to the neighbourhood of Cape Joseph Henry, 27 miles distant from the ship and were still advancing slowly; but each day was rapidly adding to the intensity of the disease and the number of sick. Under these circumstances Parr nobly volunteered to bring me the news and so obtain relief for his companions. Starting with only an alpenstock and a small allowance of provisions, at the end of 20 miles he hastily made himself a cup of tea; pushing on, he completed his long and solitary walk within 24 hours. Arrangements were at once made to proceed to Markham's assistance, and by midnight two strong parties of officers and men had started; Lt May and Dr Moss who wore snow-shoes, pushing on before us, with the dog-sled laden with appropriate medical stores. By making a forced march they reached Markham's camp within 50 hours of Parr's departure. But to our great regret they were unfortunately too late to save the life of George Porter who only a few hours previously had expired.

Commander Markham, meanwhile, wrote:

All hands appear very stiff and in pain. George Porter is very low, and is undoubtedly in a very precarious state.

June 8th. Poor George Porter is no more! He expired at ten minutes past noon. He was sensible to within a few minutes of his death, and his end was calm and quiet. This is a sad calamity although we were not totally unprepared for it, and I fear the depressing moral effect that this lamentable event will have on those who are very sick, and who consider themselves to be in nearly as precarious a condition.

With the ensign at half mast, and the Union Jack as a pall, the funeral procession, attended by all but the four very bad cases, started at nine; and the burial service being read, the remains were consigned to their last icy resting place in this world. Improvising a rude cross, formed with a boat's oar and a spare sledge baton, it was placed at the head of the grave, with the following inscription:

Beneath This Cross Lie Buried The Remains
Of
George Porter RMA,
Who Died on June 8th 1876,
Thy Will Be Done

Of all the melancholy and mournful duties I have ever been called upon to perform, this has been the saddest. A death in a small party like ours, and under the present circumstances, is a most distressing event, and is keenly felt by all. During the service all were more or less affected, and many to tears.

June 9th. A wild thick day. Invalids in a very depressed state, notwithstanding all efforts made to cheer them. All eyes eagerly directed to the southward, the quarter from which we are anxiously expecting succour. We had advanced the heavy sledge one stage, and had just returned to drag up the smaller ones, when something moving among the hummocks was espied, which from its rapid motion was soon made out to be a dog-sledge. Hoisted colours. The men appeared quite carried away by their feelings, and it was with difficulty they could muster up a cheer as May and Moss arrived and shook our hands. Our delight was enhanced on being informed that they were only the advance of a larger party coming out to our relief, headed by the Captain himself and nearly all the officers. Cooking utensils lighted, water made, and soon all enjoying a good draught of lime juice, with mutton for supper in prospective. Our spirits rose wonderfully, and as if nature also wished to participate in our joy, the weather began to break, and the sun shone out. Resumed the march, Lt May pushing on with his dog-sledge, and camping about half a mile to the southward of us, they not having rested for many hours so eager was he to afford us relief. We all, including the sick, consumed and relished our pannikan full of ox-cheek and mutton that we had for supper last night, and agreed that it was one of the most delicious repasts that we had ever partaken of. After lunch, sighted the main party coming towards us. Warm greetings were exchanged. No time was wasted in asking questions, the march renewed – my party, the lame ducks, dragging one sledge, the relief party dragging the other two, the invalids who had had to walk, much to their relief, being put on the dog-sled. Lt May went on with the dogs-sleds to the ship taking the most critically ill of the invalids, Shirley and Pearson.

Captain Nares made this observation:

It is difficult for a stranger to the surrounding circumstances and scenery to realise the condition of these men, who in spite of their truly pitiable state were yet making slow progress towards the ship, struggling along over the uneven snow-covered ice as best they could, these men whose limbs becoming daily more cramped foretold that they must shortly succumb; they were gallantly holding out to the last in order not to increase by their weight a moment sooner than could be avoided, the already heavy loads being dragged by their slightly stronger companions. These poor fellows were in the habit of starting off each morning before the main party, knowing that if they experienced a bad fall or came to an unusually deep snow-drift they could not recover themselves without help. Frequently the sledge party overtook them lying helplessly on the ice. With the exception of Markham, who dragged to the very last, and in addition had to pioneer a way for the sledges before the daily start, the others remaining on the drag-ropes were in great measure dependent on the leaders John Radmore and Thomas Jolliffe.

Although these two men were the most vigorous of the sledge crews they were greatly enfeebled; yet rather than resign the post of honour as leaders, which entailed the extra labour of treading down a pathway through the snow, they journeyed along supporting each other arm-in-arm, and by keeping the drag-rope taut afforded a means of support for their more disabled companions in the rear. Their manful and determined struggle along the roughest road imaginable, is far beyond all praise. After seeing their condition there is no difficulty in realising the statement concerning Sir John Franklin's men, as made by an Eskimo to Sir Leopold McClintock, 'They fell down and died as they walked along.'

Commander Markham resumed his narrative:

Our only difficulty is in going through deep snow, when the men, their legs being so bad, are compelled to stop and drag them out of the holes into which they sink. George Winstone, our latest invalid, with the aid of a staff manages to keep up with us.

June 13th. Men's legs very stiff, but the idea of soon getting on-board the ship is a good restorative. Observed May's dog-sled returning over Mushroom Point. Sent Winstone, Lawrence and Harley to the ship on Lt May's sledge.

Early on June 12th the whole party encamped on the shore of Cape Richardson exchanging the dreary prospect of icy desolation afforded by the confused disarray of ice hummocks, which had so frequently bounded their view for nearly 60 days. This total change of circumstances together with the anxious and unremitting care of Dr Moss, the alteration of diet, and the plentiful supply of fresh game and lime juice arrested the disease, and at once produced a marked improvement in the appearance of all.

Resumed the march on the morning of Wednesday the 14th of June. Out of my original party of 15 men, three only – namely, Radmore, Joliffe and Maskell – were capable of dragging the sledge; the remaining 11 having been carried alongside on the relief sledges.

After his return to the ship Commander Markham reported:

I feel it impossible for my pen to depict with accuracy, and yet be not accused of exaggeration, the numerous drawbacks that impeded our progress. One point, however, in my opinion is most definitely settled, and that is, the utter impossibility of reaching the North Pole over the floe in this locality; and in this opinion my able colleague Lt Parr entirely concurs. I am convinced that with the very lightest-equipped sledges, carrying no boats, and with all the resources of the ship concentrated in the one direction, and also supposing that perfect health might be maintained, the latitude attained by the party I had the honour of commanding, would not be exceeded by many miles, certainly not by a degree.

Captain Nares commented:

In this I most fully concur. Markham's journey, coupled with the experience gained by Sir Edward Parry in the summer of 1827, and more recently the memorable retreat of Lt Weyprecht and his companions after having abandoned the *Tegetthoff* off the coast of Joseph Henry Land, proves that a lengthened journey over the Polar pack ice with a sledge party equipped with a boat fit for navigable purposes is impracticable at any season of the year. The much-to-be-deplored outbreak of scurvy in no way effects the conclusions to be derived from the journey. The crippled state of Commander Markham's men raised serious apprehensions regarding the health of Aldrich's western division of travellers. They were due at the Joseph Henry Depot on the 13th, but as Aldrich's last accounts informed me that the provisions he had saved would enable him to prolong his journey six or seven days, and not expecting that his men would be called upon to undergo much more severe labour than former Arctic travellers had successfully combated, I was not greatly alarmed about him. Nevertheless frequent and anxious visits were made to the look-out hill, from whence the black pile of provisions forming his depot could be indistinctly seen, though 30 miles distant, whenever the atmosphere was clear. After seeing Markham's men made comfortable and distributing the champagne presented to us on our departure by Sherard Osborn to those among them whom the doctor permitted to receive it, I ascended to the look-out cairn. The depot looked smaller than when last seen, so I conclude that Aldrich has visited it. If so he will be at Knot Harbour to-morrow, and will signal from thence.

June 17th. The depot was distinctly in sight to-day. If Aldrich does not arrive there to-morrow a relief party must start to meet him; however he is so judicious an officer that I have every confidence in his actions whatever may overtake him. Arctic sledging is necessarily precarious work; although with specially equipped expeditions it has hitherto been attended with success, there have been many hair-breadth escapes.

All the gunpowder has been brought from the shore, but I am waiting for warm weather to dry the magazine before stowing it away. The depot being still untouched, Lt May, with well-rested dogs and three strong men, William Malley, James Self, and James Thornbeck, started this evening to meet Aldrich and his party. Aldrich was due 12 days ago. The country in our neighbourhood is so covered with snow that it would be useless for a shooting party to leave the ship. But as the hills near Cape Richardson present a more promising appearance Parr and Feilden have started for Knot Harbour in the hope of obtaining some fresh game, ready for Aldrich's men. Nelly, Markham's dog, and both the cats are suffering in health, and are supposed to have scorbutic symptoms. Bruin, an old dog that refuses to work with the sledge team, has for some time been performing very valuable service in dragging fresh water ice from the quarry to the ship. The men merely load the sled and start him on his journey, whence he runs home by himself.

June 21st. To-day Markham and I, after an hour's stay on the hilltop could see no sign of the depot or any indication of Aldrich's arrival.

Now that the ration of salt meat is reduced, the rough salt obtainable from the salt meat brine is not sufficient for our consumption. It is a curious fact that such a simple but necessary article was the only thing forgotten in our ample outfit.

Chapter XVIII

Lt Aldrich's Journey

After parting company with Commander Markham on 11 April, Lt Aldrich and Lt Gifford with their two sledges arrived at the shore of James Ross Bay four days later, having been obliged to resort to double manning the sledges for the greater part of the distance. Four hares had been shot, and traces of ptarmigan seen. Expecting to obtain further supplies the game was cooked at once; it was to be the only fresh meat meal that they obtained.

On 25 June, Gifford and his crew, after loading their own sledge, transferred to Aldrich's party the surplus supplies which he and his crew would not require to get back to the ship. After an exchange of hearty cheers and good wishes, Lt Gifford and his party took their departure.

Aldrich and his men continued to battle the rough hummocks and rugged terrain, the sledge coming to a dead stop over and over again in the deep snow. Lt Aldrich explained the difficulties:

> Had anyone been in the neighbourhood, and unacquainted with the method of progression in this detestable travelling, they would very probably have been astonished at the constant shouts of 'One, two, three, haul!' varied by 'Main topsail, haul!' et cetera, to relieve the monotony of the same old yarn. However we had the whole country to ourselves, and were at perfect liberty to expend as much of our breath in shouting as we could spare, without fear of awakening or frightening anybody.

For the next seven days, with Aldrich's sledge heavily laden, the daily advance was painfully slow, as was usual in similar journeys, and the soft snow entailed very severe labour on the crew. However difficult and unpleasant Lt Aldrich and his men's journey was, they do not appear to have encountered anything like the unending stretches of hills or hummocks which entailed so much road-making for Markham's party. Lt Aldrich reported:

The western sledge party about to start. (*Illustrated London News*, 4 November 1876.)

The men are all very much done up, the fact being that, light loads or heavy loads, this thick snow takes it out of one tremendously, and the constant standing pulls shake one to pieces. The double journeys are most discouraging to the men, and their looks of disappointment when after nine hours' labour, they find themselves only two and a half to three miles from where they started. Half our daily journey is necessarily done with the sun in our faces, causing a few cases of snow-blindness. The Sergeant-Major has just shown me a very ugly-looking red patch or blotch just above the ankle; the limb is slightly swollen.

We had Evening Service after supper.

The 29th was the last day on the outward journey that we were obliged to advance with half-loads at a time. We were then a few miles east of Cape Columbia.

May 1st. The questionable pleasure of having a man dancing on you when brushing down the condensation collected on the inside of the tent was dispensed with this morning, there was none to brush down.

As the weather gives every promise of being fine, I intend remaining off Cape Columbia to-morrow, and to ascend Cooper Key Peak, from which we shall get a splendid view. The whole crew are anxious to come, I told them to draw lots for one to remain; poor James Doidge is down on his luck, having been elected to stay behind, The Sergeant-Major's leg still gives him no pain but the angry red colour has spread considerably; I don't like the look of it all. I have given him turpentine liniment to rub in, which he uses with a will.

May 7th. The health of the crew is good, except stiff legs, which are pretty general, and only to be expected. The two worst cases are the Sergeant-Major and James Doidge.

The march continues, the crew experiencing great difficulties, which are now accepted as being inevitable.

Although an out break of scurvy was not anticipated, the unsatisfactory condition of the men was causing Aldrich much anxiety. On 10 May he wrote:

The men are nearly all suffering a great deal with their unfortunate legs, which appear to get worse every day. This we all feel to be very disappointing, as it affects the journey, and although stiff limbs were expected, everyone thought the stiffness would wear off in time. It seems, however, inclined to hang on, and sets at defiance all the limited medical skill we possess among us, and to scorn succumbing to turpentine liniment, bandages, good elbow grease et cetera. The legs get a little more comfortable after being a short time under way; but somehow the men do not appear to be up to the mark. Adam Ayles and I are the only two who eat all the pemmican we can get. I should like them to have a rest but too much time was lost at the outset to admit it. Joseph Good has been added to our list of suspected scurvy sufferers. The three invalids struggle manfully but are really not able to do much. The actual weight on the sledge is nothing comparatively, but it is the inability to walk rather than drag well which impedes the party.

A Sunday morning, with a desultory conversation going on while waiting for pemmican, now of England, now of fresh food and vegetables – a pretty constant topic – and an occasional lamentation as to the wretched state of the legs, with an expectation that they may be the only cases, and the fear that in consequence their work will not bear comparison with that performed by the other sledges and former Arctic travellers. Under way at 6.15a.m. and the sledge went merrily down the hill; but I repented my decision of last night to keep easy work for a start, for the sledge was too lively for the unfortunate cripples, some of whom were in positive agony. After proceeding about a mile we reached the level floe of a bay seven to eight miles deep, with steep cliffy shores and hills rising from 400 to 1,000 feet in height. These hills, like all those we have met with, do not run in ranges, but are scattered irregularly about, and separated and cut up by ravines in all directions. The south west point is low and shelving, and just open of it, about 20 miles distant, shows out another cape, which I have pointed out to the men as the spot from which I shall be perfectly satisfied to turn back. No snow-blindness, except my own – my eyes being extremely painful.

May 18th. Taking into consideration the state of the crew, and the quantity of provisions remaining, I think it advisable to turn back for the ship to-day. The biscuit remaining is five days' full allowance, which with a healthy crew would be ample, but looking as I must to marches not much better than we have been performing lately, it will have to last ten days. Henry Mann is not fit to march. The Sergeant and Doidge insist against my better judgement to limp along.

Halted to-day for grog and biscuit. Hoisted the Union Jack and drank Her Majesty's health. On the homeward journey the attack of scurvy became more pronounced, and the fast increasing weakness of the men rendered the daily distance accomplished so short that the provisions placed in depot on the passage out were insufficient to last them on full allowance, while travelling from one depot to another. Doubtless the necessarily reduced ration helped to accelerate the advance of the dreadful malady. On the 5th of June we passed Cape Columbia on our return; to-day we can see to within 30 miles of the ship, a fact I have impressed on the men, with good effect, and on the 7th the dreaded word scurvy was used for the first time. I have heard many mild complaints of late as to the affects of the pemmican; latterly everyone except Ayles and I suffer more or less. I attribute it to weakness; had we had the good fortune to procure game, I daresay this would not have been experienced; but where game is not to be got I believe an occasional change to preserved meat might be beneficial. Another symptom which has become apparent yesterday and to-day with four of the crew, is tender gums, which I hope may be due to the increased allowance of biscuit. Hitherto, while rather short of it, we always soaked it in tea or pemmican to make it go farther, now we eat it, or some of it, without softening it. I hope it is not scurvy, though James Doidge asked me the question to-day, is scurvy ever got while sledging, sir? I answered in perfect truth in one sense, though not in another, 'No', and attributed everything to the hard biscuit. The temperature is 3° above freezing point, and the wet snow forms a bad road. Could not get on at all; halted, unpacked, and loaded to 300lbs. This was nearly as bad. Took everything off the sledge except the cooking gear. At 10a.m. Thomas Stubbs came to me very ill, and I was obliged to excuse him from the drag ropes. Shortly after, the Sergeant became out of breath, and too weak to go on, so I sent him back ready for the second load. After taking a spell, finding Ayles and I could get on quicker ourselves, I sent them all back, while he and I dragged the sledge and tramped down a road. Halted, unpacked, and back for the remainder of the gear, which came up slowly but surely. Got along tolerably for half an hour, then came to a dead stop. Canted sledge on to the medical box, and scraped the runners, which in some places had as much as three inches thickness of ice on them underneath, which assisted in enlarging the tremendous cakes of snow the sledge forced before it. A second time we did this, and at the end of an hour we had advanced just ten yards. I ought to put Stubbs on the sledge, the Sergeant ought to be put there too, but there is not enough strength left to drag them. Came across numerous deep places which cost us much trouble to get

223

through. After lunch Stubbs and Mann both gave in, leaving five of us on the drag ropes, Ayles and I becoming permanent leading men. We had the tent pitched by the time the sick arrived. Gums very tender, which prevents the allowance of biscuit being eaten. It will be observed that it is the blue jackets who stick it out – the marine, shipwright, and the blacksmith being disabled.

June 11th. Poor Stubbs requires all his courage and endurance. Several times as we went on, Ayles and I sank nearly up to our hips. We are looking forward to news from the ship as we draw near our depot – something to give us a change to the conversation, which tumbles into the same groove pretty well every night. Read the Morning Service. Travelling very hard, which brought us abreast the Cape Colan Depot all fagged out. I walked up to it while the tent was being pitched, with the intention of getting the letters, et cetera, but found Lt Gifford had erected such a magnificent structure, that I could make but little impression on it, and contented myself with his note, which I found attached to the staff. There were several hare tracks around the cairn. Good is thoroughly knocked up again and can eat nothing. Made good five miles.

June 12th. Left the invalids in the tent. Remainder of us up to the depot, everything in order except the lime-juice jar broken in the neck. Fortunately none of the contents were spilt. Read the news to the crew. All hands glad to hear *Discovery* was all right, and communication established. Their success with the musk oxen caused our mouths to water. We are feeling the heavy load very much, the sledge is heavier by 400lbs, which with the contents, brings up the total to 1,000lbs or 200lbs per man. Breakfasted off 6lbs of preserved meat which had been forwarded to the depot, everyone relished the change, and ate well. A heavy fall of snow, and a dense fog puts an end to my only chance of getting down the inlet. Took the collapsible boat off the sledge, fitted her with drag ropes, and with a light load gave her in charge of three worst invalids, who managed to keep together and get along slowly, but causing us to lose much time by waiting for them. Got on fairly till eight o'clock, when Good nearly fainted. There appears to be utter inability to get breath, no pain and no difficulty to speak of in breathing when at rest. The least exertion brings it on. I am half afraid we shall not get on-board without assistance, for which Ayles or myself will have to walk in, an entirely lost day, one way and another. Made good a mile and a half. Notwithstanding the sickness, the consumption of food to-day has been very large.

June 14th. Made good way until within a mile of Sail Harbour, when we came into the most villainous snow, which caused nothing but standing hauls. In this our comfort greatly depended on keeping way on the sledge, and our struggles to do so would have been ludicrous to anyone not engaged in them. Ayles and I leading, often got in nearly to our middles, we could not afford to stop hauling, which we continued on hands and knees, until we got on to a firmer footing, or came to a helpless standstill. For us it was bad enough, but when the other three went in, separately or altogether, they had hardly time to throw themselves clear of the runners.

June 15th. Adam Ayles not very well to-day, the effects of being trodden on by an invalid in getting out of the tent last night. I could ill afford to lose his services. Mann and Stubbs no worse. After reaching Sail Harbour we got on but with a little trouble, being delayed only by the sick lagging behind.

Waiting as we had to do in thick fog, and with a cold east wind, was not comfortable after the violent perspiration brought about by our exertions.

Under way at eight to cross the Parry Peninsula, but found the hill too steep for the small amount of strength we could command. The strongest of us carried the gear up.

June 17th. Joseph Good and Doidge are at the drag-ropes, but not pulling an ounce, they are very plucky, but utterly unable to do anything. Despatched the invalids ahead – it is dreary work, such constant waiting. Not being able to leave the sledge, I cannot go on to see the road. I hope we shall come out all right, but to me the route is new, and whether Gifford tried it or not I do not know. Had we but one invalid, or perhaps two, we could put them on the sledge, as it is they must walk, or give in altogether, in which case I must send Ayles on from View Point Depot, trusting in his intelligence, strength, and endurance to reach the ship and ask for assistance. When I spoke to him on the subject, he expressed his readiness to start, and I have every confidence in the man. He has been with me both in the autumn and spring, and I cannot speak too highly of him. Having the blessing of health, his assistance to me throughout has been invaluable; and the anything but cheering circumstances in which we are placed enables me fully to appreciate. I keep an anxious look-out on the weather, dreading the thaw which must shortly set in, and which will soon render the route between View Point and the ship very bad if not impassable.

June 18th. Read the Morning Service. Rejoicing in a cold morning, but it is thick and inclined to snow. It is fortunate I walked ahead last night, as we followed the tracks. James Doidge collapsed soon after starting, and having brought him to, with a strong dose of sal volatile, left him to come on with the others, while Good, Mitchell, Ayles and I marched on with the sledge, poor Good complaining bitterly we were going too fast and Mitchell scarcely able to put one foot before the other. The crew showed such evident signs of giving way to their ever-increasing sickness, and that before we could reach View Point, I took Good on one side, and told them they must all try their hand at dragging again. I explained the actual necessity there was for reaching our next depot, and that, failing to meet anyone there, I should communicate with the ship. To further impress this on the men, I loaded the collapsible boat to 130lbs, and absented myself with it from the party for over an hour, leaving them to follow. I was able to do this without getting far away, as the fog was very dense. I returned to the sledge, and found

225

them hauling five or six yards at a time, and then halting for breath. The poor fellows were all struggling, and fully alive to the effort they had to make. Nothing could exceed the patience and endurance they showed; And I fell in with them, and we reached the boat and camped, the whole of them, except Ayles, thoroughly done up. Under these circumstances pitching the tent and cooking comes heavy. We divided these duties keeping to the usual turns for cooking as often as possible for the proper man to take it; but the cuisine suffered. Made good three miles (overland).

June 20th. Travelling most excellent, fortunately, and the ravine taking us down, so as to admit of the sledge following with the least possible strain on the drag belts. As the Sergeant was exceedingly ill, and I did not like the look of him at all, we put him on the sledge. I walked on with the boat well loaded. Mitchell, Good, Doidge and Ayles came with the sledge. On coming to a little bit of level travelling, which required more strain on the drag-ropes, I got the Sergeant down, and supported him along while I dragged the boat at the same time. There was nothing for it but to go on very slowly, waiting as they required, and urging on for the depot and ship news; but the fact of getting the latter does not raise their spirits, although the actual fact of getting it has been more or less talked about all the homeward journey.

At seven came to View Point. Observed a staff placed in the snow by Dr Moss, which gave us the intelligence that the Commander's party had passed but no particulars, the latter being left farther on at the depot. We were glad to hear of their safe return, but sorry they were before us, as we had half hoped to have met with some assistance from them. As events have become subsequently known, we should not have benefited one another by meeting. Little by little we crept on, but every moment made our inability to go on for the ship without assistance the more apparent. There is a silver lining to every cloud and never did one appear so welcome as that which came in the form of a shout from the hill above View Point and the discharge of a gun. It turned out to be William Malley, and what he thought of my proceedings I don't know, for on my yell of Challenger I disappeared back among the hummocks and returned to the sledge party. My news was received with a shout by the crew, and thinking it might be a shooting party, I promised them a hare supper. I then left them to pitch the tent, and walked in towards the shore. As I neared it, among the hummocks, I met Lt May and Malley. On learning that they had been despatched to our assistance by Captain Nares, on his seeing the condition of the Northern Party when they returned, the relief to my mind I cannot describe. All the difficulties seemed to vanish; and the very sight of the fine healthy and clean appearance of our visitors led me to look for a much more rapid and comfortable return on-board than I have thought about for weeks. I accompanied May to his tent at the depot, while Malley went out to the men to lend them a hand in pitching their tent and cooking. As soon as possible we sent off Thornbeck with medical comforts for their supper; and I cautioned both him and Malley about saying anything of the deaths which had occurred during our absence fearing the effect it might have on the men.

I was truly distressed to hear of the deaths of dear George Porter and Petersen; and I congratulated myself, and felt deeply grateful, that we had arrived with all hands alive, if not well. Having arranged with May to send two hands to help us along in the morning, and that the depot should be demolished, as a pre-concerted signal to the Captain, I returned to my tent, and found the social barometer had risen several inches; but I heard afterwards that Malley was received with tears.

June 21st. Under way at 9.45. The dog-sled brought on the invalids by relays, two at a time. This plan was continued until we reached the ship. As I feared inaction for the sick, I constantly made them do some walking. The only exception I made to this rule was in the case of the Sergeant, whom we kept permanently on the Challenger. Camped at 9.30p.m. Reaction had set in and the excitement of yesterday has given way to greater weakness and lowness of spirits. Regaled the crew with two pots of oysters, apple jelly and egg flips, much to their satisfaction. Ayles has shown his first sign of weakness of limb to-day; strength of will remains as before, his knee rather swollen and stiff. Made good eight miles. As I did not want my men to hear of poor Porter's death, and his grave was a short distance ahead on the floe, I sent Self on with the ostensible object of carrying the five-man baggage ahead first, but really to remove the cross which marked the spot. This he did, and returned to go on with the same work as yesterday, advancing the sick two at a time. Directed Self to replace the cross over the grave, which was accordingly done.

June 22nd. Arrived at Cape Richardson, and were welcomed by Lt Parr and Captain Feilden to their tent; they cooked for us, and gave us what we had not tasted for many long days – hare and geese. We all ate heartily of this fare, which with the port wine, made the invalids different men. The travelling has been heavy, 'one, two, three haul!' pretty constantly, and snow soft and sludgy, above the knee in places.

Sunday, June 25th. Trudged through sludge and pools of water, very hard travelling. Self had a difficult day and the last of the invalids did not reach the tent till two hours after us. No fainting to-day, but the Sergeant is very, very weak indeed, and there is no visible improvement in the others. Ayles is better, but evidently touched with the malady. The travelling is worsening, as we come to many places where the snow looks sound enough, but in which we sink down till we come to water underneath. As we were now only six miles from the ship, and we had good reason to expect good travelling, we rested for three hours and I served out the remainder of the comforts, which was sufficient to give all the sick a very fair meal. We then hauled the sledges over the land. On reaching the next bay we found to our dismay that the travelling was extremely bad, deep soft snow, water in places, and sludge, through which we had great difficulty with both sledges, the dogs being afraid of water and useless in the deep snow. It was becoming apparent we would have to camp out another night, much to the disappointment of the invalids, when we sighted the sledge in the distance. This turned out to be a volunteer party of officers and men, with Captain Nares and Commander Markham, who hurried us on. We reached the ship just after midnight, amid the cheers and congratulations of our shipmates.

Captain Nares's reaction to these events:

The return of the travellers to the *Alert* so completely broken down in health naturally caused me much anxiety. Out of 53 men on-board, 27 were under treatment for decided scurvy, four others were slightly affected, and eight had only lately recovered; five men were in a doubtful state of health from the same or other causes, leaving only nine who in addition to the officers could be depended on for hard work.

George Porter is dead, and we have no idea if Lt Beaumont's party is as badly affected with scurvy as Markham's or Aldrich's. Our great desire was to endeavour to obtain fresh meat for the invalids, and the officers diligently scoured the neighbourhood in the hopes of securing game. A small amount of mutton which had remained frozen in the rigging during the winter had fortunately been saved; this, with the birds obtained from time to time, enabled Dr Colan to give the scurvy-stricken patients a fair change of diet, on which their health rapidly improved. Although I confidently looked forward to the invalids being speedily restored to health, when I considered the magnitude of the outbreak I felt that it was my first duty to guard against its repetition. Accordingly I determined to give up all further exploration, and to proceed to the southward with both ships as soon as the ice should break up and release us. I was confirmed in this resolution when I considered the results of the spring exploration. Owing to the absence of land to the northward, and the impenetrable character of the Polar pack, it was evident that the ship could not be taken any appreciable distance farther in that direction than the latitude which we had already gained; and also that it was quite impossible to reach the Pole by sledging from any position thus attainable by the ship. The sole result that we could possibly expect to gain by remaining on the shores of the Polar Sea would be an extension of our exploration a few miles farther in an east and west direction. But I could not reasonably hope to advance the travelling parties more than about 50 miles beyond the extreme points already reached, even should the men be fit for extended journeys in the following year. The primary object of the expedition – reaching the North Pole – being thus unattainable, I considered that I was not justified in risking a second winter, which in all human probability would entail loss of life. All engines running freely, the pleasing noise of running water, with the occasional call of a bird, which has now taken the place of the winter silence is most agreeable and we linger in the ravines purposely to listen to the welcome sound. Great rejoicing this morning – Parr having shot three musk oxen.

Poor Bruin, the dog that has performed such good work in dragging freshwater ice to the ship from the quarry was to-day found drowned, having probably fallen into the water in a fit. Our invalids are improving fast; there are now only 22 under Dr Colan's care, nearly all are confined to bed.

At this stage, the *Alert* had been surrounded by the icepack for almost eleven months. Captain Nares was most anxious that all would be in readiness to facilitate a fast getaway to open water when he considered the time was right:

July 20th. A southwest gale is blowing and has driven the pack off shore, the water channel reaching to Cape Sheridan, whence a crack extends two or three miles in the direction of Cape Joseph Henry. In consequence of a slight movement in the ice, the ship became upright once more. The last of the stores have been embarked from the shore, and we are ready to start south at a few hours notice. Mr Wooton is naturally anxious to try the engines after their having been dismantled during the winter. I trust that everything will be correct when the order is given to start. To-day Parr exploded a 43lb jar of gunpowder under a heavy piece of ice closing our door of exit through the ice barrier. The effect was very great, and proves that we can make our escape at pleasure when the outer ice eases off; always provided no new floe bergs become stranded. As gunpowder only explodes upwards, guncotton is a far more effective auxiliary in ice navigation. It is now stated that there is no danger in carrying it to cold climates or in permitting it to become frozen.

July 30th. Our gateway through the floe berg barrier has been enlarged to the widest dimension advisable, and several large charges of powder are ready for a final discharge as soon as the pack gives us an opportunity to start. It is certain that we can only escape when a strong south-west wind blows the ice away from the shore. As that will be a foul wind for us in Robeson Channel, the ship has been made snug aloft, ready for steaming into the wind. No sailing ship could ever get to the southward from this position. At this time I had but slight anxiety concerning the health of the men who were exploring the northern coast of Greenland, fully expecting Lt Beaumont to obtain enough game to insure his party from attack of scurvy. The number of musk oxen procured by the crew of the *Polaris* in Hall Land was sufficient to justify this expectation.

Chapter XIX

Beaumont's Journey
to Greenland

On the morning of 20 April the temperature was -8°, with light snow falling sufficiently strong to collect in the sheltered places. The activity on the ship and on the ice around it was frenetic as the third and final sledge party of the expedition prepared to leave.

Below deck, in his hammock lay the critically ill and forlorn Neil Petersen. One can only imagine his sense of loss and utter helplessness as, for the second time in a week, he had to listen to the sounds of his excited shipmates as they carried out their preparations. Jim Hand was only one in a long line of men bidding him goodbye and wishing him well. Jim must have wondered would they ever see each other again – they didn't; Neil Petersen, who died on 14 May, was to become the first fatality of the expedition. The heroic figure of so many extraordinary expeditions, he had entered the pantheon of Arctic history.

Four sledges weighted to 218lbs a man were fitted out with provisions for fifty-six days, together with two eight-man sledges manned by seven men each, and two five-man sledges manned by three men. The sledges were christened the Sir Edward Parry, Discovery, Stephenson, and Alert.

Along with Jim Hand on Parry were Alex Gray (sledge captain), William Jenkins, Wilson Dobing, Charles Paul, Peter Craig, and Frank Jones. There was not quite the fanfare that had accompanied the departure of Markham and Aldrich, but nevertheless the men must have experienced a great sense of excitement and anticipation as they set out for the great unknown.

The men in harness, dragging their sledges, started at 7p.m. for the north coast of Greenland; picking up provisions at Cape Rawson, where they had been carried by sledge and laid down by the crews of the *Alert* while exercising preparatory to the North Pole sledgers starting their journeys. Lt Beaumont had no map of the Greenland interior. None existed. There was nothing to draw, just millions of acres of ancient ice sculpted by the wind. And they were

A sledge party from the *Alert* making a push for the Pole. (*Illustrated London News*, 4 November 1876.)

facing temperatures that defied any form of existence anywhere.

A brief review of Captain Nares's plans for the expedition show that he had despatched Markham directly for the North Pole. Aldrich had gone north-west on Ellesmere Island, while Beaumont was to go north-east on the Greenland coast. We know that Beaumont, immediately prior to leaving the *Alert*, was making preparations and provisions for 1877, which would indicate that Nares was prepared to be patient in seeking and completing his successful mission. If his three-prong attack was unsuccessful for whatever unforeseen reason in 1876, the *Pandora* under Captain Sir Allen Young and carrying fresh supplies would enable the ships to spend another winter in the Arctic prior to making a final and successful attempt to reach the Pole.

In 1875 Sir Allen was about to sail on another expedition to the Arctic seeking answers to the many remaining unanswered questions of Franklin's disappearance. But he was prevailed upon by the British Admiralty to track the Nares Expedition by seeking the cairns erected by Nares that would give details of his progress and whereabouts, and if necessary his need for a rendezvous with supplies. Lt Beaumont reported:

We started early in the morning of the 20th of April for Repulse Harbour, on the Greenland coast. The weather is extremely cold minus 40° to minus 30°. Thanks to the road made on the orders of Captain Nares, the passage of the fringe of shore hummocks at Black Cape was made in safety by the heavy sledges; one five-man sledge, however, broke down, forced a return to the *Alert* for it to be exchanged. The men are having difficulty sleeping due to fatigue and cold, their mood was not helped when the stew-pan was rendered useless on the fourth day out by the melting of the solder of the central funnel. We have also discovered in Arctic weather lamp trimming is the secret of successful and economical cooking.

The line between Black Cape and Repulse Harbour led us in a south-easterly direction, and was crossed by many bands of heavy hummocks, necessitating a good deal of road-making for the heavy sledges, and great care in the management of the five-man sledges, which are hardly calculated to stand such rough work. The entrance to Repulse Harbour is a mass of hummock ridges with small floes between them to within 200 yards of the shore, then you come to a solid barrier of immense floe bergs over which we had to find a way. This took half a day of road-cutting and bridge-making, for such large masses have wide gaps between them; our only consolation for the delay was the thought that it would be a lasting work, and might prove useful to others. The men by this time were becoming skilful road-makers, and the officers practised engineers. The tents pitched, the provisions were re-distributed amongst the three remaining sledges, a cairn built, and a site selected for the depot to be left for our return journey. Having written a letter to Captain Nares of our progress to that date, I despatched George Emmerson on his way back to the *Alert*.

On the 27th of April we started northward, having secured in the depot a few things of which we were not in want, to lighten as much as possible the now very heavy sledges. Our way led us round the harbour, which is two and-a-half miles broad and at present only half a mile deep; but if this is the Repulse Harbour of the Americans, it is no wonder that from a distance it appeared to them a desirable place of refuge; the background of the hills gives it the appearance of a large bay, nearly three miles deep, with two islands in it, the remainder of the land between the hills and the sea so flat and low as scarcely to be distinguished from the floe. No doubt it is an old harbour, and even now, some considerable distance in, the land is covered with ice. A wide and deep valley on the same level runs from the north-east corner of this dry bay. On the 28th we passed the farthest point reached by Lt Rawson in his flying visit a few days before. He certainly was justified, so far as he saw, in making a favourable report of the travelling, but another six miles would have told a different tale, for it was not until the second day that our difficulties commenced. Early in the journey we came to a point covered so deeply with drift snow that it almost rose to the level of the huge hummock mass forced on the end of the point. This drift, like all accumulations of snow which the wind makes on meeting with an obstacle left a deep and precipitous gap between it and the hummock, and our only way past was to climb the snow-hill. It was so steep and slippery that the eight-man sledge had to be partly unloaded, and then each sledge hauled over separately by all hands. This point we named Drift Point. The next point was very much the same as Drift Point, and the slopes continued for some distance beyond. We had to double man the sledges to get on at all, and even then our progress was very slow. To prevent losing ground and to clear what we took to calling the drift-pits, which existed in a greater or less degree round every hummock, we had to keep dragging up-hill as well as forward, and thus, making a great deal of leeway, the sledges were hauled along by degrees.

Next journey we started on a more level road, and hoped to make a better march, but we soon came to another point worse than either of the other two. The slope, which continued for another two miles, was so steep that it was impossible to stand on it, while towards the end of it became almost perpendicular. At the foot of this slope was a tortuous and intricate passage along and inside the hummocks, full of deep holes and covered with thick snow. The work of getting through this promised to be endless, and it was impossible to say what was beyond, so I sent Lt Rawson, accompanied by Dr Coppinger, to report on the road; in the meantime we commenced to cut through all obstacles. They returned in about two hours to say that, after two miles of a road that got worse and worse, they came to a cliff that went sheer down into the tidal-crack and which it would be impossible to pass without going out on to the ice. It had been impressed upon me that the object of keeping to the land on the outward journey was to prevent leaving an impassable barrier in the rear, which supposing the ice to break up before our return, would effectually cut off the retreat of the party. But here was a case in which it was a necessity to depart from the rule. The cliffs extended, as far as could be judged, for about four miles, and must be passed by the ice or not at all. It was too late to depend on boats being sent to meet us, so we trusted that the ice would remain and befriend us. As we had to take to the ice we took advantage of the good floes that lay in our direction, and struck the land again some distance beyond the cliffs, which in consequence of a remarkable black rock like a horn projecting from one part, we called the Black Horn Cliffs. The next three journeys were spent in crawling along the sides of the never-ending snow-slopes, sometimes halting for hours, while as many as could be employed were cutting a road in the hard, slippery snow, wide enough for the whole breadth of the sledge. The angle of these slopes – carefully taken with a clinometer by Dr Coppinger – showed that they varied from 20° to 24°. If the snow was hard it was impossible to stand on this latter incline, and here broad roads had to be cut. So direct and heavy was the pressure from the outside on some parts of these slopes that the floe bergs were forced right up on them, and left us nothing but the steep talus of the cliff by which we pass. Comfort, with our sleeping bags and tent robes frozen so hard as to resemble sheet-iron more than woollen substances, was quite out of the question. The very appearance of our coverlet, when passed into the tent was sufficient to banish all ideas of comfort or sleep.

Captain Nares, who had experienced something similar in his career, spoke of it with feeling:

> Very few can possibly realise the utter wretchedness endured by young men in their full health and strength, and full of life, when imprisoned in a heavy gale of wind within a small light tent made of no thicker material than an ordinary cricketing tent … compelled to remain lying down at full length cramped up in a compacted space between 28 to 32 inches across for yourself and your companion for one, two or even three consecutive days; packed in order to save space, heads and tails alternatively like preserved sardines. Inside the tightly closed blanket bag it is too dark to read and woe betide anyone who leaves the mouth of that tent open, for the whole interior of the tent is filled with snow drift.

Their clothes thawed, saturating the sleeping bags which then froze when packed back on the sledges, thereby increasing the weight of the load and making their next night more uncomfortable still. Each man had a double blanketed sleeping bag (of 1874 manufacture) and a pair of fur moccasins for sleeping in. The naval issue boots did not fit swollen or frost-injured feet. When sledging the men wrapped their feet in strips of blanket over which they wore moccasins. With the sole exception of those strips of blanket they had no other change of clothing, no matter how wet or frozen they became in the Arctic conditions. The sledging day lasted eight to ten hours. Depending on the size of a sledge party, a large group of eight, ten, or twelve would use their tent while a smaller team of under seven men would build a snow edifice to sleep in, a most disagreeable part of the day.

The commander arranged the schedule depending on the conditions; they travelled through the night when temperatures were lowest, which also reduced the risk of snow blindness.

Rising at 5p.m., at the commencement of a journey the men were obliged to keep moving about to prevent their feet being frostbitten. Breakfast at 6p.m. consisted of cocoa or tea and biscuit. After breakfast came the struggle to get into the now frozen boots. The sledge was packed and made ready for the days work. Harnesses were donned at 8p.m.

Frozen buffets were at midnight. Lunch was of short duration and consisted of hard frozen pemmican, biscuits and a tot of rum. These halts were most disagreeable for sledge parties. In freezing temperatures, waiting while water boiled always seemed to take an eternity. There was no shelter or seating, the men swinging their arms and stamping their feet to increase circulation, whilst they got through a few mouthfuls of almost frozen food as dexterously as they could, hampered by heavy gloves or mitts. Their feet were numbed after hauling for several hours sometimes through slush and ice-cold water. Their upper garments became frozen from the constant splashing or were saturated by rain or mist. When those conditions prevailed the sledgers suffered indescribable misery. Looking back, it is difficult to imagine how these men coped in those awful conditions. In extreme conditions they erected a makeshift shelter with a sail for protection and rested their weary bones by sitting on the sledges. The drop of grog allowance constituted the only enjoyable short period of these nightly buffets. Supper consisted of four ounces of pemmican, half an ounce of tea, two-thirds of an ounce of sugar and two biscuits.

Dr Coppinger had orders to proceed with Lt Beaumont until 5 June, but in early May the party encountered a series of delays while they cut into a long extent of road. Beaumont decided nothing could be gained by Dr Coppinger waiting around until they finished. It was agreed he should return to the ship but also that he would monitor Beaumont's impending return to the Polaris Bay Depot. Dr Coppinger handed over all the provisions he could spare and set out for the *Alert*.

Lt Beaumont, in preparation for the return journey, laid down a substantial supply depot of 120 rations or ten days' rations for twelve men, and continued the difficult task of cutting through the ice. Beaumont's narrative continued:

Not only was the travelling of the slopes very slow, but both men and sledges suffered from it. The work was unusually hard and the strain on the ankles caused them to swell and become stiff; the heavily loaded sledges, from continually resting on one runner, bent it inwards and in the case of the five-man sledge, not only exhausted the supply of uprights, but eventually proved the ruin of the entire runner. The five-man sledges are not built for these unforeseen conditions; many hummocks are the size of two-storey houses, three and four men in a five-man sledge cannot keep up. Great care was required in the management of five-man sledges. It was decided the eight-man sledge would take the five-man in tow to avoid risk of damage to the five-man sledge (no sledge replacements would be available). However, the end was near at hand and on the morning of May 5th. We encamped at Cape Stanton, which would have been in sight the whole time had not the weather been densely thick. Our next start was made in high spirits, the slopes were passed, the sun shone once more, and a wide bay lay before us, though it was infinitely better than what we had had, still soft snow made our distances travelled very short.

It was at the end of this journey, May 6th, that J.J. Hand, one of my sledge crew, told me in answer to my inquiry as to why he was walking lame, that his legs were becoming very stiff. I suggested he use some liniment; he told me later the liniment made him feel better, but the relief was only temporary. I asked him had he spoken to Dr Coppinger about the symptoms. Dr Coppinger attributed the stiffness and soreness to several falls that he had had, they both agreed it might just wear off. Dr Coppinger did not pay much credence to Jim Hand's symptoms. Now however, there was pain as well as stiffness in his joints – and both were severe and increasing.

Lt Beaumont was busy carrying out his orders, charting the coast and christening the various geographical locations:

In our next journey we passed another fine bay. I observed here also that from Cape Stanton the shore had been lined with floebergs of great size, particularly at this bay, which I called Franklin Bay. This aspect of the country promised better travelling, and I was anxious to push on; but as usual more hurry less speed, for after crossing Franklin Bay, and dragging the sledges over a hill 150 feet high – the only practicable route – both Lt Rawson and myself came reluctantly to the conclusion that the men were very much done, and required a day's rest; as we had been dragging ourselves all the time, we were better able to judge of their feelings. J.J. Hand, who had thought himself better at starting, was now quite lame; so we camped, determined to wait for a day, in the hope that the rest would restore both the lame and the tired. We had to travel through fresh snow two and a half feet deep in harness, which made the task of lifting your foot out of each hole physically exhausting. It was too much for Hand in his deteriorating condition. It had become too plain to be misunderstood: stiffness, pain, sore and inflamed gums, loss of appetite – all pointed too clearly to scurvy.

On coming into camp I examined Hand's legs, and from his description of the stiffness and pain I suspected scurvy. I had no reason to expect it, indeed I had never thought of it, but the striking resemblance of the symptoms to the ones described in the voyage of McClintock's *Fox*, as being those of Lt Hobson, who suffered severely from scurvy, suggested it to my mind; and my suspicions were confirmed by Gray, my ice quartermaster, who in his whaling experience has seen much of it. He, however led me to believe at the same time, that it would probably wear off. Thus from the 7th until the 10th I waited, hoping that his words might prove true.

It seems odd that when one of his crew members on the *Discovery* had been

Hand Bay.

afflicted with scurvy in January, that Lt Beaumont had no reason to suspect it, or had never thought of it, as the symptoms would have been similar. (An excellent overview on the disease is given in 'A Paper on Scurvy by Dr Donnet and Dr Frazer, which can be read in Fergus Fleming's *Ninety Degrees North*.)

On the 10th of May, Lt Beaumont ascended Mount Wyatt 2,050 feet called after Lt Wyatt Rawson; all to the eastward was smooth and level, while to the westward lay the Polar pack, with its flows and hummocks. I was very reluctant to order Lt Rawson to return; it was like sending back half the party; it would be, I felt a great disappointment as the loss of his advice and assistance would be considerable; but on the 10th of May it was arranged Lt Rawson should take Hand back, deciding on his arrival at Repulse Harbour, whether to cross over to the *Alert* or go on to Hall's Polaris Bay Depot.

I at the same time called upon the remainder of my men to say honestly if they suspected themselves to be suffering from the same disease, or could they detect any of its symptoms, as in that case it would be better for the party to advance in reduced numbers than to be charged with the care of sick men. I did this because two of them had complained of stiff legs after the hard work on the snow-slopes; but they all declared themselves to be now perfectly well, and most anxious to go on. I did not take one of Lt Rawson's men to fill up my crew, for I feared that the time might come when he would have to carry Hand, and I suspected that George Bryant, the captain of the sledge, was already affected with the same

237

disease. Thus it was that early on the 11th of May Lt Rawson left me, much to my regret, he making the best of his way back, whilst I continued to advance with six men. I was glad for Rawson's sake that he had obtained a good view of this unknown country.

The next Cape and Bay Lt Beaumont encountered, he named Cape Bryant and Hand Bay, after George Bryant and Jim Hand, the two stricken scurvy victims.

Chapter XX

Jim Hand's Final March

On 11 May the party set out on their return journey. With Lt Rawson were George Bryant, Michael Regan, Elijah Rayner, and Jim Hand. They had only travelled a short distance when it became more evident that George Bryant was a victim of scurvy. This was a most unwelcome turn of events. Lt Rawson's naval discipline demanded a daily record or log. His narrative noted:

> Saturday May 13th. Don harness, temperatures are rising. Hand very done, spread a sail and gave him a knapsack for a pillow and he slept a little. I climbed a high peak 1,500 to 2,000 feet which I called after Egerton. I got a very good round of angles. Started down, reached East Cape of Hand Bay, made good four and a half miles. It was a warm day, no duffles or coverlet on. We had bread dust pemmican to-night which Hand seems to be able to eat better than the ordinary stuff as he say it does not taste so greasy. Apart from his legs being black and blue and a red rash around the calves, he cannot eat any biscuit unless it is soaked in tea or cocoa as his gums teeth are very sore.

Jim Hand was now, in medical terms, the classic case of a patient in the advanced stage of scurvy affliction, when the skin grows sallow and takes on a leaden hue and the countenance becomes bloated. A general debility and apathy of manner is noticed. The patient becomes feeble in the knees, ankles and wrists which are swollen, rigidity is observed in his hams, for which a predilection seems to exist in the case of men engaged in exercise. In this appalling state of health Jim Hand continued on what would be his death march.

The party retraced their sledge route on reduced rations. Needless to say Jim Hand's condition continued to deteriorate under the strain of dragging the sledge, and his body began to decay, both on inside and from the numerous sores on his body. His gums became swollen and spongy and his breath fetid; his shipmates found the smell uncomfortable when close to him. He was afflicted with flying pains resembling rheumatism which attacked various parts of his body. The sledge team struggled manfully against the elements. Soft fresh snow about eighteen inches deep made travelling most difficult and strength-sapping. George Bryant also began to show increasing symptoms of scurvy. Now there were two of the sledge crew weakening and not really able to pull their full weight. The conditions continued to worsen, with heavy falls of soft snow each day accompanied by heavy and freezing fog. Lt Rawson's narrative continued:

Hand was unable to pull, was reduced to walking, and through shortage of breath he was unable to keep up with the pace, which sometimes left him far behind. When we stopped for lunch he would catch up with us, he suffered a great deal to-day in the legs, and has a cough that troubles him a great deal, and makes his breathing very short, he tries to be as cheerful as he can, and never complains. My men do all in their power to cheer him. Bryant is now unable to share the load, thus we are reduced to hauling a heavy sledge with only three men.

Sunday May 14th. 7.30p.m. Breakfast and preparations, donned harness 10.20p. m., started across the flow; not bearing and most of hand-over-hand or 'one, two, three, haul'; Bryant is stiffer than ever. It is a cloudy day with no sun. Pitched for lunch on the flow in Hand Bay. We have not made more than three-quarters of a mile this march. Let Hand have half a pipe before starting. Bryant's legs are as stiff as pokers; and he is very little use along these slopes but he tries his level best.

I am sorry to say we have no pickaxe, as we gave ours to Emmerson who had lost his down a ravine, so now we will have to use our pemmican chopper to make a road with, took to the floe (or rather hummocks) and by dint of much hauling, tumbling, and the use of the pemmican chopper (which we could not have done without) made only one and a half miles to day. Temperature +10°.

J.J. Hand very sick, giddy and he has got the shivers, vomits his cocoa, he is scarcely able to crawl, he craves lime juice. He talks a great deal of what he will eat when he gets home, and constantly talks of vegetables.

May 19th. J.J. can only walk about five yards without resting. He has been carried on the sledge part of the way.

Not being able to pull he walks between the drag ropes, legs very stiff. Nausea, very thirsty, continues to eat his pemmican. He cannot eat biscuit unless soaked as his gums are very sore, he has a cough which troubles him and his breathing is very short, the least exertion makes him perspire; he cannot walk more than 30 yards without lying down for a five or ten minute rest. He stuck out very pluckily, it will soon be a case of carrying Hand I am afraid; but that I want to put off as long as possible, but we should not make a mile a day if we waited for him, Bryant is no better so there are only three of us who can pull. Hand seems to suffer a great deal of pain, and seems to have a strong craving for lime juice. I only wish I had a ton of it to give him.

May 21ˢᵗ. J.J. Hand is always carried on the sledge, is very low, groans a great deal, face very swollen, hardly eats any pemmican, he is in low spirits, he indulges in the gloomiest of ideas, the fetidness of breath is intolerable; his gums protrude as spongy masses from his mouth, his teeth became loose in their sockets, and frequently fall out.

Carrying Hand, we had to go through some heavy snow, shade +18°, made good five and a half miles in nine and a half hours. Arrived at Repulse Harbour, visited the cairn, a letter from Egerton. Coppinger has gone to Polaris Bay to see if there are any cracks in the Robeson Channel. I intend to follow him to Thank God Harbour. I am glad to see they have left my pickaxe and some gold leaf tobacco, also a five-man sledge runner, a thing we are greatly in need of as one of our runners has been very shaky lately since we have had to carry Hand who is a big man. I also collected 20 rations (without rum), four rocket staffs and a saw. Left a letter for Beaumont.

9.15p.m. Donned harness, started, a very thick cloudy day and snowing, I expect we will have very tough work along here. Rayner's eyes are very sore from snow-blindness, mine are also beginning to trouble me. This thick dull weather is very trying on one's sight. We all look a dirty unwashed and unshaven crowd. Reached Gap Valley, Rayner's and my eyes are both bad, so we each had a drop of wine of opium in them, or as the men call it a drop of 'open eye'. Only those who have not undergone this operation can fully appreciate it. We do look a miserable set. Raynor's left leg is also giving him trouble.

Sunday May 22ⁿᵈ. Made good three and a half miles in seven hours forty minutes, I can't see to write more.

A week later, Lt Rawson's vision was impaired. He was unable to write without great difficulty and for that week his diary simply records the weather, temperatures, and climatic changes:

I have been blindfolded on account of my eyes. I have been stumbling about in the most absurd manner. Our travelling has been very rough, particularly on Hand on the sledge and he seems rather down on his luck and seems not to care what becomes of him. Weather blowing hard from the north with a great deal of drift. My eyes are still too bad to take any angles, but the travelling is by far the best we have ever had. Hoisted a sail on the sledge; it helped us a great deal as the top of the ice is perfectly hard, and I don't wonder at the former expeditions travelling 20 or 30 miles a day if they had ice like this and a healthy crew.

Saw the sun to-day which is a very unusual event. Made good 10 miles in nine and a half hours Temperature +10°. A beautiful day, made sail, saw a snow bunting.

There are thousands of seashells on the land, two or three species I got from a height of about 300ft above sea level. I am glad to say both Rayner's and my eyes are serene again.

Sunday May 29th. Donned harness, snowing hard again to-day, so thick that you can't see above a 100 yards. George Bryant has hardly been able to keep up with us to-day. Hand still on the sledge, his teeth are beginning to fall out, two fell out this morning. Snowing hard again and fog is as thick as pea soup, it makes the work very hard. I have decided on depoting all the gear I can here, as this heavy snow makes hauling very hard and I am afraid Rayner or Regan may get laid up.

I have left five knapsacks (60lbs), one lower robe (30lbs), Beaumont's spare cooking stove (25lbs), one sextant (12lbs), Boatswain's bag (30lbs), a bag of gear belonging to Hand, one spare tent pole (5 lbs); total 182lbs. Depot is marked by tent pole with a blue comforter as a flag. Temperature is +19° today, melting the snow and making travelling more difficult, all our gear is soaked through and Bryant is rapidly getting worse, he is now at the stage when Hand was only able to crawl and I am afraid we shall have to carry Bryant as well. We have only two more days provisions left; that is counting to-day.

More deep snow, have to bandage Rayner's leg, Bryant in severe pain. All of us suffering from cramp, we felt the want of our coverlet which we depoted the other day. A five-man tent for five good-sized men, two of which are scurvy patients, is rather close stowage. Made good two and a half miles in eight hours. None of us has been able to eat our full allowance of food, which is fortunate, for we are only provisioned up to day, but now we can run on at least two days more. Temperature in tent last night was + 15° which without a coverlet is not pleasant.

May 31st, journey 39. Donned harness, started under sail, Rayner blind in the left eye again. Hand is giddy and breathing very heavy so much so that I thought he was going to choke to-day, he is delirious, he is unable to change his clothes, or reach his footwear, someone must dress him every morning and put him to bed at night, everything has to be done for him.

Our appetites are failing, we still have enough pemmican, biscuit tea and cocoa for another day. The men are all done in but I trust we shall be in Thank God Harbour before long. It is snowing so hard, added to which I am snow-blind entirely in my right eye and partially in my left and have to walk between the guide ropes.

As our provisions will be finished tomorrow at breakfast, and there is no sign of the Polaris Bay Depot, although we are now exactly at the place where the chart marks it, I intend going on with Regan and Rayner tomorrow to try to find the depot and bring back some more provisions.

Friday 2nd June. 6a.m. Blowing hard from the NE, started with Regan and Rayner with a light sledge to bring back provisions but after we had gone 400 yards I saw we could not get even the light sledge through the heavy snow, so we left the sledge and got on top of the raised beach, where we were able to walk better.

At 8a.m. sighted Captain Hall's grave and at 8.30 reached the depot. I found the records in the house. Coppinger and Fulford were up in Petermann Fiord with the dog sleds, but would be back in three or four days; I sincerely wish Coppinger was here to see to my two sick men.

I took from the depot four pounds of pemmican, four pounds of preserved meat and vegetables, four pounds of biscuits, one ham, two gills of rum, and half a pound of lime juice (frozen).

Started back to camp, my eyes have stuck together and had to walk between the two men. Rayner's leg is now black and blue. The day's rest did Bryant much good but had the opposite affect on Hand. We gave them some preserved meat, lime juice, and a little of the rum. I shall be glad to turn my two invalids over to Dr Coppinger.

We are now on our 42nd journey, June 3rd. We are too weak to carry Bryant on the sledge, he can only travel 30 yards without lying down for breath. I have given him the rifle and if he is very far behind we shall have to come back for him with an empty sledge. Had a head wind all day making it rather unpleasant. Pitched for lunch, after over an hour later Bryant came up.

Reached Thank God Harbour at 4p.m. Pitched tent close to the depot. Read prayers. Hand was very bad when we helped him into the tent, his breath came in such short gasps, and he clenched his teeth so tightly that I thought he was going off, his mind wanders now and then.

8.30. Hand seems much worse. He gets hot and cold fits. I don't know if scurvy affects the lungs, but I suspect his were gone altogether. He was unable to eat food but drank a little soup. We covered him over with a sail and one lying as close to him as we can to keep him warm, but when he gets a hot fit he tries to throw everything off.

We have no grog to-night, and will have none now till Beaumont comes back. Hand is much worse, his mind wanders greatly, in his hot fits he breathes 40 times a minute.

11p.m. J.J. Hand is dead. He had a hot fit about five minutes after my last entry, his breathing stopped for so long that I roused the men. I was able to get a little brandy and about 20 drops of sal volatile between his teeth which seemed to revive him a little but he lost his breath again and died at about a quarter to eleven.

Sunday June 4th. We have placed the body of poor Hand in Hall's Depot this morning. I do not intend burying him till after Coppinger has returned, as I wish to know whether it is entirely owing to scurvy as I have never heard of any man dying in so short a time from this cause.

Read the Morning Service. I hope the preserved meat, vegetables, lime juice, and a good rest will pull Bryant through, but he seems to be much worse today and I think he has got a little nervous about himself. We have found an old mattress belonging to the *Polaris* and this we have put in our tent for Bryant.

Monday 8a.m. June 5th. I have picked out a place for Hand's grave close to the grave of Captain Hall; but we have got to get through two feet of snow first, so I don't know yet whether the ground is soft enough in that place to get down. It is blowing hard from the north with a great deal of drift.

3p.m. We have to pick a new place for the grave, as we found it was frozen clay at the first place I chose and so tough that the pick would hardly make a mark in it; but the place we are digging now is much softer. We have been able to dry our sleeping bags and night gear to-day, which is a great comfort, as a wet bag is anything but a warm thing in this weather.

Blowing hard from the north all night and had to turn out twice to re-secure the tent. Wind is falling light, so we were able to continue digging Hand's grave.

Wednesday June 7th. Dr Coppinger, Lt Fulford, Frank Chatel, Hans Hendrik and the dog team turned up from Petermann Fiord. I am sincerely glad we have now a doctor for Bryant. They were very surprised to see us here and to hear our sad news. Dr Coppinger examined the body of J.J. Hand and said it was a clear case of scurvy, he also said Bryant was in a critical state, and Michael Regan also has scurvy.

Chatel, captain of Fulford's sledge, also has scurvy symptoms. Fulford had a seal and several dovekeys which they had shot at Petermann Fiord, so we shall have fresh meat for the sick men. It is coming on to blow again from the north.

Thursday June 8th. Buried Hand. Dr Coppinger conducted the religious service as Hand was an R.C. We have placed stones all around the grave and Dr Coppinger has planted some dwarf willow and saxifrage over it; he intends to cut an inscription on a mahogany table top which is the best thing we can find here for a headstone.

Bryant is very weak, and as the doctor wishes to be near him he is going to sleep in my tent and I am going to sleep in Fulford's.

Bryant, Regan, and Chatel are living off the seal meat. Fulford has given us a week's allowance of rum out of his stock. All the preserved potatoes which he has are to be kept for the scurvy patients.

Chapter XXI

Beaumont's Journey Continued

Lt Rawson had left Lt Beaumont's party on 10 May to return to the ship with J.J. Hand. Lt Beaumont's report on his exploration continued:

On the 11th of May we arrived at the end of the unbroken coastline along which we had hitherto travelled in a north-easterly direction; this must have been our highest northern point reached. Unfortunately, though we twice halted here, each time it snowed heavily, I was unable to get a meridian altitude. With a crew reduced to six and a probability of my not being able to drag, which I had done hitherto, I came to the conclusion that to do good work in the wide field of operations opening before us, we must lighten the sledge at all cost; so here at this point, we left a depot 180lbs of equipment including, a rifle, ammunition, knapsacks and pemmican, and thus lightened we started for Cape Fulford, which is the north extremity of the line of cliffs on the west side of St George's Fiord. The snow varied from two and a half feet to four and a half feet in thickness.

Beaumont described in great detail his efforts to chart as much as was humanly possible under the most difficult conditions, and to reach and climb Mount Hooker. The following is an edited version of his report:

I considered that from its summit I should not only see the islands to the north, but get the best idea of the trend of the mainland; at the same time I felt I could not leave these wide and deep fiords behind me, any one of which might be a through passage. We were advancing without incident when the five-man sledge got jammed. With a great deal of difficulty William Jenkins lashed it together with skin-hide lashings, the only tools were a knife and a snow saw, the same sledge lasted for the whole of the season.

16th May. On our way we passed some most remarkable ice-hills, which from a distance we had taken for islands. Some stood singly, huge masses of solid blue ice rising gently, with rounded outlines, from thirty to forty feet above the floe; others grouped together, looked like a mountainous country in miniature, and formed far too formidable a barrier for us to overcome.

We pushed on, hoping for better things, the travelling had become worse and worse, the snow varied from two and a half to four and a half feet in thickness, and was no longer crisp and dry but of the consistency of moist sugar; walking was most exhausting, one literally had to climb out of the holes made by each foot in succession, the hard crust on the top, which would only just not bear you, as well as the depth of the snow preventing you from pushing forward through it, each leg sank to about three inches above the knee, and the effort of lifting them so high to extricate them from their tight-fitting holes, soon began telling upon the men.

William Jenkins, Peter Craig and Charles Paul are beginning to show scurvy symptoms, and all of us were very tired.

Our next march was made under a hot sun, though snow never less than three feet thick; we were parched with thirst, and obliged to halt every 50 yards to recover breath. The shore for which we were making did not seem more than two miles off, so I went ahead to see if the travelling was better under the cliffs. I got about a mile and-a-half ahead of the sledge in three hours and then I gave it up. I was nearly done; so I hailed them to go to lunch, but would rather have missed three meals than gone back all that distance, so I had a good rest and made a sketch instead; and seeing that the sledge would never reach me that day I started back for them, walking in my tracks. In the meantime the men had been struggling on as best they could, sometimes dragging the sledge on their hands and knees to relieve their aching legs or hauling her ahead with a long rope and standing pulls. When we encamped we had hardly done two miles, and Jones was added to the stiff-legged ones.

May 19th. The men could hardly bend their legs. We tried every kind of expedient. We made a road for the men to walk in, and tracked the sledge. Then we tried a broader one for both sledge and men, but all to no purpose; and at last went back to the usual way, tugged and gasped on, resting at every ten or twelve yards.

Today I decided to return to the *Alert*, after reaching 82°54'N, L.48°33'.

In my journal I find this entry: No one will ever be able to understand what hard work we had during those days, but the following may give some idea of it. When we halted for lunch, two of the men crept on all fours for 200 yards, rather than walk through the terrible snow. But although tired, stiff, and sore, there is not a word of complaint; they are cheerful, hopeful, and determined. Since the 12th of May it is my birthday; but I can safely say I never spent one so before, and I don't want to be wished any happy returns of it. On that march we did not make much more than a mile. Everyone was very tired with the unusual exertions of the last few days, and the work was pain and grief to those with stiff legs. Quite a foot of snow had fallen since we had passed, and it was rotting the old crust beneath, which gave way under the weight of sledge and men, and made the sledge seem a ton weight.

Matters did not look promising at all. I had started across the channel first to see down past Cape Buttress, and after reaching Reef Island the northern shore looked so near that I came to the conclusion that we had better push on, reaching the land, and coast along to Mount Hooker. So we went on for two days, until going back seemed as hard work as going on. Our provisions would compel us to start homeward on the 23rd. We could not do two miles a day, and the men were falling sick. I did not encourage inspection of legs and tried to make them think as little of the stiffness as possible, for I knew the unpleasant truth would soon enough be forced upon us.

We started again on the evening of the 19th and worked away as before; but our progress was ridiculously small and something had to be done; so leaving the sledge we started in two ranks, four a-breast, to make a road to the shore, for the actual dragging was nothing compared to the exertion of making the road. The shore still looked about one mile off; it had looked the same for two days past, and, to our astonishment and dismay, we walked for five hours without reaching it. It was evidently impossible, on a floe so level that there was nothing in sight the size of a brick to estimate the distance of the high and precipitous cliffs in front of us.

I altered my plans and sent the men back to lunch and rest, while Gray and I went on. It took us two hours more to reach the cliffs, and when we did, it was to find the same deep snow reach their very foot; for a hundred yards from the shore the ice was seamed with wide cracks covered by snow, into which the sledge itself might have disappeared. These had water in them, the surface of which was quite fresh, probably due to the glacier which we knew to be close by, though now everything was hidden by a thick fog.

I saw to my great disappointment that we could not make Mount Hooker, and I came to the conclusion it would be useless to advance any farther with the sledge, as turn which way we would, there was the same smooth, treacherous expanse of snow and only two days' provisions, which would not have enabled us to reach any part of the shore; so I went back to the tent after a nine-and-a-half-hour hard march, and found two men, J. Craig and Wm Jenkins, unmistakably scurvy-stricken.

I therefore decided to wait where we were, if necessary, for two days in hopes of being able to ascend a high peak just over the glacier, and from that elevation decide the question of the channel past Mount Buttress, as well as a view of the distant islands. It seemed too cruel to have to turn back after such hard work, without seeing land or seeing anything, and I was pleased and encouraged by the anxiety the men showed to make the end of our expedition more successful. But it was not to be.

May 21st it snowed hard all day; May 22nd the same, and a strict survey of the provisions warned us that we must start homewards. We left on the evening of the 22nd, a mournful and disappointed party. The feeling was shared by all, with two men walking by the drag ropes, and none of the others, Alexander Gray and myself excepted, any better for the long rest. We then pushed on through the thickly falling snow, which had not stopped for an instant.

Just before camping on the 24th a north wind rose, as if by magic the sky cleared, it became a beautiful morning; there lay Mount Hooker once more in sight, distance about 16 miles, from which I believed, we should see everything; it was too tempting, so the men agreeing eagerly, the plan was arranged. Craig and Jenkins were to remain with the tent, provisions, and gear, whilst the remainder, with one robe, bags and five days' provisions, were to make a dash for the mountain; rations were neatly packed, we turned in for a good rest.

When we awoke it was snowing hard, as if it would never stop. Not a word was said, we packed up and started homewards more disappointed than I can say. The weather eventually cleared and one of the highest mountains in the neighbourhood was only six miles off. I determined on one more effort. Alexander Gray and I set off for the mountain; it took us six hours to reach the top; the view was magnificent, elevation 3,700 feet, but I did not see what I wanted.

Lt Beaumont described in detail the many significant geographical landmarks of this panorama; Cape Britannia, Stephenson Land, St George's Bay, St Andrews Bay. His report continued:

The view was so immense that to sketch it would have been the work of a day, rising clouds warned us to descend to the camp, it was blowing fresh with thick snow and fog. After a short rest we once more started, making for Cape Fulford; the gloomy and unfavourable weather had a depressing influence on the men's spirits, who, poor fellows, were already rather desponding, for out of seven only Gray and myself were perfectly free from scorbutic symptoms, while the two first attacked kept up with great difficulty. We arrived at Cape Bryant and camped below the depot.

During the very bad weather, which continued about this time for many days, I pitched the tent over the sledge when halted for lunch, thus keeping the men under shelter and the gear dry, and providing a comfortable seat for the sick; by putting the sledge quite on one side of the tent there was room enough for all the rest to sit alongside it on the sail on the other side. This comfortable rest of two hours with an extra half-pint of tea, was thought more of, and seemed to do them more good, than anything else we could devise, and so was adhered to for the remainder of the time.

On the 28th of May, finding we could not go on dragging the full load (with four men) through the heavy snow, we made up a depot consisting of pemmican, a coverlet, all the knapsacks and gear, in all about 200lbs, and got on much better afterwards. We gradually retraced our steps.

June 3rd. Up to this time the weather had been one continuous snow-fall with thick fogs; the sun once or twice came out for an hour or so and then snow fell again. The sick were getting worse steadily; for the last few days neither Paul nor Jenkins could keep up with the sledge, but crawled after it, and often kept us waiting, I would not let them get too far behind. Craig was very bad, but still hobbled along with us.

Dobing and Jones were getting stiffer and stiffer, but still pulled their best. Gray and myself were the only sound ones left. The sick hardly ate anything. They could not sleep or lie still, and the offensiveness of their breath made the tent almost unbearable. We started out again in the evening, and had not gone ten yards before Paul fell down quite powerless, and from that time until the end he was like one paralysed, his legs were so completely useless to him. Jenkins still crawled along but his time was drawing near, and on the 7th he took his place alongside Paul on the sledge. We now had to make two journeys a day, taking the provisions and baggage on for half the time and then coming back for the tent and the sick. With great labour we got around Snow Point, but Drift Point was impassable to us, and we had to go out on the ice.

On the 10th of June we reached Repulse Harbour Depot, the weather having once more relapsed into a steady snow-fall. Feeling the urgent necessity of getting the sick under medical care, for both Paul and Jenkins were alarmingly weak and short of breath, I read the records carefully, and having considered the matter in all its bearings to the very best of my ability, I determined to cross over to the *Alert* at Cape Sheridan. Everything was to be sacrificed to getting over quickly; so we again made up a depot and left everything we could possibly spare, including the tent and gun, the sextant and knife the only two things I had left.

We started on the 11th of June and had not gone a mile from the shore hummocks before we came to water. It was a large black-looking pool, surrounded for some distance by ice so rotten that the sledge, sick and all would have gone in at the first step off the thicker floe; we had to turn back.

This obstacle at the very outset, where I so little expected it, made me stop short knowing the strong tides and currents that existed on the other shore. I felt that with a sick and enfeebled crew the risk was too great, so we turned back and landed again.

We had considered leaving from the depot with eight days' provisions; that would have been ample to cross with. Now we had to make the best of our way to Polaris Bay, 40 miles off. The question was how much more to take; we ate so little, that eight days would last us twelve I knew, and if we went on as we had done that would be enough; so taking the tent and gun from the depot we started along the coast.

Next march Dobing broke down altogether, and Jones felt so bad he did not think he could walk much longer. Poor fellows! Disappointment at the change of routes had much to do with it. This was our darkest day. We were 40 miles off Polaris Bay at the very least, and only Gray and myself to drag the sledge and the sick, the thing did not seem possible. However it was clear that we must take all the provisions, and then push as long and as far as we could. So we went back to the depot, Gray, Jones and I and brought the remainder, ten days making us to eighteen days; then on we went.

Craig now could barely walk, but his courage did not fail. Dobing became rapidly worse, but fortunately Jones revived, and there were still three on the drag ropes. We toiled painfully through McCormick Pass, a very hard road, all rocks and water but very little snow. The work towards the end became excessively severe on account of the narrowness and the steepness of the passes. The sledge had to be unloaded and the sick lowered down separately in the sail. We were travelling very slowly, Jones dragged with difficulty and it was evident would be too ill to pull at all. Craig could hardly stand and he and Dobing had to be waited on constantly. I did not exhibit any of the well-known symptoms as yet though I did feel stiff and sore about the body from constant over exertion.

On the 21st of June we camped. It soon came on to blow a gale, and the squall so violent and changeable in direction that all our efforts to keep the tent standing were unavailing, and we had to put the sick on the sledge and cover them over with the sail; but the drifting snow which whirled around us penetrated everywhere, and soon wet them through, and they caught colds, which made Paul much worse afterwards. In the afternoon of the same day the wind lulled, and by using the guys, sledge lashings, and drag ropes, we managed to pitch the tent after an hour's hard work. We put the sick in, and tried to make them comfortable; but the tent was badly pitched, and the squall from the cliffs, more like whirlwinds, sometimes made the two sides meet in the middle. We were huddled up in a heap, wet through, and nobody could sleep.

This went on until noon of the 22nd when, the wind having gone down, we repitched the tent and had a few hours rest, which we so much needed. At 9.30p.m. we started; but the wet and cold had stiffened our limbs, and for the first time I felt the scurvy pains in my legs.

Craig and Dobing, but especially Paul and Jenkins, were in the advanced stage of the disease, almost dragged themselves along, their breath failing entirely at every ten yards, this appears to be the most marked feature of the advanced stage of the disease. All four now, but especially Paul and Jenkins, gasped for breath on the slightest exertion; it was painful to watch them.

We were a long way from the Polaris Depot; I did not see how we were to reach it under the circumstances.

On the 23rd of June it became necessary to carry both Dobing and Craig, to enable us to advance at all; and although this, in our weakened state, made three trips each day necessary, and limited our advance to a mile, yet we were still moving on.

On the evening of the 24th we started our last journey with the sledge, as I thought; finding Jones and Gray were scarcely able to pull, I had determined to reach the shore at the plain, pitch the tent, and walk over by myself to Polaris Bay to see if there was anyone there to help us; if not come back, and sending Jones and Gray, who could still walk, to the depot, remain with the sick and get them on as best I could.

But thank God it did not come to this, for as we were plodding along the now water-sodden floe towards the shore, I saw what turned out to be a dog-sled and three men, and soon after had the pleasure of shaking hands with Lt Rawson and Dr Coppinger. Words cannot express the pleasure, relief and gratitude we all felt at this timely meeting; it did the sick men all the good in the world, but once again the relief was tempered by the news of the death of their shipmate J.J. Hand.

Lt Rawson had informed Lt Beaumont of Nares's decision to abandon the expedition completely, of his intention to rendezvous with *Discovery*, and of his plan to return to England forthwith. Hearing this news Beaumont must have been bitterly disappointed. He had had no way of knowing of the scurvy affliction that had also struck the Markham and Aldrich sledge parties, or of the death of Naval Gunner George Porter. He continued:

Lt Rawson had in my opinion, acted with great judgement in planning his relief expedition, for had he come sooner he not only might have missed us altogether, but the small force at his disposal would not have been of so much service. As it was he came in time, with sufficient provisions, and by one great effort got us all into safe quarters, as I shall explain.

We met early on the morning of the 25th of June, and with the help of his party reached the Newman Bay Depot the next day, Dr Coppinger watching the four now utterly prostrate sick with unremitting attention. Half a day was spent here in an attempt to obtain a seal, but without success, and so next morning we started for the depot at Polaris Bay, the dogs, with the assistance of the three officers, dragging both sledges.

It is mainly due to Hans's clever management of the dogs, and his skill as a driver, that we were enabled to advance so rapidly with such a heavy load. That evening when we camped, we were only 12 or 13 miles from the depot. Charles Paul is dangerously ill, he had caught a fresh cold the day before and has terrible fits of coughing; his efforts to breathe were most distressing, and Jenkins in a critical condition.

I felt the importance to them both of a state of complete rest as quickly as possible, an opinion in which Dr Coppinger concurred; so on the morning of the 28th Dr Coppinger and Hans, with the two men on the eight-man sledge drawn by the dogs, started for Polaris Bay Depot. Soon after, Lt Rawson and myself, having placed Craig and Dobing on the five-man sledge, as well as the tent and all the gear, but only two days' provisions, also started for the same destination. Jones and Gray who could still walk, though slowly, came on behind. Fortunately for us two, the wind helped us for some time; but later on, the travelling became very heavy, we were obliged to camp, having accomplished a little over three miles.

Next day as we supposed the sledge was on its way back to us, I was anxious to move the sick men as little as possible, I determined to await its arrival. This did not occur until 3a.m. on the 30th of June; and the whole party was so done, dogs and men, that they had supper and turned in. They brought me a letter from Dr Coppinger saying that he had had a very arduous journey, and had not reached the depot until midnight. The extremely rapid thaw of the snow of the plain obliged them to cross broad strips of bare shingle, while the floe was so seamed with cracks that they must have doubled the distance in looking for a road. The sick had borne the journey well and eaten with good appetite on their arrival; but from noon on June the 29th, Paul had gradually grown weaker and weaker until he died at 5.15 p.m. Jenkins was no worse.

I was very much grieved at Paul's death. I had watched him and cared for him so long, and had hoped so, that we might not be too late, I felt his death very much.

Monday 3rd of July we buried the remains of C.W. Paul, AB, beside those of J.J. Hand, who had died on the 3rd of June. The sledge flags were half-mast high on each tent and three volleys were fired.

Now there are three at graves at Hall's Depot at Thank God Harbour; lying side by side are the remains of J.J. Hand, C.F. Hall, and C.W. Paul.

However, we were not far from the end of this arduous journey; the thing was to get the remainder in as soon as possible. Lt Rawson and his party taking the sick on the eight-man sledge round by the sledge route, while I took Gray and Jones round by the foot of the hills. We three reached the depot at 7a.m. Lt Rawson with his party, arrived at 11a.m. after a very heavy journey, having travelled nearly all the way on bare shingle. We were all safely in, in good hands and comfortable quarters.

The next day being Sunday, I read the Morning Service, all of us joining most heartily and fervently in rendering thanks to Almighty God for His gracious mercy and protection towards us.

Dr Coppinger set up a mini hospital, where the scurvy victims remained for several weeks recuperating. Hans Hendrik hunted fresh meat and game to feed the invalids. Both sledge parties were extremely fortunate, firstly by being rescued, and secondly with the availability of fresh meat and game (earlier or later in the season so far north there would have been none). Finally, the ice-craft and hunting ability of Hans Hendrik was the key to their survival.

Jim Hand could not be saved, but after a week George Bryant and Michael Regan, with rest and fresh food were able to stand and take a few steps unaided. They both recovered fully and were deemed fit for duty five weeks later. Dobing, Jenkins, Jones and Craig all recovered fully, as did all the other scurvy patients from the Markham and Aldrich sledge parties.

Lt Beaumont rested, revised his sketches, drawings and charts. and put names on the various geographical landmarks. In almost every respect Lt Beaumont's graphic report of his men's sufferings reflected Lt Rawson's nightmare return sledge journey.

Meanwhile, the *Alert* was still trapped in the frozen ice at Cape Sheridan and Captain Nares had yet to break out. Captain Nares's story continued:

In the evening Lt Rawson and two seamen arrived from the *Discovery*, and brought me the distressing news concerning the Greenland division of sledgers. He informed me that Lt Beaumont's party were still at the Polaris Bay Depot. They intended starting on August 5th for Discovery Bay.

Although I had the fullest confidence in Lt Beaumont, I was naturally most anxious concerning his crossing the strait when the ice was so much broken-up and the spring tides at their greatest height.

Consequently, in addition to our incessant watch for an opening in the ice by which we might advance, many an anxious look was directed towards Polaris Bay, our thoughts were chiefly engrossed on the perilous position of our comrades there.

After several unsuccessful attempts we broke through the barrier of ice with the aid of explosives, with no greater damage than two boats having been stove in against the ice floes. Snow storms and squalls continued and the ship sought sanctuary at Cape Beechey.

There, while the ship was detained Captain Feilding obtained some Eskimo relics. The spot where he found them is evidently the northern limit of the migration of these people on the west side of the channel. From thence they have crossed to Polaris Bay, where their traces are again met with. In the same neighbourhood several rings of stones marking the sites of summer tents were found; and in one locality numerous flakes of rock crystal which had been broken off in the process of making harpoon heads. During our detention at Cape Beechey, the ice in the Robeson Channel, which is only 13 miles wide at that part, drifted up and down the strait with the tide, the wind having the effect of increasing the speed of the current and the duration of its flow both towards the north and the south. As Captain Stephenson, by the last orders, conveyed to him via Polaris Bay in May, supposed that the two ships would probably pass a second winter in the neighbourhood of Discovery Bay, it was necessary to send him instructions to prepare the *Discovery* for sea, and to inform him of my intention to proceed to England. I despatched Mr Egerton with the necessary orders.

On 12th August the *Alert* joined the *Discovery*, after a separation of eleven and a half months. As there were no tidings of Lt Beaumont and his party, preparations were immediately made for the *Alert* to cross the channel to Polaris Bay.

The ice not permitting us to start, I visited the look-out station, obtained a magnificent view, but to our regret and increasing anxiety, nothing was to be seen of the travellers. A white object was plainly visible at Hall's Rest, but whether it was Beaumont's tent or the second boat which he would be obliged to abandon and leave there, it was impossible to say; with such fine weather it was most probable that he would have started.

On the 14th of August our anxiety concerning Beaumont's party was put to an end by our seeing his encampment on the ice. A relief party was immediately despatched to his assistance. I had the satisfaction of seeing the members of the expedition collected together again. This satisfaction was however considerably marred by the thought that Petersen, Porter, Hand and Paul, four of our original number, had sacrificed their lives in the performance of their duties.

Chapter XXII

The Ships Sail South

Captain Nares explained:

Aware of the large depot of supplies at the Polaris Bay Depot of preserved meat, vegetables, lime juice and everything necessary for the party to survive, I could not foresee such a calamity as the total collapse of so large a party of men and officers as were then on the Greenland shore, which included three lieutenants, one surgeon, twelve men and a dog sled (Fulford's), until Fulford reached me with the intelligence on the 25th of July, 25 days after they were due to board ship.

Lt Beaumont, Dr Coppinger and the remainder of his men arrived safely onboard from Polaris Bay on the 15th of August. All the shooting parties were recalled to their vessels. They have been highly successful in replenishing our provisions. On the day the crews of both ships reunited, officers and men experienced the full gamut of emotions, sadness at leaving four comrades buried in the ice, disappointment at their failure to complete the mission, huge relief felt by the scurvy survivors and amputees.

The Revd Pullen penned this beautiful poem:

'The Return of the Sledge Journeys'

Welcome home to the wished-for rest,
Traveller to North and traveller to West;
Welcome back from bristling floe,
Frowning cliff, and quaking snow;
Nobly, bravely, the work was done;
Inch by inch was the hard fight won;
Now the toilsome march is o'er –
Welcome home to our tranquil shore;

Rough and rude is the feast we bring;
Rougher and ruder the verse we sing.
Not rough, not rude are the thoughts that rise
To choke our voices and dim our eyes,
As we call to mind that joyous sight
On an April morning cold and bright,
When a chosen band stepped boldly forth
To the unknown West and the unknown North;
And we from our haven could only pray –
God send them strength for each weary day;
He heard our prayer – He made them strong,
He bore their stalwart limbs along;
Planted their sturdy footsteps sure;
Gave them courage to endure.
Taught them too, for His dear sake,
Many a sacrifice to make;
By many a tender woman's deed
To aid a brother in his need.
And safe for ever shall He keep
In His gentle hand the four who sleep.
His love shall quench the tears that flow
For the buried dear ones under the snow.
And we who live and are strong to do
His love shall keep us safely too;
Shall tend our sick, and soothe their pain,
And bring them back to health again.
And the breath of His wind shall set us free,
Through the opening ice to the soft green sea.

Captain Nares continued:

The dead crew members are all buried, a rough cross overlooking the Arctic marking
a new northernmost grave is erected, and if the ship does not escape soon there will
be additional funeral services. The men have been enjoying the fresh meat and game.
The two ships were prepared for their voyage southward. Our main concern was
for our store of a few tons of steaming coal left, and after it was gone we would have
to use the coal necessary for warming the ship during the coming winter. It is now
September, if we are unable to clear the Arctic for whatever reason, its expenditure
had become a very serious matter. I need hardly say no ashes were ever thrown
overboard. All our invalids are now so far recovered that they are doing duty on deck,

merely being excused from going aloft or working on the boats; but as I must expect a recurrence of the disease to manifest itself during the coming winter, the quickly advancing season makes me rather anxious lest we fail to escape from the ice.

Eventually we reached blue water and considering the small amount of coal there was on-board either ship it was a great relief to me and I trust that I was not unthankful to God for His merciful care of us and for the great success that had attended us in the truly perilous navigation north of Smith Sound. We arrived at Cape Isabella, and found a package of letters and newspapers left there by Sir Allen Young a few weeks previously. The officers and men of the *Alert* and *Discovery* can scarcely feel sufficiently grateful to Sir Allen Young and his companions for their determined and persevering efforts to open communication with them over the two seasons. Sacrificing so great a part of the short navigable season of 1875 and paying two visits to the Cary Islands on our account alone, when Sir Allen's purpose was to explore in a totally different direction, was stretching a friendly action to the utmost. Such consideration can only be fully appreciated by persons situated as we were.

Not a word was spoken until the mail-bags were sorted and the lucky ones received their news; along with the mail was a large number of newspapers which to some extent consoled those who were not the fortunate recipients of letters.

After our long sojourn within the Polar ice it was a strange transition to feel the ship rise and fall once more on the north water of Baffin Bay, and to look astern and see Cape Isabella, one of the massive portals to Smith Sound, fading away in the obscurity of snow and midnight darkness; whilst an ice-blink stretching across the northern horizon reminded us forcibly of the perils, dangers and anxieties that we had contended against for so many months. In comparing the voyage of the *Polaris* and that of the *Alert* and *Discovery* it is evident that the navigation of the ice which is to be met with every year in Kane Sea is entirely dependent on the westerly winds. Both in 1875 and 1876 we met navigable water off Cape Victoria in latitude 79°12', with only a narrow pack 15 miles in breadth between it and Grinnell Land, which a westerly wind of a few hours' duration would certainly have driven to the eastward. The same wind would have opened a channel along the shore, and any vessel waiting her opportunity at Payer Harbour could under those circumstances have passed up the channel with as little difficulty as the *Polaris* experienced in 1871.

The quantity of one season's ice met with in the bays of the south-east coast of Grinnell Land in 1876, proves that on the final setting in of the frost, after we passed north in 1875, the pack had been driven from the shore, leaving a navigable channel along the land. Nevertheless I do not recommend future navigators who wish to attain a high northern latitude by this route to wait for such a favourable occurrence. Certainly no one could have made a passage through the ice in 1876 before the 10th of September by doing so. At that date the season had advanced so far that the attainment of sheltered winter-quarters would have been extremely problematical.

The ships continued to sail south approaching the land occupied by the Arctic Highlanders:

We were extremely anxious to land to communicate with the Eskimo, but the gale was blowing so fiercely and the sea breaking so heavily against the shore that it was dangerous to send a boat away from the ship. We looked forward to landing the next morning, and a number of presents were prepared, but during the night the wind shifted, blowing directly into the bay. The thick snow-storm, dark night, and rocky shore compelled me to think more of the ships than the unfortunate Eskimo. We afterwards gladly learnt that Sir Allen Young in the *Pandora* had visited the same family only a fortnight previously, and given them many valuable gifts.

On the 25th of September we entered the well-known anchorage of Lievely. We were warmly welcomed by our kind friends Mr and Mrs Krarup Smith and Mr and Mrs Fencker, who informed us that the *Pandora* had left for England four days previously.

We remained two days at Disko, Mr Smith kindly supplying us with a small quantity of coal. Hans Hendrik and Frederick were landed and the few remaining dogs were given to them. Hans was to remain at Disko until the following spring, when the ice would permit him to journey north and join his family at Proven.

Frederick in his excitement at returning home could scarcely find time to look after his own goods, but his numerous friends on-board took care that he was not the loser; with his many riches he has doubtless long since found a wife.

On the 29th we arrived at Egedesminde. Governor Bolbroe kindly supplied us with 20 tons of coal, but owing to a bad season he could only give us one haunch of venison. This was however sufficient for a meal for the former invalids, who by this time were, to all intents and purposes, well and strong.

Our visit to Egedesminde was rather opportune, as there were numerous cases of scurvy among the Eskimo and the few Europeans. I accordingly landed a large quantity of lime juice and all the remaining stock of sundries belonging to the officers, not the least acceptable present being a quantity of music and mittens.

On the 4th of October we crossed the Arctic circle, after experiencing 15 months of unnatural division of light and darkness. Encountering a succession of strong and contrary gales very slow progress was made to the southward.

On the 16th of October we fell in with the *Pandora*, the only vessel we met with during the voyage. The three ships kept company for two days but we lost sight of each other during a strong gale.

The *Alert* entered Valentia Harbour on the 27th October, the *Discovery* arriving at Queenstown two days later. The two ships having again joined company

HMS *Alert*, homeward bound. (*Illustrated London News*, 4 November 1876.)

entered Portsmouth Harbour on the 2nd of November; the *Pandora* arriving at Falmouth on the previous day. I will not here dwell on the warm and hearty reception which the officers and men received from all classes of their countrymen, notwithstanding the somewhat natural disappointment that the North Pole had not been reached.

The Lords Commissioners of the Admiralty were pleased to express their warm approval of the conduct of all engaged in the Expedition, and we were honoured by receiving the following letter addressed to the First Lord of the Admiralty by direction of Her Most Gracious Majesty the Queen.

Dear Mr Hunt,

I am commanded by the Queen to request that you will communicate to Captain Nares, and to the officers and men under his command, Her Majesty's hearty congratulations on their safe return.

The Queen highly appreciates the valuable services which have been rendered by them in the late Arctic Expedition, and she fully sympathises in the hardships and sufferings they have endured, and laments the loss of life that has occurred.

The Queen would be glad if her thanks could be duly conveyed to these gallant men for what they have accomplished.

Yours very truly,
Henry F. Ponsonby.'

Open Polar Sea

The theory of an Open Polar Sea that had been expounded in England appeared to be a myth to Captain Nares:

As not a speck of water could I see, I peered north through my telescope but saw only frosted hummocks of ice clambering towards the horizon. Nothing but ice, high, tight and impassable, was to be seen – a solid impenetrable mass that no amount of imagination or theoretical belief could ever twist into an Open Polar Sea. A Polar Ocean; a frozen sea of such character as utterly to preclude the possibility of its being navigated by ship; a wide expanse of ice and snow, whose impenetrable fastness seem to defy the puny efforts of mortal men to invade and expose the mysteries.

On 30 December 1876 *The London Times* published a letter:

Sir,

With reference to the recent letter of a distinguished German geographer to the Royal Geographical Society on the subject of Arctic Expeditions, I really cannot help expressing my amazement that anyone should still be found to maintain the existence of an open Polar ocean round the Pole.

As I have passed five seasons in the Polar Seas, my opinion may perhaps, be

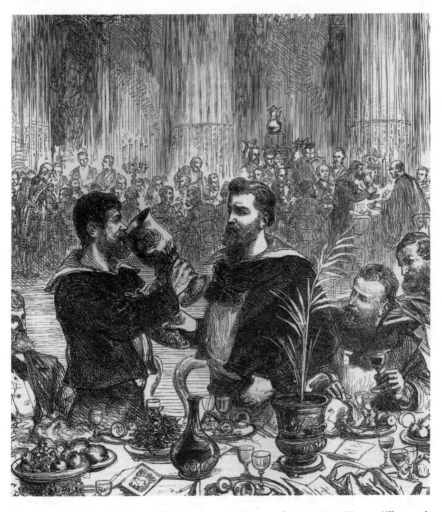

Entertainment for the sailors of the arctic expedition at the Mansion House. (*Illustrated London News*, 16 December 1876.)

considered worth heeding on the point. After my first two voyages in 1858 and 1859, I formed a very strong opinion – and published that opinion, 'Seasons with Sea-horses' (1861), to the effect that no open Polar ocean did or could exist.

Years after that I was partially argued out of my own practically formed opinion by one or two learned men who had theoretically formed a different opinion; and I fitted out, entirely at my own expense, a costly and very well-adapted vessel, with which I passed three more seasons amid the polar ice, in hope that by combining my practical knowledge with the theories of my learned friends I might make at least some approach towards the Pole. The result was that I returned with my own previous convictions strongly fortified; *viz* that no approach can possibly be made to the Pole by water.

In the course of my voyages I have talked long and earnestly with scores of practical men who have passed their lives in ransacking the Polar Ocean, and who would run any risks to get across to fresh hunting grounds to the north, and I never met one of these men who had not an utter contemptuous disbelief of an open ocean to the north. Now after all that, is it not enough to take one's breath away with astonishment to be told by a learned philosopher who has never, so to speak, left his own library, that we ought to have had no difficulty whatever in sailing straight away to the Pole; and through pack ice so dense and heavy that the strongest ironclad afloat could not force her own length into it.

Every now and then it makes me laugh to hear or to read of someone who says that someone else had got to the edge of this open Polar Ocean and saw nothing before him but open water – 'a vast illimitable open ocean reaching to the Pole' – is I think the usual expression; and that nothing but the want of time, or want of provisions or want of something else had prevented him – the informant's informant – from sailing to the pole direct. Now surely it is time that all this nonsense about an open Polar Sea was knocked on the head. I have been deceived 20 times myself by what looked like an open sea when in reality it was only a pond of water a few miles broad. We all are liable to be deluded in like manner, because, in our eagerness to see what we wish to see, we are apt to lose sight of three very simple facts. First, as the ice lies very low in the water; secondly, that it is only a very small horizon that one sees from the masthead of a vessel; thirdly, that only half a mile beyond our horizon may lie, not 'a vast illimitable ocean' but a vast illimitable ice-field reaching to the Pole.

To conclude I beg to express my firm belief, founded on all I have seen, on all that I have heard, and all I have read, that all around the North Pole, as around the South Pole, there lies an eternal mass of ice, a thousand miles in diameter and perhaps miles thick in the centre. And further, I do not believe that either ship, sledge, bird or balloon will ever get across it.

I am your obedient servant.

James Lamont, FGS, FRGS.

Chapter XXIII

The Inquiry

In Britain and indeed in Ireland, jubilation was unconfined at the safe return of the expedition. The media and public perception was that although four men died, it had been a much more successful expedition than the Franklin disaster. Medals were struck, splendid banquets arranged, rousing speeches were given, and promotions awarded. Captain Nares was awarded the Royal Geographical Society's Gold Medal. Even if the Pole had not been reached, the expedition had broken the record for the farthest north; it had produced charts which would not be bettered for fifty years; it had brought back scientific findings which where later to give rise to some forty published articles and reports; it had taken more than 100 photographs. There was a small number of fatalities, which under the circumstances were deemed acceptable, but by and large the expedition had arrived home intact.

Nevertheless, along with the unfortunate civilian Neil Petersen, three naval seamen (Jim Hand, Charles Paul and George Porter) had died on land, and in peacetime. Some one had to explain the reason why. This was the responsibility of Captain George Nares. Despite Nares's defence that 'The Open Polar Sea did not in reality exist, to enable us to reach it', which was contrary to what he was led to believe before sailing, some newspapers were critical of him for not having reached the Pole.

Captain Nares was not court-martialled. Instead the Admiralty set up an Inquiry. From 10 January until 3 March 1877 the Board heard evidence from 1p.m. to 5p.m., six days a week.

Captain Nares had to sit through a number of uncomfortable and heated exchanges. He was questioned at length as to why his men should have died from scurvy when he had adequate supplies of antiscorbutics, including lime juice available on-board. He answered that sledge parties previous to his had been away for longer periods and had not caught scurvy. Furthermore he had doubled the dosages of lime juice in the previous weeks. Also Aldrich's and

Markham's crews had taken their lime juice according to their journals and their men still contracted scurvy.

And so the sessions continued. But Nares was fighting a losing battle. If fresh meat or game had been available to the sledge parties, he said, not only would they have survived but the expedition would have made history the following summer by reaching the Pole. The Board of Inquiry was not interested in Nares's claim that the expedition was so far North that neither fresh meat nor game were obtainable and conditions were so excruciating for the sledgers that scurvy was unavoidable. The Board of Inquiry considered Nares's response lame and feeble.

The findings were published by HM Stationery Office in a 500-page tome, the leather-bound spine of which carried the words 'Scurvy Report'. The Report asked such questions as: Why hadn't he trained his sledge crews better? But he had trained them he said. Then why hadn't he given them more antiscorbutic? The two ounces of dried potato per man per day which they had been allocated wasn't much. The Navy's leading medical expert, Dr Armstrong, had advised him to issue lime juice as well. Why hadn't he? Few sledge expeditions in the past had taken lime juice, he replied, and they had not caught scurvy despite being out for far longer than his men. Anyway Markham's and Aldrich's journals revealed they had taken bottles of lime juice and it had done them little good. Then why hadn't he given them extra lime juice before they left? But he had, he replied, he'd doubled their rations in the preceding weeks. Why then, since the disease had obviously taken hold before the sledgers left, hadn't he followed a healthier dietary regime? Because that was the regime he had been instructed to follow – a standard regime which he had been promised would keep scurvy at bay for at least two years and probably three. So why had his men got scurvy when other expeditions hadn't? All Captain Nares could suggest was that previous expeditions had misreported the disease; they had said they were suffering from exhaustion when really it was scurvy in disguise – the sledge captains had made the same mistake. The Board hammered away at Captain Nares. Finally, to his intense relief, the torment ended. The Inquiry delivered its verdict:

> We find that the orders of the Commander of the Expedition for provisioning the three extended and principal spring parties did not include lime juice, thereby deviating from the 11th Article of the Memorandum of Recommendations and Suggestions of the Medical Director-General, furnished by their Lordships for his information, and that the reasons assigned for such deviation being insufficient, the said orders were not proper.

In fact, Navy regime was inadvertently to blame; previous expeditions had found that ordinary lime juice froze in its bottles and burst them, so the Navy had supplied Nares with a concentrated version. The concentrating process involved boiling the juice in a copper kettle. Copper leaches Vitamin C and heat destroys it. Therefore the lime juice with which Captain Nares had dosed his men had been stripped of most of its antiscorbutic properties. The sledger's body store of Vitamin C would have been depleted long before they started.

Whatever lime juice they carried did them little good, as in the conditions they encountered, even the concentrate froze. Having neither the time nor the fuel to thaw it properly, they slept with the bottles clasped to their chests. The meagre essence settled at the bottom and the sips they took from the top had as much effect as tap water. Ironically they were victims of a technology designed to save them. None of this would be known however, until the discovery of Vitamin C in the twentieth century. In the meantime, Captain Nares was considered to be the culprit.

Captain Nares did not come out of the Inquiry very well, and was publicly censured.

Chapter XXIV

Later...

When I began to research this story I knew little about scurvy, and was highly critical of Captain Nares. I felt Jim Hand's excruciating death had been unnecessary. But I was wrong. Further research illustrated that the much-vaunted lime juice was a myth and was only effective up to a point. Yes, in different circumstances lime juice is a preventative. If Jim Hand, Charles Paul and George Porter had remained on-board the ship they would in all probability have survived, but working their way through ice, snow and slush, often in blizzards, harnessed, pulling up to 300lbs per man for ten hours a day, seven days a week, week after week, having mainly diet of pemmican alone, burning up thousands of calories each day, trying to sleep on a tarpaulin canvas on ice in an unheated tent in minus temperatures – it is obvious that if the sledge parties had continued, every single one of them would have perished.

But one other question remains unanswered: should Aldrich, Markham and Beaumont in particular, have returned immediately when they saw the first indications of scurvy? The following is an a abbreviated report written by the Scandinavian explorer Vilhjalmur Stefansson who made a study of scurvy on three expeditions to the Arctic:

> Scurvy has been the enemy of explorers. When Scott's party of four went to the South Pole in 1913 their strength was sapped by scurvy and they were unable to maintain their travel schedule and died. [This was over thirty years after Jim Hand and his shipmates had died from scurvy.]
>
> In 1936 an American doctor reported that one hundred Ethiopian soldiers a day were dying of scurvy.
>
> The medical profession and laity equally believed that they knew exactly how to prevent and cure the disease, yet the method always failed when severely tested. The premise from which the doctors started was that vegetables, particularly fruits, prevented and cured scurvy. They named lime juice as a sure cure. Lawmakers

followed the doctors. It is on the statute books of many countries that on long voyages the crew is to be supplied with lime juice or compelled to take it.

Ignoring the decimation of armies, and the burden of this disease in many walks of civilian life through past ages, we turn to the explorers, the class most publicised as suffering and dying from scurvy.

The explorer James Cook in the late 1700s was credited with having discovered how to prevent and cure scurvy. He demonstrated that with vegetables and fruits scurvy could be prevented on the longest voyages. From this developed the knowledge according to which we extract and bottle the juice of the lime, and stock ships with it to prevent and cure scurvy. As shown above however, the good physicians, with their faith in lime juice as a specific, overlooked its constant failure on severe tests.

How stoutly the faith was kept is shown by the British polar Expedition of Sir G. Nares. When he returned to England in 1876 after a year and a half, he reported much illness from scurvy, some deaths and a partial failure of his programme as a result.

In his view fresh meat could have saved his men. But the doctors as we shall see when we consider how they later advised Scott, soon forgot whatever impression was made by Nares. They seemed to have frightened themselves with the old doctrines by a series of assumptions; that the lime juice in the Nares Expedition might have been deficient in acid content, that some of the victims did not take as much as needed, and that perhaps it was too much to expect of even the marvellous juice to cope with all the things which tended to bring on scurvy – absence of sunlight, bad ventilation, lack of amusement and exercise, insufficient cleanliness.

Particularly because Nares's medical Court of Inquiry had closed on a note of cleanliness and 'modern sanitation' you would think the medical world might have felt a severe jolt when they read how Nansen and Johansen had wintered in the Franz Josef Islands in 1895/6.

They had lived in a hut of stones and walrus leather to conserve fuel; the fire smoked, so the air was additionally bad. There was not a ray of daylight for months, during this time they practically hibernated, seldom going outdoors at all and taking as little exercise as was humanly possible. Yet their health was perfect all winter and they came out of their hibernation in as good physical condition as any men ever did out of any kind of Arctic wintering. Their food had been the lean and the fat of the walrus.

Therefore it remained for my own expedition to demonstrate, so far as polar expeditions are concerned, to call to the medical profession the most practical and only simple way of curing scurvy. For no matter how good the juice of limes (or lemons). it is difficult to carry, it deteriorates, and you may lose it, as by shipwreck. The thing to do is to find antiscorbutics where you are, to pick them up as you go along.

Stefansson relates an expedition he organised:

> Three men came down with scurvy, they had disobeyed instructions, were
> afflicted and became classic cases of scurvy [similar to Jim Hand]. Unable to walk,
> every joint in their bodies ached with stiffness, their teeth fell out, their gums
> became spongy, and lastly, descended into gloom. One had to be carried on the
> sledge he was so weak. They reached an island with an abundance of caribou and
> ate only cooked meat and within four days the gloom was replaced by optimism.
> In a week their recovery was remarkable. In four weeks, apart from gums prob-
> lems they had made a complete recovery.

The following is a letter from Admiral Robert Hall to Sir George Nares at the
conclusion of the Inquiry:

Admiralty, 5 June 1877

Sir,

1. With reference to the 8th paragraph of my letter to the Commander in Chief at
Portsmouth, of the third of November last, in which their Lordships stated that
they refrained at present from expressing any opinion on the cause of the outbreak
of scurvy in the Arctic Expedition under your command, I am commanded by my
Lords Commissioners of the Admiralty to acquaint you that, after the receipt of
the Report of the Director General of the Medical Department on the outbreak
of scurvy, and your letters of the 30th of November and 14th December last, my
Lords thought it desirable that the questions discussed therein should be referred
to the judgement of a Committee.

2. My Lords desire me to forward to you a copy of the Report of the Committee,
and I am to state that they accept the conclusions at which the Committee have
arrived, after a careful investigation of the matter.

3. I am to observe that my Lords make full allowance for the great practical difficulties that you had to contend with in deciding upon the best scheme for
provisioning the sledge parties, and that they appreciate the reasons which guided
your action in the matter, but at the same time, their Lordships must express
their regret that you did not attach due weight to the recommendations of the
Director General of the Medical Department upon the subject.

(signed) Robert Hall.

The Inquiry revealed the answer to one final question which may have puzzled
the reader: why did not a single officer become a scurvy victim? A two-fold

answer can be given. The first was provided by the army captain Feilden, 'We brought additional private supplies of food of greater variety such as butter, cheese, sardines, potted meats, jams and wines.' This information was corroborated by Lt Beaumont when he referred to additions to his 'ordinary rations', and Lt Rawson refers to 'what private stores they had'.

The second answer of course is that only in extreme circumstances or in the most difficult conditions did officers man-haul. Their role was to scout the way forward, navigate, sketch and chart their progress. They did not expend anything like the amount of calories as did the men in harness.

Nares's Report of the expedition is a truly remarkable work. Massive in quantity, masterful in detail and absolutely priceless for future Polar expeditions, Nares covered every item of clothing down to the last stitch, and explained how Arctic apparel could and should be improved. In painstaking detail he covered the food, diets and rations, admitting the shortcomings, their harmful effects and how these should be remedied. His report went down to the last nail in the equipment, the ship's timbers and the stitches in each sail.

A huge problem – and a cause of great vexation – was the lack of ventilation and the amount and the degree of freezing condensation, which made living conditions intolerable in high minus-degree temperatures chiefly due to the icy polar wind and air. The draughts and the close confinement of the men did not help. Cooking in freezing condensation made life very difficult for the unfortunate cooks.

There was one-eyebrow raising sentence in his report: Captain Nares was quite happy with the wearing apparel and the footwear. This is most surprising when it is remembered that some of the crew were confined to bed for a period of four months recovering from frost bite and amputations to hands and feet. Captain Nares himself mentioned the problem of canvas boots. The men spoke unfavourably about the woollen clothing. When they perspired the perspiration froze on their bodies, in sharp contrast to the clothing worn by the Eskimo. Whatever maladies the natives suffered from, and there were many, rarely did they suffer from serious frostbite.

The following are some comments made by the crew to give a flavour of their experiences:

Dr Colan: washing – the men were supplied with the usual tubs, the medical team were satisfied as to the cleanliness of most of the men.

Wm Jenkins: the provisions were more than sufficient. I did not eat the salt meat and the preserved meat pemmican was monotonous.

Crew continuously complained no butter.

General consensus: two-ounce ration of preserved potato per man grossly insufficient.

Dr Colan: the salt meat was hard and tough.

Captain Fielding: there was ample food but the salt beef was tough.

Lt Egerton: cooking apparatus cooked too slowly.

Dr Ninnis: when sledging, water bottles carried in waistbands of trousers froze.

Lt May: when sledging, lighting the matches was a constant cause of frustration.

Captain Nares: insufficiency of beer and the ingredients to make a ship's brew.

Commander Markham: crew was healthy except for frost bite. Lt May had a toe amputated.

Other interesting observations include:

Sleeping hammocks had to be stored to dry out after being soaked by condensation, but it was almost impossible to dry them in the very difficult circumstances.

Cooking the main meal took up to three hours.

There were no special regulations for the changing of clothing on the *Alert*.

The crew changed no clothing for sleeping, but changed only their foot and headwear.

Advice for future Polar explorers: the ideal age is between 25 and 32. Officers may be a little older necessarily because of experience.

When sledging, the cooking job had to be a duty one would dread. Exhausted after man-hauling for eight or ten hours the cook had to work another two to three hours more before the unfortunate man could rest.

When arranging for a daily change of cook, the officers took care that no officer would cook.

It would appear that there was an adequate supply of food on the ships, but not sufficient food or variety for the overworked sledge parties.

Time and time again, the men lost their appetites, being totally fed up with the diet of pemmican.

To summarise:

- The expedition was aborted due to the scurvy attack. Captain Nares was publicly censured for ignoring or failing to implement the procedures to deal with the disease.
- Many of the officers were decorated and promoted, some went on to become Admirals.
- Neil Petersen was among those who did not survive. He died on 14 May and was buried on land at Cape Sheridan. His wife and children returned to Copenhagen. Captain Nares arranged a pension for Petersen's dependants even though Petersen had not officially been in the British Navy.
- Hans Hendrik died on 11 August 1889 at Godhavn. Hans had made quite a name for himself when he returned home. He wrote his life story, an account of his Arctic experiences on the Kane, Hall and Nares expeditions. He wrote it in Greenlandic. Henry Rink, a Danish geologist and colonial administrator transcribed it into English in 1878 under the title *Memoirs of Hans Hendrik, Arctic Traveller*. It is claimed he was the first Inuit to write his life story, and to have it published. He also had an island named after him, Hans Island, believed to have been so named by Charles Francis Hall on his 1871 Expedition. It is a small knoll in the middle of Kennedy Channel and Nares Strait at 80°49'N. The island is claimed by both Canada and Greenland. The dispute may turn into a test case on sovereignty. His last expedition was in 1883 when he accompanied Alfred Gabriel Nathorst on a scientific exploration to West Greenland.
- George Porter died on 8 June from scurvy on Commander Markham's sledge party. He was buried on an ice floe.
- Charles Paul, sledge mate of J.J. Hand on the sledge Parry, also died from scurvy on 29 June, the day before Lt Beaumont reached the depot. He is buried beside J.J. Hand and Captain Hall.
- What became of the heroic Lt Wyatt Rawson? Looking back on his contribution, he appears to have been the unsung hero of the expedition. It is hard to realise that he was only twenty-three years of age at the time. Sadly he died in 1882, a mere six years later, on the hospital ship *Carthage* at Malta. There is a memorial dedicated to him at the English Heritage Store, Fort Brockhurst,

Arctic medal, 1875–1876.

Gosport, England. It reads, 'He fell while acting as guide to the Second Division at the Battle of Tel-El-Kebir, Egypt, 13 September, 1882, aged 29. He served in the Ashantee War, 1873-4, and in the Arctic Expedition, 1875-6.'

- The medal roll for HMS *Discovery*, *Alert* and supply ship *Pandora* records that the Arctic Medal was awarded to all the officers and men, including a posthumous award to James Hand, which his father John Hand received on 19 November 1877.

- In the years following the Nares expedition, Dr Coppinger rose through the ranks and in March 1901 was appointed Inspector General of Hospitals and Fleets. He retired in 1906 and died on 2 April 1910. In 1883 Dr Colan was promoted to Inspector General of Hospitals and Fleets. He died in August 1885. Coppinger Mountains on the north-west coast of Canada and Cape Colan on Ellesmere Island are geographical reminders of both surgeons' Arctic service.

- Adam Ayles died in early April 1912, while mowing the green at Rocky Nook Bowling Club in Auckland, New Zealand. Adam was one of only two teetotallers on the Expedition.

- The expedition discovered much more about the Polar Sea than was previously known, and charted 300 miles of new coastline. Hourly tidal observations had been recorded for seven months aboard the *Discovery*. Hourly data was also observed for two months on the *Alert*. Both sets of data were reported upon by Revd Samuel Haughton MD, DCL, FRS of Trinity College, Dublin. From the observations, Haughton was able to state, 'The tidal observations made during the recent Arctic Expedition were of great value, and confirm the opinion formed on other grounds that Greenland is an Island.'

- Henry Hart had also been toiling away. We are told that the vicinity of Discovery Bay, as far north as 81°50'N was subject to careful botanical study by Hart and from that latitude to the eighty-third parallel, the collections were undertaken by H.W. Feilden. In Britain, scientists were impressed at the variety of information gathered, and identified a new species of fungi from Hart's collection (*Urrula Harti*). Hart was not involved in the main sledge journeys, but concentrated on his work as the expedition's naturalist.

- Commander Albert Hastings Markham received a Knighthood and is credited as the designer of the New Zealand National Flag, he died on 28 October 1918.

- On the extreme north-west tip of Greenland lies Cape Bryant and a little south of it, is Hand Bay.

- Dr Belgrave Ninnis MD (1837–1922) signed Jim Hand's death certificate. He was born in London in 1837, joined the Royal Navy in 1861, and was naturalist to the Northern Territory of the Southern Australian Surveying Expedition of 1864–6. Dr Ninnis became Inspector Surgeon General of the Royal Navy.

  His son Lt Belgrave Edward Sutton Ninnis (1887–1912) died tragically while on the 1911 Sir Douglas Mawson Antarctic Expedition. He fell into a crevasse and although his fellow explorers attempted his rescue their valiant attempts to save his life were unsuccessful. A nephew of Dr Ninnis, Aubrey Ninnis was a member of Shackleton's Ross Sea Party in 1914.

  Dr Ninnis died in London, aged eighty-five.

- In the early 1970s the Danish Government implemented plans to rehouse the Greenland Inuit in settlements. Attractive inducements and subsidies were offered to the natives and were broadly accepted. The Inuit were provided with new heated homes, all having modern conveniences. The plans included a health care service and an education programme. However, urban living changed their nomadic lifestyle and unfortunately a fairly high percentage were unable to adapt, causing a serious social problem for the authorities who are dealing with a troubling alcohol problem. The centuries-old Inuit communing-with-nature way of life has changed utterly. That is called progress.

- What eventually became of the HMS *Alert*? On her return from the expedition she was despatched to the Pacific as a surveying ship, visited Esquimalt and was employed in charting Canadian and Australian waters before being paid off in Chatham in 1882.

The American Government sent an expedition (1881–1884) under the command of army captain Adolphus Greely to establish an observatory at Fort Conger (a little south of Cape Sheridan) on Ellesmere Island as part of the first International Polar Year. A three-man sledge party of the Greely Expedition, comprising Lt J.B. Lockwood, junior officer David Brainnard and an Eskimo Frederick, made an attempt on the Pole. They reached a new farthest north of 83°23'8" breaking the Nares Expedition record by a fraction of a degree before to being driven back by blizzards.

When they returned they found Greely and his men were starving. Due to lack of communications and the failure of two rescue missions, the twenty-four-man team attempted to march to safety. By the time they were rescued only six survived, some of whom had resorted to cannibalism. The history-making Lt Lockwood unfortunately did not live to enjoy his new-found fame in America, having been one of the fatalities. In 1884 the *Alert* was offered to the United States Navy to assist in a third attempt to rescue Greely and his men. Under the command of Captain George W. Coff, US Navy, she set up supply dumps for an expedition under Captain Schley who finally managed to extricate Greely and the other survivors. On completion of this service, it was decided that the *Alert* was the ideal vessel for the Canadian Government survey of Hudson Bay.

When the ship was first built, prior to the Nares Expedition, the crew numbered 175. For the Hudson Bay work the *Alert* was manned by the master, two mates, two engineers, a carpenter, two boatswains, twelve able seamen, six engine-room crew, a lamp trimmer, five cooks and stewards, some scientists and a medical doctor.

In 1894 after nine years service in the department, she was laid off, deemed unfit for further use. From 1886 and the completion of the Hudson Bay survey, the *Alert* had been used as a lighthouse supply vessel and boat tender, first in Nova Scotia and latterly, as the wooden hull was beginning to deteriorate, sailing from Quebec for service in the Gulf. For this work she was stripped of her former glory, topmasts and yards were sent down and with stump masts and an odd-looking wheelhouse she became simply a low-powered steamer. She had never been purchased from the Admiralty, only borrowed, and was finally sold by public auction for breaking up; she was sold to the highest bidder for £814 2s 7d. This amount was forwarded to the Admiralty for the credit of the Imperial Navy fund.

Chapter XXV

The Geographical North Pole

The question posed at the beginning of the 1875 Nares Expedition was, 'What is the Geographical North Pole?' The answer to that is now known, but who was credited as being the first to reach it? The answers to that is not to everyone's satisfaction.

The first serious claim was made on 21 April 1908 by an American veteran Polar traveller named Dr Frederick Cook. Five days later, another veteran Arctic traveller, Navy civil engineer Robert E. Peary announced that he and five companions had reached the Pole on 6–7 April 1909. Peary dismissed Cook's claim, labelling him a fake. Doubts still linger in many quarters about the veracity of Peary's claim, but ultimately the recognition was bestowed upon him. Doubts arose because of the time factor. His detractors were adamant that he could not have made it to the Pole and back to where he started from in the time he claimed. It is argued that Peary at best could only have got to within 50 miles of the Pole. The debate continues to this day.

The unfortunate Dr Cook became known as a liar and his claim was considered a hoax. Cook went to his grave still claiming he had reached the Pole.

There are several factors that greatly complicate the question of who was first at the Geographical North Pole, a question that on the surface one might think should have a simple answer. But it must be borne in mind that the Geographical North Pole is an imaginary point in the Arctic Ocean that is covered by floating ice, which is constantly in motion. There is no means to permanently mark its location. The proximity of the magnetic pole complicates matters. The use of modern technology to ascertain pinpoint accuracy is quite a recent phenomenon.

Today, travellers to the North Pole can reach it by balloon, parachute, motorised sleds supplied from the air and other modes of transport. Most appealing of all is a vacation on a monstrous icebreaker.

What a contrast from the days of James Hand and his fellow explorers.

Epilogue

The Mystery of the Jim Hand Memorial Markers

I had sought the help of my cousin Noel Dunne in the unearthing of pictures, and it was simply out of idle curiosity that he discovered a website in Canada, which revealed a relic I did not know existed. It was a photograph of an inscribed memorial plaque to Jim Hand and fellow sledger Charles Paul. There was a problem with the photograph – it was spoiled by the reflection of a ceiling fluorescent light. One could see that it was two sections of a headboard with a small piece of wood joining the two plaques together and it was in a display case in the Customs Examining House in Winnipeg. But why was it in Canada, rather than in Thank God Harbour, north-west Greenland where the remains of James Hand and Charles Paul lay buried?

Noel then discovered a photograph of a different memorial plaque to the two men. It was on another website and it was different memorial plaque altogether, much more professionally manufactured but with the exact same wording as was on the original and clearly made at a later date. This was a most surprising turn of events; what explanation could there be for two pictures of two different plaques and from where did they originate?

We ran into a dead end when seeking information on the picture of the replica. We had found the website of one Tim Christie, but received no response when we emailed. However, another cousin of mine, Dr Leo Metcalfe, a scientist in the European Space Agency in Madrid, succeeded in finding a different email address for Tim Christie. Christie was a pilot for the Canadian Meteorological Service at Station Alert.

Cape Sheridan/Station Alert, on the most northerly point of Ellesmere Island was the anchorage of HMS *Alert* during the unsuccessful G.S. Nares expedition. Fort Conger, in Discovery Harbour on the shore of Lady Franklin Bay on Ellesmere Island, is associated with the ill-fated 1881-84 US Army Scientific Expedition to Lady Franklin Bay led by US Army Captain Adolphus

Tim Christie's aerial photo of Fort Conger, showing the markings in the ground after Peary dismantled it. (Photo courtesy of Tim Christie.)

Washington Greely, which ended in one of the worst debacles in polar history. Approximately fifteen years later, the American explorer Robert Edwin Peary (a civil engineer in the United States Navy) arrived at Fort Conger and he used the wooden structure as a base camp to make several attempts to reach the North Pole. After two failed attempts he finally succeeded and in 1909 he was acclaimed the first man to have reached the North Pole after he had set out from Fort Conger. Station Alert is now a Canadian Forces outpost named after HMS *Alert*.

On his blog, Tim Christie describes how, on a mission to Station Alert on a summer's day in 2003, he had flown over the Greely's/Peary's huts at Fort Conger. Tim sought permission to land which was granted (providing he was accompanied by officials of the Environment of Canada) and he landed the next day and took dozens of photographs of the Heritage Site, including the replica of the memorial plaque.

On contact, Tim was most helpful and he emailed Jennifer Hamilton, Collections Archaeologist at Parks Canada, explaining that I would like a

The replacement markers at the graves of James Hand and Charles Paul. (Photo courtesy of Tim Christie.)

photograph of the original memorial for my book. Jennifer Hamilton set in motion a process among her colleagues in the Department and a Mr Douglas McGregor then photographed the original memorial plaque in the Custom Examining Warehouse in Winnipeg.

However, I still had not solved the mystery of its origins or why it was housed in that particular building. I then asked Jennifer if she could contact a historian who might help to fill in the details. She in turn spoke to Caroline Phillips, the archaeologist who, in 1977, removed the memorial boards for preservation and safe keeping in Ottawa at the Parks Canada Conservation Lab (they were later moved to Parks Canada's Archaeology Lab's Humidity controlled room in Winnipeg). Apparently there was increased activity at Fort Conger, with artifacts being removed by treasure seekers, and the fear was that these memorial boards would disappear. The decision was made to remove them from the site for conservation treatment, store them in an environmentally controlled environment and place a replica of the boards back on site at Fort Conger.

The boards had been found lying on the ground in 1965 by Robert L. Christie of the Geological Survey of Canada, who was doing work at Fort Conger at this time. They had suffered damage from snow and dampness so Mr Christie secured the boards to the east wall of the south hut (one of three at

Fort Conger), which was presumably built and used by Robert E. Peary and his party during the winter of 1900–1901.

When the ill-fated Greely Expedition of 1881–84, which led to the deaths of nineteen of its twenty-six men (mostly through starvation and execution), arrived at Lady Franklin Bay, the men built a single-storey structure, which was named Fort Conger. While there, a small party crossed the Robeson Channel to Thank God Harbour, where they visited the tombs of Captain Hall, J.J. Hand, and C.W. Paul and found them to be in excellent order.

Around the turn of the twentieth century Peary (*b.*1856) arrived at the abandoned Fort Conger. He planned to use the encampment as a base station from which to reach the North Pole. Peary dismantled it and built three smaller and more comfortable huts, one for his own use, one for Matthew Henson, and one to house his four Inuit guides. It was from Fort Conger in 1909 that Peary and his five-man team accomplished his lifelong dream of reaching the North Pole.

When asked about the memorial itself, Caroline Phillips explained that it consists of two separate headboards joined side by side in a frame. The left board is made of Honduran mahogany. The other board is made of white oak and is inscribed J.J. Hand. A third inscription runs across the bottom of both boards. Each board has a sculptured top edge with a radiating sun motif in the upper corners. All inscriptions and designs have been incised and appear to have been painted black. The boards are fastened together by two horizontal wooden strips at top and bottom and one vertical strip where they join. Nail holes indicate that vertical strips were also fastened to the sides. An artificial leather flower has been nailed to the centre of the upper cross-piece. It still bears traced of blue dye.

The wooden strips do not appear to be original since markings on the surface of the boards indicate that narrower, more carefully finished strips were used previously. Upon removal of the top strip by the Conservation Division, the letters USA were found stencilled to the back. This suggests that the frame was replaced by one of the American parties. The memorial is slightly incomplete; a piece has split off the length of the right edge.

It was surmised that Greely's party must have been responsible for fastening a new frame to the boards since official papers from the expedition show that the leather flower on the upper strip was placed on the memorial by Frederick and Long on 30 May 1882. Jennifer found this Greely reference in their library:

May 30th. It being Decoration Day [now known as Memorial Day], we observed it as a general holiday. Happily we have no graves of our own but on this occasion, Frederick and Long were inspired with the thoughtful idea of decorating the head-boards of the dead of the British Arctic Expedition, set up at this place in 1876. In default of regular flowers they made an elaborate artificial bouquet,

The memorial board to Jim Hand, housed at Fort Conger. (Photo courtesy of D. McGregor, Parks Canada, Western and Northern Service Centre, Winnipeg.)

which, with our camp colors, were tastefully draped over the head-boards. These marks of appreciation and honor to our dead predecessors must be considered of greater value thus coming from the rank and file of the expedition than if the initiative had been taken by the officers.

At long last we solved the mystery of the two memorial plaques.

When the crew of the *Discovery* learned of the deaths of their shipmates Jim Hand and Charley Paul, they made the original plaque and before they set sail for England they placed it in the hut/workshop or a cairn at Lady Franklin Bay along with records of the expedition. Five years later Lt Greely collected the items from the hut/cairn and stored them in Fort Conger. Robert Peary arrived at Fort Conger and when he dismantled it to suit his own needs he brought the plaque with him to the new location, where it was found after his acclaimed first to the North Pole by the authorities and taken to Winnipeg for preservation. Fort Conger was designated a Heritage Site and the replica was erected there to commemorate the deaths of these two most courageous of sailors.

A Chronology of Arctic Exploration

870AD   Floki Vilgerdarson discovers Iceland.

893   Erik the Red discovers Greenland.

1000   Leif Eriksson seeks America, crosses the Atlantic to Newfoundland.

1594-1597   William Barents makes three journeys to the north and discovers Spitzbergen.

1607-1610   Henry Hudson makes three journeys to Greenland, Spitzbergen, Jan Mahen, Hudson River and Hudson Bay.

1615-1616   William Baffin and Robert Bylot make two voyages to Hudson Bay and Baffin Bay.

1725-1742   The Great Northern Expedition takes place led by Bering, Chirikov, Khariton, Dmitri Laptev, Chelyuskin, and others, to the Bering Sea and Arctic Siberia.

1778   Captain James Cook goes to north-east Siberia and Alaska; establishes the separation between the Asian and American continents.

1819-1820   William Edward Parry's first voyage in search of the Northwest Passage reaches Melville Island.

1819–1822   John Franklin's first overland/canoe expedition down the Coppermine River and east to Point Turnagain in search of the Northwest Passage (in conjunction with the Parry voyage). It ends disastrously with eleven members of the expedition losing their lives.

1821-1823   Parry's second voyage in search of the Northwest Passage reaches Fury and Hecla Strait from Hudson Bay.

1824-1825   Parry's third and final voyage to the Canadian Arctic, again in search of the Northwest Passage, ends in disaster, with the shipwrecking of one of the vessels on Fury Beach, Somerset Island.

1825-1827   John Franklin's second overland/canoe expedition to the Arctic Sea coast of the Canadian mainland. His parties explore and map more than 1,000 of coastline from Coronation Gulf to Prudhoe Bay Alaska.

1827   Parry's attempt to reach the North Pole via Spitzbergen; he reaches 82°45'N and establishes a farthest north that will stand for fifty years.

1831   James Clark Ross is the first to locate the Magnetic Pole.

1837–1839   Peter Dease and Thomas Simpson of the Hudson Bay Company overland/boat expedition to fill in the gaps on the coastline left by Franklin from Point Barrow in the west to Castor and Pollux Bay (Rae Strait) in the east.

1845-1847   Sir John Franklin's expedition aboard the vessels *Erebus* and *Terror* in search of the Northwest Passage. Neither he, his ships, nor his crew were ever seen again.

1848-1849   James Clark Ross's expedition in search of Sir John Franklin with the vessels *Investigator* and *Enterprise*.

1848-1851   John Richardson, accompanied by Dr John Rae, leads land expedition to the Mackenzie River, Wollaston Peninsula and elsewhere on Victoria Island in search of Franklin.

1848-1851   Plover and Herald reach Bering Strait; Lt W.J.S. Pullen leads expedition by boat in search of Franklin, exploring the Arctic coastline to the Mackenzie Delta.

1850-1854   Robert McClure leads expedition in *Investigator* through the Bering Strait in search of Franklin. He establishes the last link in one route of the Northwest Passage and claims the parliamentary award for its discovery.

1850–1855   Richard Collinson commands the *Enterprise* part of the expedition through the Bering Strait in search of Franklin.

1850–1851   The William Penny expedition with the *Lady Franklin* and the *Sophia* to the eastern Arctic in search of Franklin.

1850–1851   Horatio T. Austin commands official four-ship Admiralty expedition to the eastern Arctic in search of Franklin.

1850–1851   Sir John Ross, aged seventy-three, leads a private expedition in search of Franklin.

1850   Charles Codrington Forsyth leads Lady Franklin's privately financed expedition in search of her husband on the *Prince Albert*.

1850–1851   Edwin J. De Haven leads the first US expedition to the Arctic in search of Franklin. Elisha Kent Kane is surgeon on one of De Haven's vessels.

1851–1852   William Kennedy, accompanied by Joseph Rene Bellot, leads another expedition privately financed by Lady Franklin in search of her husband.

1852–1854   Sir Edward Belcher leads a five-ship Admiralty expedition in search of Franklin.

1852   Commander Edward Ingerfield, RN, discovers Smith Sound to be navigable. His *With a Peep into the Polar Basin* suggests that ships might be able to sail through Smith Sound to a theoretical Open Polar Sea and from there to the Pole itself.

1853–1855   Elisha Kent Kane leads the second US search aboard the *Advance* in search of Sir John Franklin, choosing Smith Sound. He announces he has found the Open Polar Sea. He is mistaken.

1853–1854   Dr John Rae is sent by the Hudson Bay Company to complete a coastal survey in the area of King William Land and Boothia, hears of relics of the Franklin Expedition in the possession of the Eskimo.

1857-1859　　Francis Leopold McClintock leads the *Fox*, financed by Lady Franklin to verify if Dr Rae's claims are true.

1860-1861　　One of Kane's officers, Isaac Hayes, takes another expedition up Smith Sound in search of the Open Polar Sea. He too is mistaken when he identifies it. In reality he has found only a stretch of water that happens to be temporarily ice-free.

1860-1862　　American Charles Hall makes his first Arctic journey in search of Franklin survivors.

1864-1869　　Hall's second expedition reaches King William Island.

1869-1870　　Germany launches a polar expedition under the command of Captain Carl Koldewey. The *Germania* and *Hansa* reach the east coast of Greenland, whereupon they become separated. Sledgers from the *Germania* explore the coast, reaching 77°01'N. The *Hansa* is crushed and its crew drift south on a floe for 600 miles before reaching safety.

1871-1873　　Charles Francis Hall reaches 82°11'N aboard the *Polaris*.

1872-1874　　Captain Karl Weyprecht and Lt Julius von Payer of Austria-Hungary on the *Tegetthoff*. The ship becomes trapped in the ice, they drift north to discover a group of islands which they name Franz Josef Land. Threatened by scurvy, they abandon ship and drag their boats south until they meet open water.

1875-1876　　Captain George Nares leads the British Navy's last attempt in search of the North Pole.

1878-1879　　Baron Nils Nordenskiöld, in command of a Russian ship the *Vega*, completes the first successful navigation of the North-East Passage.

1879-1879　　Sponsored by the US newspaper magnate James Gordon Bennett, Lt George Washington De Long commands the ill-fated *Jeanette* expedition search for the North Pole. The ship sinks and twelve men including De Long perish in the Lena Delta.

1881–1884   Adolphus Greely of the US Army leads an expedition to Ellesmere Island as part of the first International Polar Year. His junior officer Lt Lockwood reaches a new farthest north of 83°23'8"N, breaking the Nares Expedition record. When supplies fail to arrive, Greely evacuates his men overland. By the time they are rescued only six of the twenty-four-strong team are alive, some of them having resorted to cannibalism.

1883   Nordenskjold tries to cross Greenland and fails.

1886   Robert Peary attempts to cross Greenland and fails.

1888   Fridtjof Nansen, a Norwegian, makes the first crossing of Greenland. In doing so he introduces skis as a tool of Arctic exploration.

1891–1892   Peary's first large Arctic expedition to North Greenland is mistaken when he believes Independence Bay to be Greenland's northernmost point.

1893–1896   Nansen, with Otto Sverdrup in the *Fram*, a ship specially designed to resist ice pressure. Nansen and a crew member, Hjalmar Johanssen, on skies reach a new farthest north 86°10', before being rescued by Samuel Jackson after retreating to Franz Josef Land.

1893–1895   Peary achieves nothing new on his second expedition to Greenland.

1897   Salaman Andree flies aboard the balloon *Eagle* from Spitzbergen for the Pole. At 82°93'N the Eagle is driven down by bad weather. The remains of those aboard were not found for another thirty-three years.

1898–1902   Peary's third Arctic expedition reaches 84°17' N (not as far as Nansen). Peary loses two of his toes to frostbite.

1899–1900   The Duke of Abruzzi leads an Italian expedition from Franz Josef Land in search of the Pole. Captain Umberto Cagni reaches a new farthest of 86°33'N. Three of the support team vanish in the ice.

1903-1905 Roald Amundsen completes the first successful navigation of the Northwest Passage.

1905-1906 Peary's fourth expedition reaches a new farthest north 87°06'N.

1907-1909 Frederick Cook claims to have reached the North Pole; but fails to convince his claim is genuine.

1908-1909 Peary claims to have reached the North Pole, but unlike Cook his claim is believed. Peary has been recognised as the first to reach the Pole, but to this day there are doubts cast on the claim.

1925 Roald Amundsen and Lincoln Ellsworth leaves Spitzbergen on two German-designed Dornier flying boats. They reach 88°N before engine failure forces them down. They leave one flying boat on the ice and after two weeks spent on repairs, narrowly escape on the other.

1926 Richard E. Byrd flies over the Pole from Spitzbergen in a Fokker trimotor plane.

1926 Roald Amundsen, Lincoln Ellsworth and Umberto Nobile fly from Spitzbergen to Alaska on the airship *Norge*. They claimed to have been the first to actually see the North Pole.

1948 A team of Russian scientists led by Alexander Kuznetsov claimed they were the first to set foot on the Pole. Again doubts have been expressed by Arctic experts on the claim.

1958 USS *Nautilus* nuclear submarine passes under the Pole.

1968 Ralph Plaisted reaches the Pole using snowmobiles with air support.

1968-1969 British explorer Wally Herbert leads a dog sled on foot with air support to reach the Pole.

Sources

Appleton, Thomas E., *Usque Ad Mare: A History of the Canadian Coast Guard and Marine Services* (Department of Transport: Ottawa, 1969).

Beattie, O. & Geiger, J., *Frozen in Time The Fate of the Franklin Expedition* (Bloomsbury: London, 2004).

Fleming, Fergus, *Barrow's Boys* (Granta: London, 2001).

Fleming, Fergus, *Ninety Degrees North* (Granta: London, 2002).

'Geological Survey of Denmark and Greenland' (www.geus.dk).

Guttridge, Leonard F., *Ghosts of Sabine: The Harrowing True Story of the Greely Expedition* (Putnam: New York, 2000).

Hall, Charles Francis, *Arctic researches and life among the Esquimeaux being the narrative of an expedition in search of Sir John Franklin, in the years 1860, 1861 and 1862* (Harper: New York, 1865).

Henderson, Bruce, *Fatal North: Murder and Survival Aboard the U.S.S.* Polaris, *the First U.S. Expedition to the North Pole* (New American Library, 2001).

Kane, Elisha Kent, Papers, American Philosophical Society (http://www.amphilsoc.org/library/mole/k/kaneek.htm).

Kinealy, Christine, *This Great Calamity* (Gill & Macmillan: Dublin, 2006).

McGoogan, Ken, *Ancient Mariner The Amazing Adventures of Samuel Hearne, the Sailor Who Walked to the Arctic Ocean* (Harper Collins: Ontario, 2004).

McGoogan, Ken, *Lady Franklin's Revenge* (Bantam Books: New York, 2007).

Nares, Captain George S., *Voyage to the Polar Sea* (Two Volumes) (Kessinger: Montana, 2007).

Nugent, Frank, *Seek The Frozen Lands. Irish Explorers 1740–1922* (Collins Press: Cork, 2004).

Paine, Lincoln P., *Ships of the World: An Historical Encyclopedia* (Houghton Mifflin Harcourt: Boston, 1997).

Parliamentary Papers: 'Lt Wyatt Rawson records Jim Hand's death, 3 June 1876.'

Parliamentary Papers: 'The Inquiry.'

Parliamentary Papers: 'The Scurvy Report.'

Smith, Michael, *Captain Francis Crozier: Last Man Standing?* (Collins Press: Cork, 2007).

Spufford, Francis, *I May Be Some Time: Ice and the English Imagination* (Palgrave Macmillan: New York, 1999).

Taylor, Andrew, 'Arctic Blue Books: online index to 19th Century British Parliamentary Papers concerned with the Canadian Arctic' (http://www.umanitoba.ca/faculties/arts/anthropology/bluebooks/index.html).

Tyson, Captain George E., *Arctic Experiences: Aboard the Doomed Polaris Expedition and*

Six Months Adrift on an Ice-Floe (Cooper Square: MD, 2002).

Williams, Glyn, *Voyages of Delusion The Quest for the Northwest Passage* (Yale University Press, 2003).

Index